Divorce FOR DUMMIES®

2ND EDITION

by John Ventura and Mary Reed

WILEY

Wiley Publishing, Inc.

Divorce For Dummies®, 2nd Edition

Published by
Wiley Publishing, Inc.
111 River St.
Hoboken, NJ 07030-5774
www.wiley.com

Copyright © 2005 by Wiley Publishing, Inc., Indianapolis, Indiana

Published by Wiley Publishing, Inc., Indianapolis, Indiana

Published simultaneously in Canada

For general information on our other products and services, please contact our Customer Care Department within the U.S. at 800-762-2974, outside the U.S. at 317-572-3993, or fax 317-572-4002.

For technical support, please visit www.wiley.com/techsupport.

Wiley also publishes its books in a variety of electronic formats. Some content that appears in print may not be available in electronic books.

Library of Congress Control Number: 2005923741

ISBN-13: 978-0-7645-8417-6

ISBN-10: 0-7645-8417-0

Manufactured in the United States of America

10 9 8 7 6 5 4 3 2 1

2B/QW/QW/QV/IN

WILEY

About the Authors

John Ventura is an attorney and a nationally known authority and advocate on consumer law and financial issues. As a boy, he dreamed of becoming a Catholic priest so he could help others. To prepare for that career, he spent his high school years in a seminary. After graduation, John decided he could best pursue his dream by combining journalism with the law, so he earned a degree in both from the University of Houston.

Today, John has an interest in four law offices in the Rio Grande Valley, where he offers legal advice in the areas of bankruptcy and consumer law. His goal as an attorney and as an author is to provide individuals with the information and advice they need to make the laws work for them, not against them.

John has written 12 books on consumer and small-business legal and financial matters and is the author of *Law For Dummies* (Wiley). He has written for *Home Office Computing* and *Small Business Computing* magazines and has written a regular column for a Texas business journal. John also has hosted a weekly radio program on legal issues.

John has been a frequent network TV show guest on CNN, CNN-fn, CNBC, the Fox News Channel, and the Lifetime Network and has done numerous national and local radio programs. He has provided expert opinion for publications including *Money, Kiplinger's Personal Finance Magazine, Black Enterprise, Inc., Martha Stewart Living, The Wall Street Journal,* and *Newsweek.*

Mary Reed writes about financial and legal issues affecting consumers and small-business owners. She coauthored *Divorce For Dummies* (Wiley), *Good Advice for a Bad Economy* (Berkley), and an e-book entitled *Stop Debt Collectors Cold* (www.stopebtcollectorscold.com). She has ghostwritten 11 other books for consumers and small-business owners and has also written for *Good Housekeeping Magazine, Home Office Computing Magazine, Hispanic Business,* as well as for several Texas newspapers.

Mary is the owner of Mary Reed Public Relations (MR•PR), an Austin, Texas-based public relations firm. She counts book publishers, attorneys, financial professionals, healthcare professionals, nonprofit organizations, retailers, and restaurants among her clients.

Prior to starting MR•PR, Mary was vice president of marketing for a national market research firm, public affairs and marketing director for a women's healthcare and advocacy organization, public relations manager for *Texas Monthly Magazine,* and aide to an Austin City Council member. She also worked as a consultant to state and federal agencies while living in Cambridge, Massachusetts, and Washington, D.C.

In her free time, Mary enjoys being with her many friends and family, gardening, bike riding, reading, volunteering, and taking care of her cat.

Dedication

John's Dedication
To Lisa Taylor, the best divorce attorney I know.

Mary's Dedication
To my parents. Your words and deeds have taught me what a successful, happy marriage is all about and have provided me with a model to strive for. Thank you!

Authors' Acknowledgments

Thanks to Alissa Schwipps, our project editor, and Michelle Dzurny, our copy editor, for their help in reshaping the material in *Divorce For Dummies*. They made us work hard but, as a result, this second edition is even more helpful for readers who are faced with the possibility of divorce or are in the middle of one than the book's first edition. Their input and advice was invaluable.

Publisher's Acknowledgments

We're proud of this book; please send us your comments through our Dummies online registration form located at www.dummies.com/register/.

Some of the people who helped bring this book to market include the following:

Acquisitions, Editorial, and Media Development

Senior Project Editor: Alissa Schwipps

(Previous Edition: Nancy DelFavero)

Acquisitions Editor: Tracy Boggier

Copy Editor: Michelle Dzurny

(Previous Edition: Tamara Castleman, Elizabeth Netedu Kuball)

Editorial Program Assistant: Courtney Allen

Technical Editor: John T. Reed, Attorney at Law

Senior Editorial Manager: Jennifer Ehrlich

Editorial Assistants: Hanna Scott, Melissa Bennett

Cover Photo: © K-PHOTOS/Alamy

Cartoons: Rich Tennant (www.the5thwave.com)

Composition Services

Project Coordinators: Adrienne Martinez, Shannon Schiller

Layout and Graphics: Carl Byers, Andrea Dahl, Joyce Haughey, Julie Trippetti

Proofreaders: Laura Albert, Leeann Harney, TECHBOOKS Production Services

Indexer: TECHBOOKS Production Services

Publishing and Editorial for Consumer Dummies

Diane Graves Steele, Vice President and Publisher, Consumer Dummies

Joyce Pepple, Acquisitions Director, Consumer Dummies

Kristin A. Cocks, Product Development Director, Consumer Dummies

Michael Spring, Vice President and Publisher, Travel

Kelly Regan, Editorial Director, Travel

Publishing for Technology Dummies

Andy Cummings, Vice President and Publisher, Dummies Technology/General User

Composition Services

Gerry Fahey, Vice President of Production Services

Debbie Stailey, Director of Composition Services

Contents at a Glance

Table of Contents

Introduction

· ·

Nearly half of all marriages in the United States end in divorce. That adds up to more than a million divorces a year — the highest divorce rate in the industrialized world despite a general increase in divorce among all industrialized countries! Despite divorce having become so commonplace, most people are almost completely at a loss over what to do first if *their* marriage is breaking up. (An understandable situation — most of us go into marriage expecting the best but not usually being prepared for the worst.)

Overwhelmed by confusion, anger, fear, and resentment, many divorcing spouses turn what could be an amicable breakup into a cutthroat battle. Others panic over the changes occurring in their lives (and the lives of their children) and end up making costly mistakes that they could have avoided if they had had more information about the divorce laws in their state. They end their marriages bitter, angry, and a whole lot poorer.

But divorce doesn't have to be about winners, losers, and huge legal bills. With the right information and advice (and the proper attitude), most couples can work out the terms of their divorce with a minimum of expenses, hassles, and emotional upheaval. In this book, we tell you how.

About This Book

Welcome to the new edition of *Divorce For Dummies*. Like the first edition, this book helps demystify the divorce process using plain English (and not a bunch of confounding legalese). However, this second edition features updated information and lots of new resources. Want to know exactly what you find in the chapters ahead? Dip into this book and you can find out about

- ✔ Alternatives to divorce
- ✔ How to be financially prepared for the possibility of divorce
- ✔ What to do first before you file for divorce
- ✔ The difference between a fault and no-fault divorce
- ✔ The basics of family and divorce law and how divorce laws may vary from state to state
- ✔ What to consider when you and your spouse are making decisions about the division of your property, spousal support, child custody and visitation, and child support

✔ Mistakes to avoid, trade-offs to consider, and insights for effective negotiating

✔ Tips for finding a divorce attorney who's competent *and* affordable

✔ What to expect if you're able to negotiate the terms of your divorce with an attorney's help or through mediation

✔ Divorce-related resources, including Internet sites, support groups, and publications

We also offer you advice for keeping your emotions as well as your legal expenses under control. And, for the small percentage of you who are involved in hostile divorces and have to go through a divorce trial, this book prepares you for the courtroom experience. Plus, we offer invaluable advice for minimizing the potential negative effects that divorce can have on your young children, provide guidance on how to resolve common post-divorce problems, and suggest ways to rebuild a new life for yourself after divorce.

The great thing about *Divorce For Dummies,* 2nd Edition, is that *you* decide where to start and what to read. It's a reference that you can jump into and out of at will or whenever you have a question about divorce. Just head to the table of contents or the index to find the information you need.

Conventions Used in This Book

We use the following conventions throughout the text to make things consistent and easy to understand:

✔ All Web addresses appear in `monofont`.

✔ New terms appear in *italics* and are closely followed by an easy-to-understand definition.

✔ **Bold** highlights the action parts of numbered steps and other important information you should know.

What You're Not to Read

We know that reading a whole book about divorce can be a pretty overwhelming proposition, so we separated the stuff you really need to read from the information that may be interesting but isn't essential reading to make using this book easier for you. The shaded boxes of text called sidebars elaborate on information in the rest of the chapter, provide extra tips and advice, or highlight useful resources. You may want to return to this information later when you have a better grasp of the basic facts of divorce and are ready to add to your body of divorce knowledge.

Foolish Assumptions

As we wrote this book, we made some assumptions about our readers. We hope what we had in mind reflects you.

- You're either going through your first divorce or made a mess of your previous divorce and want to do a better job of ending your marriage this time.
- You don't have a lot of experience with the legal system and are somewhat intimidated by attorneys, laws and legal terms, and judges.
- You haven't been to law school, and you don't read legal books for fun.
- You want to get divorced with a minimum of angst and expense.
- You want to protect your legal rights and get your fair share.
- You want to make your divorce as easy as possible on your children.

If our assumptions about you are right on the money, we're certain that you'll find this book to be a valuable resource. It can't mend your broken heart or take away your pain and worries, but it can help you feel more informed about divorce and that you have more control of your life as you plan for the end of your marriage, go through the divorce process, and begin to put the pieces in place for a happy, fulfilling post-divorce life.

How This Book Is Organized

You can use *Divorce For Dummies,* 2nd Edition, in one of two ways: You can sit down and read it from cover to cover or pick it up when you want to read about a certain topic or need an answer to a question. For easy reading, this book is organized into six parts; the following sections explain what information you can find where.

Part I: Trouble in Paradise

Part I helps prepare you to deal with your marriage when it's in serious trouble. In this part, we provide an overview of the key issues and decisions in divorce and the divorce process itself, whether you work out the terms of your divorce outside of court or turn your divorce over to a judge. We also review various alternatives to divorce and provide detailed information on getting separated, whether you separate in an effort to save your marriage or use the separation as a prelude to divorce. This part also educates you about how to become an informed manager of your finances, whether you want to stay married or plan to divorce. For example, in this part, you find out about the kinds of financial skills you need, the various financial records and documents you should have access to and understand, and why, whatever the state of your marriage, you have to have a credit history in your own name and know how to build one. Finally, we offer advice and resources for maintaining your employability if you're a stay-at-home spouse so that you can earn a good living after your marriage ends.

Part II: Moving Forward with Your Divorce

Part II tells you how to initiate a divorce, with specific advice about how to break the news to your spouse. This part also helps you set your divorce goals and priorities. For those of you who anticipate a hostile divorce, we include a chapter that provides essential advice and guidance for protecting yourself financially and we give you the specific steps you should take to protect yourself and your children if your spouse becomes violent or threatens violence. We also include a chapter that discusses your emotional needs and those of your kids, with advice on how to cope with the inevitable ups and downs that the breakup of a marriage brings and how to break the news about your divorce to your children. We also prepare you for the kinds of questions that your children may ask you about your divorce and provide advice for how to keep the lines of communication open with them.

Part III: Decisions, Decisions

After your divorce has begun, you have some important and sometimes difficult decisions to make. For example, you and your spouse have to decide how to divide up your marital property as well as all the debts you acquired during your marriage. You also may need to decide about spousal support — whether you will receive it or pay it and how much the payments will be. If you and your spouse have young children, you must also figure out how to handle child custody and visitation and child support. After you read the chapters in this part of the book, you should find resolving these issues much easier.

Part IV: Coming to an Agreement: Negotiating the Terms of Your Divorce

Part IV gives you a real appreciation for the value of staying out of court by negotiating the terms of your divorce, whether you and your spouse do most of the negotiating yourselves or you each hire attorneys to do the negotiating for you. You also find out about the benefits and the drawbacks of using mediation to help settle your divorce. We tell you how to locate an affordable attorney, what you should expect from the attorney you hire, what your attorney expects from you, and how you and your attorney can work together to get you a good divorce settlement. For those of you headed for divorce court, the final chapter in this part tells you what to expect before, during, and immediately after your divorce trial.

Part V: Looking Toward the Future Now That Your Divorce Is Final

After your divorce gets wrapped up, you still have paperwork to deal with and money matters to think about. For example, you must manage your own money and take care of your estate planning. Plus, you may need to earn your own living or find a job that pays you more than you're making now. This part helps you address those issues, and it also offers advice and guidance for how to get the emotional support you may need after your marriage has ended, how to have fun again, and how to rebuild a sense of family for yourself and your children. In addition, this part features a chapter to help you grapple with some of the most difficult problems that people often face after their divorce, including problems with visitation, unpaid child support and/or spousal support, falling finances, and emotionally troubled children. Finally, if you're thinking about marrying again, we include a chapter that explains the value of proactive planning through the use of prenuptial and postnuptial agreements.

Part VI: The Part of Tens

This part points you to some great Web sites where you can find out more about divorce, get your questions answered by divorce experts, and chat with other individuals who may be struggling with the same divorce-related problems as you. We also offer advice on how you can help your kids cope with the aftermath of your divorce. Finally, the last chapter focuses just on you by offering practical tips for how to put your divorce behind you and move forward, emotionally, financially, and socially.

Part VI also features a handy, dandy glossary so you can understand the terms that your attorney uses or that you hear in divorce court.

Icons Used in This Book

To make this book easier to read and simpler to use, we include some icons that can help you find and fathom key ideas and information.

We use this icon to draw your attention to some of the more technical but very important financial details of getting a divorce.

This icon points out important information you should squirrel away in your brain for quick recall later.

This icon calls your attention to aspects of divorce and family law that may differ from one U.S. state to another.

This icon clues you in to something especially useful that can save you time, money, or energy as you're going through your divorce.

Stop and read this information to steer clear of common divorce-related mistakes and pitfalls.

Where to Go from Here

We organized this book so you can jump in and out wherever you want — you don't have to start at the very beginning and work your way to the end to find out about divorce. For example, if you're particularly concerned about child custody and child support, start with Chapters 10 and 11. If you're not sure where to begin reading, turn to the book's table of contents or the index at the end of the book. Another good starting point is Chapter 1, which introduces you to the book's key concepts and topics.

Part I
Trouble in Paradise

The 5th Wave   By Rich Tennant

"I don't know if we have irreconcilable differences or not. We never talk."

In this part . . .

Not all marriages are made in heaven. If your marriage is on the rocks and you think that you and your spouse may be headed for a split, this part of the book provides you with a quick overview of divorce. This part introduces you to the legal and financial issues that you and your spouse must resolve before your divorce is final, the laws that apply to divorce, and the likely costs of your divorce. It also gives you an idea of what to expect if your divorce ends up in court.

If you want to try to save your marriage or if divorce isn't an option for you, this part also reviews various alternatives to divorce. Many couples separate as a last-ditch effort to save their marriages or in lieu of divorce, so this part pays special attention to separation.

You also find a chapter on your family's finances, which discusses the whys and hows of becoming fully informed and actively involved in the management of your family's finances. Whether you divorce, separate, or save your marriage, pay close attention to this chapter.

Chapter 1

Understanding What Divorce Is All About

*T*he thought that a divorce is in your future may make your stomach churn and cause you to lie awake at night worrying about what the process will be like, especially if your only knowledge of the legal system comes from watching courtroom dramas on TV. Understandably, the prospect of dealing with lawyers, courts, and legal mumbo jumbo may intimidate you.

Like most people in your situation, you're probably also concerned about what the divorce will do to your finances. You may worry about how much you'll have to spend to get divorced and whether after your divorce is final, you'll have to pay every penny you earn on spousal support and/or child support (or whether you'll receive enough spousal support or child support from your spouse). You may also lose sleep wondering about the kind of post-divorce lifestyle you will be able to afford.

And, if you have young children, you probably have worries about how your divorce will affect them. You're right to be concerned because studies show that when parents don't work together to make their children feel safe and to keep their lives as normal as possible during and after their divorce, the children are apt to suffer emotionally. Studies also show that these same children have difficulty establishing healthy relationships as adults.

But, after you read this book, you should sleep better at night and worry a little less because you'll be armed with the information and advice you need to help you and your children get through your divorce and prepare for life afterward.

This chapter highlights the kinds of pre-divorce planning you should do, provides you with a peak at the divorce process, explains the differences between a fault and a no-fault divorce, helps you calculate the cost of your divorce, and reviews the main money-related issues that you have to resolve in most divorces. In this chapter, we also touch on the emotional aspects of divorce. In addition, we introduce you to some of the professionals you may need to call on to help with your divorce and to the role that mediation and the collaborative law process can play in a divorce.

Considering Whether You Have Cause for Concern

If your marriage is going through tough times, you may find yourself wondering whether it's an example of the "for better or for worse" alluded to in your marriage vows or whether your relationship is truly on the rocks. Although no test exists that can tell you whether your problems are typical reactions to the stress and strain that most marriages experience at one time or another or whether they point to more serious issues, troubled marriages do tend to exhibit many of the same characteristics. How many of the following statements apply to your marriage?

- In your mind, your spouse just can't do anything right anymore.
- You fight constantly.
- You've lost the ability or the willingness to resolve your marital problems.
- Resentment and contempt have replaced patience and love.
- You've turned from lovers into roommates.
- One or both of you is having an affair.
- You go out of your way to avoid being together and, when you are together, you have nothing to talk about.
- Your children are reacting to the stress in your marriage by fighting more, having difficulty in school, getting into trouble with the police, abusing drugs or alcohol, or becoming sexually promiscuous.
- You have begun having thoughts about divorce.

Don't panic if you find that your marriage exhibits some of these characteristics because you're not necessarily headed for divorce court. However, you do have cause for concern; you and your spouse need to assess your options — first separately and then together — and decide what to do next.

Marital problems can trigger depression, feelings of vulnerability, powerlessness, anger, and sleep disturbances, any of which can impede clear thinking and sound decision-making. A mental health professional can help you or your spouse deal with these problems so that you can move forward. If your spouse is struggling emotionally, suggest that he or she get mental health counseling, assuming that you think your spouse will be receptive to advice coming from you given the state of your marriage.

Getting Prepared Financially for a Divorce

Pre-divorce financial planning is essential to minimizing the cost of your divorce and increasing the likelihood that when your divorce is over, you will have a settlement agreement that meets your short- and long-term post-divorce financial needs. (We discuss how to prepare yourself emotionally in the "Surviving the Emotional Roller Coaster" section, later in this chapter, as well as in Chapter 7.) The amount and type of planning you need to do depends on how involved you have been in managing your family's financial life, whether you have a good credit history in your own name, and whether you have maintained a career outside your home during your marriage. See Chapter 3 for advice about evaluating your family's finances.

If your spouse totally surprises you with plans for a divorce, pre-divorce planning may be impossible, especially if you're clueless about your family's finances. If that's the case, your divorce teaches you a painful lesson: That not being an informed and active partner in your family's financial life is risky because you're at an immediate disadvantage if your marriage ends (or if you become widowed).

Ideally, before your divorce begins, you will have

✔ **Built a good credit history in your own name.** In other words, all or most of your credit should not be *joint credit* — that is, credit that you share with your spouse. Without a solid credit history of your own, you will have a difficult time qualifying for credit that has affordable terms after your divorce. You may even have a difficult time qualifying for certain kinds of jobs or promotions because some employers check your credit history as part of their decision-making process. You may also have a difficult time renting a nice place to live because some landlords review their potential tenants' credit histories as part of their screening process. Finally, without good credit, you may not be able to obtain adequate insurance.

✔ **Cleaned up your credit history if the one you built in your own name was full of negatives.** To improve your credit history, make all future credit payments on time, don't go over your credit limits, and don't take on new debt. Within a matter of months, your credit history should begin to improve.

✔ **Begun to update your job skills and/or to develop new ones if you've been a stay-at-home parent or a full-time homemaker during your marriage.** In this current economy, having the right job skills is critical to being competitive in the job market. You may have to return to school to get the skills that you need.

TIP

✔ **Considered taking a part-time or full-time job while you're married.** By taking a job while you're married, you can begin adding recent work experience to your resume and begin building some professional relationships that may help you after you're out of your marriage.

✔ **Taken a basic class in personal finance at your local college or university or through some other resource if you know next to nothing about money matters or feel that you need a refresher course.** Having the right money-related information and skills is essential to negotiating the financial aspects of your divorce and to managing your money wisely when you are on your own.

✔ **Created a written inventory of all your family's assets and assigned an approximate value to each one.** Going into a divorce, having a complete record of everything you and your spouse own is important so that you know what assets you have to divide up between you. Without a record, you may overlook an asset and not get all that you're entitled to in your divorce. When compiling your list, don't worry about listing items of little value; instead, focus on financially significant assets like real estate, stocks, mutual funds and bonds, vehicles, antiques, fine art, and so on. Also, when valuing each asset on your inventory, write down its *market value* — what the asset is worth now, meaning what someone would pay for it if you were selling it right now. Market value isn't what you or your spouse paid for the asset when you first purchased it or what you wish the asset were worth.

✔ **Inventoried all your family's debts.** Your inventory should note the name of each creditor and how much you owe each one as well as which of your assets may secure your debts. For example, your home secures your mortgage loan. In other words, if you default on the loan, the mortgage holder is legally entitled to take back your home. Creating an inventory of all your marital debts is just as important as inventorying all your marital assets because you have to divvy up those debts during your divorce negotiations, too.

✔ **Located all the ownership papers for your assets.** These documents include deeds to property; titles to vehicles; documentation for stocks, bonds, mutual funds, and other investments that you and your spouse may own; life insurance policies; estate-planning documents that you and your spouse prepared; information about your respective retirement plans; and so on. You need these documents for two reasons. First, you need them to help determine the value of the assets that you and your spouse are dividing between yourselves. Second, after you've divided everything, you need the documents so that you can properly transfer the titles to you or your spouse, depending on who gets what. Without the title to the assets you're taking away from your marriage, you will not be their legal owner.

✔ **Obtained copies of important documents, such as your family's tax returns for the past five years and your real estate tax bills for the most current year.** Also have a record of all your bank accounts — the accounts that you and your spouse share as well as your individual accounts — including the types of accounts, the financial institutions where the accounts are located, and the account numbers.

✔ **Have begun thinking about your post-divorce financial needs — the money and other assets you will need to live a financially secure life after your marriage ends.** Consider what trade-offs you're willing to make with your spouse to ensure that your needs are met.

Making It Official

Before your divorce can begin, you must take care of some preliminary divorce matters. For example, you must make certain that you meet the divorce requirements of the state where you want to get divorced. Also, you or your divorce attorney must file legal paperwork with the court to officially set your divorce in motion and you must decide whether you will file a no-fault or fault divorce, assuming fault divorces are permitted in the state where you are divorcing.

If you don't want to live with your spouse anymore, but you don't want to get divorced, either, you and your spouse can *separate.* You can separate temporarily while you decide what to do about your relationship or you can make your separation permanent and finalize it with a *legal separation agreement,* which addresses the same kind of issues you would address in a divorce. We discuss the pros and cons of separation in Chapter 4.

Meeting the requirements

To get a divorce, you must meet certain minimum requirements set by your state. Although those requirements vary somewhat from state to state, the most common ones are

✔ **Residing in your state for a certain period of time.** A handful of states have no residency requirement — your obvious destination for a "quickie divorce" — but most states require that one or both of you be a resident for a minimum amount of time before you can file a petition for divorce or before your divorce can be granted. Six months is the most common residency requirement, but some states' requirements are weeks, months, or even a year. Also, some counties have their own residency requirements.

- ✓ **Getting divorced in the state where you live.** You must get divorced in the state you call your permanent home — and not in the state where you got married.

- ✓ **Being separated.** Before you can get a no-fault divorce, some states require that you live apart from your spouse for a certain period of time — six months to a year in most of these states, but as long as two to three years in some states. The theory behind this requirement is that, with enough time, you and your spouse may have a change of heart and reconcile. See Chapter 4 for information about legalizing a formal separation.

You can find out the particular divorce requirements in your state in several ways. You can do an Internet search using key words like "requirements for divorce in [your state]." You can call your local family court, check with your local bar association, or contact a divorce attorney in your area. If any of these resources can't or won't provide you with the information that you're looking for, they should be able to tell you where you can get it.

Filing a divorce petition

No matter what state you live in and regardless of whether you and your spouse agree that ending your marriage is for the best, your divorce begins when one of you files a divorce petition with the court. If you and your spouse have already hired divorce attorneys, one of the attorneys files the divorce petition. (See the later section in this chapter, "Involving a divorce attorney," as well as Chapters 13 and 14, for more information about working with a divorce attorney.) Otherwise, one of you can go to your local court-house and file a divorce petition yourself.

After someone files a divorce petition, the nonfiling spouse is legally notified about the petition, which usually involves a sheriff or constable hand delivering the notice or the nonfiling spouse receiving it in the mail. The nonfiling spouse isn't served at all if he or she waives notification, which is most likely to occur if both spouses agreed to an amicable divorce and are already familiar with everything in the divorce petition. If the nonfiling spouse disagrees with anything in the petition, such as the grounds for the divorce, the request by the filing spouse for sole custody of the couple's children, and so on, he or she will file an *answer* with the court, stating his or her side of those issues.

Deciding who's at fault

Depending on the state you live in, if you initiated your divorce, you must decide whether to file a fault or a no-fault divorce. As of this writing, about 70 percent of all states allow couples to get either an old-fashioned *fault divorce* or a *no-fault divorce,* which is a kinder, gentler type of divorce.

When you file a fault divorce, you must provide a very specific reason, or *grounds,* for wanting to end your marriage. In other words, you must accuse your spouse of some sort of unacceptable behavior, such as adultery, physical abuse, mental cruelty, drunkenness, drug addiction, or insanity. Depending on your state, you may also be able to get a fault divorce if your spouse has been in prison for a minimum period of time or has deserted your marriage.

When you allege fault, you must also prove that the grounds actually exist. Proving fault can involve having a friend or relative who witnessed your spouse's bad behavior testify to it, although they may be reluctant to get involved in your divorce, especially if they like your spouse. Or you may need to hire a detective to document your spouse's bad behavior on video. Although a fault divorce can provide the grist for a lurid soap opera, some spouses feel that the drama is worth it because if they can prove that what they allege about their partner is true, they can get a better divorce settlement.

Currently, all states recognize some form of no-fault divorce. If you opt for this kind of divorce, you don't have to prove that your spouse did anything to cause you to seek a divorce. Instead, all you really need to do is acknowledge that things "just didn't work out" between the two of you. Common grounds for obtaining a no-fault divorce include "incompatibility," "irretrievable break-down," or "irreconcilable differences." Because you don't need to prove fault, this kind of divorce is usually less expensive, quicker to complete, and easier on spouses and their children than most fault divorces. As a result, no-fault divorces are much more frequent than fault divorces.

Fault used to play a major role in alimony decisions, but many states no longer consider that factor. About half the states consider fault when dividing up a couple's property. In those states, fault has an impact on the final details of a couple's divorce, including the amount the spouse who's *not* at fault eventually receives in the divorce settlement. To find out whether your state permits fault divorces, call your local or state bar association or a divorce attorney in your area.

Knowing What's Up with the Divorce Process

In the end, all divorces have the same result — a marriage legally ends. But you can achieve that result in a number of ways. For example, you and your spouse may work together to negotiate all the terms of your divorce without legal help; if neither of you can stand to be in the same room with one another, much less make any concessions to the other regarding the terms of your divorce, your divorce attorneys will do the negotiating for you with your input; or you may choose a path that's somewhere in between these two extremes.

If you and your spouse have been married for a very brief amount of time, have no young children from your relationship, and have amassed little or no marital property and debt, your state may have an abbreviated divorce process for which you may qualify. To find out whether your state has such a process and the criteria you must meet to use it, contact your state or local bar association or a family law attorney.

Choosing which divorce path to take

Although every divorce has one goal — to end a marriage — you can achieve that goal in several ways. For example, you and your spouse can work together to make your divorce as quick, easy, and inexpensive as possible, or you can turn your divorce into a costly battle characterized by anger, unreasonable demands, uncompromising attitudes, and a big price tag.

Just which path your divorce takes is up to you and your spouse. Your basic options include

- ✔ A cooperative divorce
- ✔ A contested divorce
- ✔ A courtroom divorce

Your divorce can actually combine two or even all three of these options. For example, you and your spouse may work out some aspects of your divorce together, but you may hire attorneys to negotiate other aspects of your divorce and have a judge resolve the issues on which you're deadlocked. The following sections describe each divorce path in detail.

A cooperative divorce

A *cooperative divorce* is easiest on your pocketbook and on your emotions. In this type of divorce, you or your spouse files a no-fault divorce petition, and the two of you work out the terms of your divorce together (Chapter 12 provides negotiating tips). When you've decided everything, one of you files the divorce paperwork. You can also achieve a cooperative divorce if you both hire attorneys to help with the negotiations, but you stay committed to keeping things friendly. (You and your spouse cannot share an attorney. You both need your own.)

After you and your spouse have drafted a divorce agreement that both parties feel is fair (with or without the help of attorneys), your divorce should move forward relatively quickly because less bureaucratic red tape and legal paperwork is involved to slow the process. After you, your spouse, or the attorneys have made any final changes to the agreement, the spouse who initiated the divorce by filing a divorce petition, or one of your attorneys if you're working with attorneys, files the agreement with the court. The spouse who initiated the divorce may have to make a brief court appearance. Soon after, your divorce becomes official.

A contested divorce

A *contested divorce* occurs when you and your spouse can't agree on all the key issues in your divorce. For example, you want sole custody of your kids, but your spouse wants to share custody, or you want to receive spousal support, but your spouse doesn't want to pay it. Because a contested divorce can get messy, lawyers are almost always involved to help handle all the legal paperwork and formalities. A contested divorce takes longer to complete than a cooperative divorce, costs a whole lot more, and is harder on your emotions. Spouses can contest fault and no-fault divorces.

You may be able to avoid a trial by resolving your differences with the help of attorneys or through a dispute-resolution technique such as *mediation* (discussed in Chapter 15).

A courtroom divorce

A *courtroom divorce* (discussed in Chapter 16) is an extreme version of the messy contested divorce. A courtroom divorce is more emotional, more time-consuming, and more expensive than a divorce decided outside of court. The process also involves a lot more paperwork and legal red tape. Your divorce goes to court when you and your spouse are unable to resolve all the terms of your divorce. In a courtroom divorce, a family law judge decides how to handle all the outstanding issues.

Although a litigated divorce may be unavoidable in your situation, it's a risky option because no matter how much time the judge spends trying to understand your marriage, he or she can never have a complete grasp of your relationship with your spouse and the intricacies of your divorce. Also, although we like to think that all judges decide legal issues with unbiased minds, the truth is, sometimes their own prejudices, preferences, and real-life experiences color their decisions. For example, if your divorce goes to trial, the judge who hears your case may have just gone through his or her own divorce and may feel that he or she was "taken to the cleaners." Or maybe the judge's daughter is a single, divorced mom who struggles to make ends meet because her ex-spouse doesn't meet his support obligations. As a result, neither you nor your spouse may be happy with the outcome. In fact, research shows that when a judge decides a divorce, the spouses involved are less likely to be happy with the final outcome of their divorce and less committed to making the terms of their divorce work than couples that arrive at a negotiated settlement.

A litigated divorce can exhaust you emotionally and financially, plus it can create so much animosity between you and your spouse that years may pass before it abates. If you have children together, this animosity can be a serious problem because your anger toward one another may seriously harm your children's short- and long-term emotional well-being. Also, don't forget that if you both want to be actively involved in their lives after your divorce, you will run into one another at their after-school games, recitals, graduations, weddings, and so on. The last thing you want is for your estrangement with your ex-spouse to overshadow or color the important events in your children's lives.

If your divorce ends with a trial, you're more apt to revisit the final terms of your divorce in your lawyers' offices and in court. Doing so not only takes money and time, but it also means that you never really put your divorce and your failed marriage behind you. Also, you can appeal a judge's decision, but appeals are hard to win. Plus, appealing means spending more money on an attorney and then, if you win your appeal, more money on a new trial. Also, a new trial may unleash emotions that you thought you had come to terms with. No one wins when you have to litigate your divorce, so do your best to settle without a trial. Sometimes giving up a little during your negotiation is the wisest thing to do.

Involving a divorce attorney

When most people think of getting divorced, they automatically assume that they need a divorce attorney's guidance from start to finish. That's the way people have handled divorce traditionally. But you have other options, though you may need to consult an attorney at various stages.

For example, you and your spouse may negotiate all the terms of your divorce and draft a divorce agreement with the help of Chapter 12, not attorneys. If you decide to do all the negotiations yourselves, meeting with an attorney before the negotiations begin is still a good idea for each of you in order to get briefed on the divorce-related laws of your state and advised about the particular issues that relate to your divorce. After you and your spouse work out a divorce agreement, the attorney reviews your draft to make sure that you haven't overlooked anything important, that your interests are protected, and that you haven't unwittingly created the potential for future problems.

Hiring a CDP to help you negotiate the financial stuff

A certified divorce planner (CDP) analyzes your family's finances and provides you with a specific plan for resolving the financial issues in your divorce, such as property settlement, spousal support, and child support, taking into account your earnings potential, age, lifestyle needs, and so on. A good CDP considers not only what's best for you in the immediate years after your divorce but also your financial needs in 5, 10, and 15 years.

You and your spouse can hire a CDP together if your divorce is amicable and you're both committed to working out an agreement that's fair, or you can each hire your own. A CDP uses software programs to run the numbers and to produce charts and graphs that illustrate the dollars and cents of various financial settlement options for your divorce. Not only do these charts and graphs clearly illustrate which options are best for you and highlight the trade-offs you may have to make to get them (or something close anyway), but they also help bring you and your spouse back to reality if one of you is refusing to back off a particular position and your negotiations are in jeopardy of ending in a stalemate. Charts and graphs have a way of making points in an emotionally free dollars-and-cents way that's difficult to argue with.

For more information about how a planner can help you and for a referral to one in your area, contact the Institute for Divorce Financial Analysts, a national organization that certifies divorce planners. You can call the Institute at 800-875-1760 or visit its Web site at www.InstituteDFA.com.

If you and your spouse can hardly stand being in the same room with each other or if you don't trust one another, you need attorneys to negotiate the details of your divorce agreement and to help prepare your final agreement. Similarly, if you're afraid of your spouse, have a hard time asserting yourself, or are unsure of your ability to negotiate a good settlement for yourself, don't go it alone — let an attorney handle your divorce. (See Chapter 13 for more information about hiring a helpful divorce attorney.)

If you want specific help working out the financial aspects of your divorce but don't want to pay attorney-level prices for the assistance, you can consider hiring a *certified divorce planner* (CDP), who's a CPA or a certified financial planner that specializes in helping couples resolve the financial aspects of their divorces. A CDP will help you not only get the best settlement possible under the circumstances but will also recommend how to manage and invest the assets you end up with in your divorce so you can maximize your return on their value in the future. A CDP isn't a substitute for an attorney but is another player on your divorce team. In fact, CDPs and divorce attorneys often work hand in hand, especially when a couple owns a substantial amount of assets. Read the "Hiring a CDP to help you negotiate the financial stuff" sidebar in this chapter to find out more about the services that a CDP offers.

Exploring alternative ways to reach an agreement

Hiring attorneys to do the negotiating for you or turning your divorce over to a judge aren't the only ways to end up with a divorce agreement if you and your spouse don't want to do the negotiating on your own or if you're dead-locked on certain issues. Depending on the circumstances, you can also use mediation or the collaborative law process. Both options emphasize working things out in a civil manner and minimizing costs.

Getting to "yes" with mediation

When you and your spouse just can't see eye to eye on some of the issues in your divorce, mediation may be able to help you move forward. In mediation, a trained facilitator helps you hear what your spouse is saying, moves your negotiations forward, and provides you with a safe place to discuss the sticky issues in your divorce. The facilitator doesn't take sides or tell you or your spouse how to decide the issues in your divorce; instead, the facilitator helps you and your spouse arrive at a mutually acceptable solution to the issues that you're struggling with.

If you and your spouse are already working with attorneys, but you've reached a stalemate on certain issues, your attorneys may suggest that you and your spouse give mediation a try because it tends to be less stressful than a trial and a lot less expensive. If your mediation efforts are successful, the mediator puts everything you agreed to in writing and sends a copy to your attorney so he or she can review it. If mediation doesn't work, you and your spouse go back to the drawing board and continue working with your attorneys to figure out a resolution to your differences. You can also go to court and let a judge decide. Chapter 15 provides more information on mediation.

Capitalizing on the collaborative law process

The *collaborative law process* is a relatively new option for spouses to work out the terms of their divorce outside of court in a friendly, low-stress atmosphere with their attorneys' help. The collaborative process was the brain child of an attorney who was worn out by the adversarial nature of litigated divorces and wanted to find an easier way for attorneys to help their clients come to an agreement about the terms of their divorce. Texas was the first state to legalize the collaborative law process. Since then, 34 other states have followed suit.

Collaborative law involves you, your spouse, and your respective attorneys (who must be trained in the collaborative law process) sitting down together to negotiate, focusing on the future, not the past. Like mediation, collabora-tive law emphasizes problem-solving. However, unlike mediation, no neutral third party facilitates your discussions.

If the collaborative process breaks down, your attorneys may suggest that you and your spouse try mediation. But because collaborative law attorneys have pledged not to take a divorce case to trial, if you refuse mediation or if you give mediation a try and it doesn't work, and you decide that your only option is to go to trial, you and your spouse must hire new attorneys, which means that you go back to square one.

Here are some important benefits to using the collaborative law process:

- ✔ It costs less than a traditional divorce — especially one that ends in court.
- ✔ It's usually a faster way to reach an agreement on the terms of a divorce.
- ✔ It tends to be less stressful for everyone involved.
- ✔ It's apt to yield creative solutions to the issues in your divorce.
- ✔ It encourages cooperation between you and your spouse and helps build a positive foundation from which to build a post-divorce relationship, which is especially important if you have young children together.

Point, click, divorce

People are conducting more and more transactions on the Internet, so why not get divorced there, too? At least, that's what a growing number of dot.coms, state courts, and even attorneys are encouraging spouses to do, touting the ease of the process, the convenience of divorcing from the comfort of your own home, its speed, and its low cost. Although getting a divorce online is okay for the simplest of uncontested divorces — a couple that has no minor children and no significant assets or debts to divide up — it's not appropriate for more complicated divorces.

Here's how most divorce Web sites work: If you're the one initiating the divorce, select your state of residence and answer a series of questions related to your marriage and divorce. After you complete the questionnaire and pay a fee — usually about $200 — using a national bankcard like MasterCard or Visa, the site sends you your completed legal divorce documents. After you and your spouse sign them, one of you must file the paperwork with the court in your area

according to the instructions that accompany the paperwork.

Be sure that whichever do-your-own-divorce Web site you're using has clear directions for completing the forms. The site should also maintain a help line if you get confused. Also, look for an online divorce Web site that provides answers to frequently asked questions and links to other sites that provide information about relevant laws. Two of the most popular online divorce sites are www.completecase.com and www.legalzoom.com.

Critics of online divorces complain that such quickie divorces trivialize marriage. Others worry that some couples will get divorced without adequately considering the issues in their divorces and, as a result, experience problems later and regret that they didn't get a more traditional divorce with the help of an attorney. One way to avoid the potential for future problems is to consult an attorney before getting an online divorce to make certain that it's an appropriate option for your situation.

Assuming that your state recognizes the collaborative law process, you can find an attorney who uses this method by contacting your local or state bar association or by going online to find out whether your state has a collaborative law institute. If it does, the institute may provide referrals.

Understanding the Basic Issues in a Divorce

Regardless of which kind of divorce you file and which path your divorce goes down, you must resolve certain issues before your divorce can be final. (If you get a legal separation before you divorce, you must work out these same issues; see Chapter 4.) The basic issues are

- **How you will divide up your marital property and debts (see Chapter 8):** Complex laws, including state property laws, federal tax laws, plus the numerous interpretations of those laws, can make deciding who gets what a complicated undertaking, especially if you and your spouse have managed to amass a considerable amount of assets. If you have debt from your marriage, you and your spouse must also decide how the debts will get paid. You may decide, for example, to sell some of your marital assets and pay off debts with the proceeds, or one of you may agree to assume all or most of the debt in exchange for more assets.

- **Whether one spouse will pay spousal support (or alimony) to the other (see Chapter 9):** If one of you will pay spousal support, you must also decide how much the support payments will be and for how long they will continue. These days, a spouse rarely receives spousal support for life or until he or she remarries. Usually if spousal support gets paid, the payments continue long enough to let the spouse acquire some job skills or to rebuild his or her career.

- **How you and your spouse will handle child custody, visitation, and child support if you and your spouse have minor children from your marriage (see Chapters 10 and 11):** Decisions related to custody and visitation are some of the most contentious and emotional in a divorce, especially when couples try to use their children as a means of getting back at one another. Although how much one spouse will have to pay the other in child support can also be a highly emotional issue, state child-support guidelines dictate the minimum amount of payment.

When deciding the issues in your divorce, certain state laws and guidelines apply to provide a framework for your decision-making. However, these laws and guidelines also allow a considerable amount of flexibility in your decision-making, though they have some limits. When making decisions about the terms of your divorce, assuming that a family law judge is looking over your shoulder is best. What we mean is that whatever you decide should be fair to you and your spouse given the laws of your state and should reflect an appreciation of what a judge would probably decide if your divorce was to end in a trial.

So What's All This Going to Cost You?

Almost as soon as your divorce begins, one thing will become painfully clear — that divorce is all about dollars and cents. In fact, the thousands of dollars you probably spent on your wedding and honeymoon may be a mere drop in the bucket compared with what your divorce could end up costing you.

Ordinarily, both parties in a divorce pay their own legal and court costs; however, you can request that your spouse reimburse you for all or a portion of your divorce-related expenses. It never hurts to ask, especially if you feel you have a strong argument for why your spouse should pay. For example, your spouse makes a lot more money than you do or your marriage is ending because your spouse was unfaithful. Whether your spouse agrees to pay your legal and court costs depends on how amicable your divorce is, his or her own financial resources, and whether your spouse thinks your request is reasonable, among other things.

The deciding factors

Exactly how much you spend to end your marriage depends on a number of factors:

- **Whether your divorce is amicable and cooperative or bitter and contentious:** The more you and your spouse agree on, the less you have to spend on attorneys, legal fees, and court costs.

- **The cost of the attorney you hire to help with your divorce:** Chapter 13 reviews the key factors that influence how much you will spend on an attorney.

- **How many divorce decisions you and your spouse are able to work out together without the involvement of your attorneys:** The more issues in your divorce you can resolve together without your attorneys' help, the less your divorce will cost.

- **Whether you and your spouse end up in a custody battle, which can be very expensive:** For example, in a custody battle, you may have to pay for the assistance of a social worker, a child psychologist, and other experts.

- **The amount of marital property and debts that you have to divide up and their complexity:** Depending on the debts and assets involved, you may need to hire a real estate appraiser, art appraiser, CPA, pension expert, or other professionals to help determine a fair property settlement.

- **Whether you believe that your spouse is hiding any of your marital assets:** If you believe that your spouse is hiding assets, you will have to hire financial experts to try to determine what has happened to them, and that help doesn't come cheap.

  ✔ **Whether you and your spouse are willing to settle your divorce out-side of court or whether one or both of you is determined to go to trial:** If you end up in divorce court, you can expect to pay substantially more to your attorney, not to mention the fees of any experts you may call to testify on your behalf, the court reporter's fees, court fees, and a whole lot more.

  ✔ **The legal strategy of your attorney and your spouse's attorney:** If either of your attorneys employs an aggressive, adversarial strategy, the cost of your divorce is apt to skyrocket because your divorce will take up more of your attorney's time. Your attorney also is likely to file more legal motions and call more expert witnesses to testify, which adds more onto the price tag of your divorce. However, you and your spouse control the strategy that your respective attorneys use by carefully screening potential attorneys to find ones who aren't attack dogs.

The least it will cost

If your divorce is extremely simple — meaning you and your spouse have little or nothing to negotiate, no minor children, no marital property, few debts, neither of you is asking for spousal support, and you're both willing to complete most, if not all, of the legal paperwork yourselves — you can get divorced for just a few hundred dollars, maybe even less, if you don't use an attorney.

Even if you own some marital property or have some debt from your marriage, your divorce may cost you no more than a few thousand dollars, assuming that you and your spouse can work out the terms of your divorce together after an upfront consultation with your individual attorneys. Your attorneys should also review your final agreement. Chapter 12 provides helpful information if you and your spouse want to do most of your negotiating.

The most it will cost

Be prepared to spend a whole lot of money on your divorce if you and your spouse fight like cats and dogs, are unwilling to give and take, or if the issues in your divorce are complicated and the active involvement of your attorneys from start to finish is essential. In this case, you may be looking at legal bills in the five figures — or even more. For example, at the end of a prolonged child-support battle, your legal bills can easily be $50,000 because your divorce will involve a lot of fact-finding, which causes your legal bills to escalate. If you and your spouse end up in court over the custody of your children, those bills can *triple!* Yikes!

The hourly rate of an experienced family law attorney ranges from $150 to $500 or more. If you hire an attorney, you have to pay a down payment, sometimes called a *retainer,* that's likely to be between $500 and $10,000, depending on the attorney's hourly rate.

Surviving the Emotional Roller Coaster

Despite the fact that you may know that getting divorced is the right thing for you and everyone else involved and, even if your divorce is amicable, assuming that you're not made of stone, you will almost inevitably experience a range of emotions as you move through the divorce process. You will probably experience a variety of emotions including shock, disappointment, regret, sadness, anger, depression, and fear, among other feelings. This mix of emotions should come as no surprise given that you're ending an important relationship in your life (see Chapter 7).

Having an idea of what's ahead and putting an emotional support system in place can help you get through the tough times ahead. Your support system may include close and trusted friends and/or relatives, your religious advisor, and a mental health professional.

Consulting a therapist as soon as you know that you're getting a divorce (if not before) is a good idea so that he or she can provide you with ongoing emotional support and advice. Alternatively, you may want to consult a therapist only when you're having a particularly difficult time with a specific problem.

Controlling your emotions so you can stay on an even emotional keel is critical when you're going through a divorce. If you don't keep your emotions under control, making wise decisions about matters that can affect your financial well-being and happiness and that of your children for years to come can become difficult. Although letting your emotions take over and allowing yourself to express your anger and to say hurtful things to your spouse or trying to extract revenge from him or her because your marriage is ending may be tempting, in the end, that approach is apt to backfire and likely to hurt everyone involved, not just your spouse.

In addition to establishing a support system and getting therapy, here are some other things you can do to help yourself stay emotionally balanced before, during, and after your divorce

- Keep a journal
- Exercise
- Take up meditation
- Begin practicing yoga
- Pursue a hobby you enjoy

Divorce can be hard on kids, too. Don't directly involve your children in your divorce — for instance, by fighting about the terms of your divorce with your spouse in front of them, by bad-mouthing your spouse to them, and so on. And don't involve them indirectly, either, by crying in front of them, by not doing the things that you've always done for your children while the terms of your divorce are being negotiated, and so on.

Although your divorce will certainly affect your children, your responsibility is to protect them as much as possible, to keep their lives as normal as you can, not to scare them, and to reassure them that you and their other parent will continue to love them after your divorce and that you and their other parent will continue to be involved in their lives. You do a grave injustice to your children if you don't give them the sense of security that every child needs, especially when his or her family life is falling apart and if you don't stay actively involved in their lives despite the distractions of your divorce. Doing everything you can to shield them from the emotions that you're feeling is critical.

Despite your best efforts to protect your children, they may begin to experience emotional problems during and after your divorce. Exactly how they express their problems depends on their ages and individual personalities; problems can range from bedwetting and temper tantrums to depression, problems in school, defiant behavior at home, among other behaviors. If you're unsure how to respond to your child, read some books about children and divorce, talk to your child's teacher or counselor, or consult a mental health professional. You may also want to consider scheduling time for your child with a child therapist. For more details on how to help your children cope with your divorce, see Chapters 6 and 21.

Chapter 2

Considering Divorce Alternatives

- -

In This Chapter

▶ Working out your problems to avoid a divorce

▶ Separating

▶ Annulling your marriage

- -

Marriages rarely die overnight. Almost always, they die little by little over time. Ideally, if serious problems begin to develop in your marriage, you and your spouse can work through them before they harm your relationship so that you can stay together. However, if you and your spouse are unable to work things out, or if you don't even want to try to save your marriage, you must decide what to do about your relationship. Although divorce is the option that many couples pursue when their marriage falls apart, it isn't the only option. Some couples decide to stay married despite their troubles — maybe until their kids move out of the house — whereas others separate rather than divorce or, under certain conditions, have their marriages annulled.

When you have marriage problems, the sooner you acknowledge them and decide what to do about them, the better. Pretending that they don't exist doesn't make the problems go away. In fact, the problems will more than likely grow worse. Furthermore, if a divorce or legal separation is in the cards, the sooner you acknowledge that your marriage is on the rocks, the better prepared you'll be for what's to come, both emotionally and financially.

This chapter highlights the nondivorce options that you have for dealing with your relationship problems. Just knowing that you have choices can be reassuring and helpful. This chapter also addresses steps that you can take if the pressures in your troubled relationship cause your spouse to turn violent, because it isn't uncommon for violence to accompany serious marital problems.

The Old-fashioned Alternative — Sticking It Out

The pressure (whether societal, religious, or economic) to stay married used to be so great that when a couple's marriage failed, divorce was almost inconceivable, no matter how miserable the couple may have been. Although times and attitudes about marriage have changed, many of today's couples also opt to stay married after their relationships have failed. They may have young children and feel that raising them in a two-parent household is important or they may not be able to afford to get a divorce right away. Some couples experience implicit or explicit pressures from their family, friends, or church to stay together, whereas other couples come to an understanding that allows them to lead separate lives but remain under the same roof. Finally, some couples don't divorce because they're afraid of what life will be like if they were single again; fear of the unknown may motivate them to tolerate a situation that would be unbearable to others.

If you decide to stay in your marriage, you have two basic options: You can try to improve your relationship or you can grit your teeth, shut down your feelings, and grin and bear it by putting up with things the way they are. The first alternative is almost always the better choice. Three options for improving your marriage include taking a short break from one another, getting marriage counseling, and trying mediation, which we discuss in the following sections. None of these alternatives are mutually exclusive, so you may want to give them all a try.

If your home is full of tension and anger because of your marital problems, you may be doing your children more harm than good by staying together. Also, if your spouse threatens to physically harm you or has already harmed you or your children, at the very least, separate and give your spouse an opportunity to get professional help. If you're fearful that leaving may trigger violent behavior in your spouse, contact your local domestic abuse shelter or the National Domestic Violence Hotline (800-799-7233; if you're hearing impaired, call 800-787-3224) for help in developing a safety plan. Also, the end of this chapter provides additional advice about how to protect yourself.

Taking a short break from each other

Sometimes what you really need when you just can't get along with your spouse and when your emotions are running high is a short time apart — a day or two, a long weekend, maybe even a vacation on your own. At the end of your time apart, you may have a whole new attitude toward your relationship and a renewed commitment to it.

Use the time apart to calm your emotions, assess your situation, and put your marital problems in perspective. Try to assess why you're not getting along and your role in those difficulties. Analyze the kind of arguments you've been having — what you tended to argue about, how often you argued, and when — to determine whether any patterns emerge. Think about whether your problems stem from the fact that you've grown apart and/or whether they exist because of things one of you did to the other that caused you to lose trust in the other or to feel hurt and misunderstood. Ask yourself if your marital problems developed because you stopped giving your spouse enough attention and affection. Think about the complaints you have both voiced about the other and try to decide whether they're truly valid. Also, try to identify the changes that you'd need to make to save your marriage and the changes you would want your spouse to make. Then think about whether you and your spouse are capable of making those changes and are willing to make them.

Don't use the vacation time to go on shopping sprees or to merely entertain yourself by going out at night and spending time with friends. Also, avoid short romantic flings and don't try to forget your troubles by using drugs or alcohol. If you spend your time apart with a close friend or family member, choose that person carefully. Avoid anyone who doesn't like your spouse or resents your marriage. If you look for advice from that person, he or she must be impartial and have good judgment.

Spending even a short period of time apart when your marriage is floundering can give both of you an opportunity to clear your heads and examine how you feel about one another and your marriage. You may both conclude that you're committed to your relationship and really want to save it. On the other hand, after removing yourselves from the emotional stresses and strains of living together, one or both of you may decide that you want to make living apart a permanent thing.

If you would like to try to save your marriage, take a look at *Divorce Remedy: The Proven 7-Step Program for Saving Your Marriage* by Michelle Weiner Davis (Simon & Schuster).

Getting marriage counseling

Saving your marriage may require more than taking a break from your spouse. (If only it were that easy!) The two of you may need to work with a therapist to get help improving your communication so you can begin a productive dialogue about what has gone wrong in your relationship, why, and what you can do to improve things. You may need to learn whole new ways of relating to one another as well. Also, if one of you was unfaithful to the other or did something else that damaged the trust you used to have in one another, you may need counseling to rebuild your lost trust. However, when your marriage is in serious trouble, your emotions can run so high that a calm, rational discussion to identify the roots of your marital problems and what to do about them can be next to impossible. Instead, you may withdraw from each other to nurse your wounds in silence or argue constantly.

When your marriage has derailed, one option to help get it back on track is to seek the help of a trusted and experienced therapist, marriage counselor, or religious advisor. The right advisor creates an environment that promotes discussion and mutual understanding. He or she can also offer insights into your problems, help you and your spouse come to agreements about what to do about those problems, and even teach you new marriage skills.

If you decide to consult a marriage counselor, choose your counselor carefully. Although nearly all states require marriage counselors to be licensed, licensing requirement standards for education and experience vary by state. Therefore, just because a marriage counselor is licensed by your state, don't assume that he or she has the experience and training necessary to help you make sense of your marriage and decide what to do about the relationship. See the "Finding a qualified marriage counselor" sidebar for advice on locating a counselor that's right for you and your spouse.

If money is an issue for you, check your local phone book to see whether or not a Family and Child Services, Inc., office is nearby. This nonprofit organization offers counseling on a sliding-fee scale for couples, families, and individuals.

If your spouse won't go with you to talk to a marriage counselor or a religious advisor, go by yourself. You may discover things about yourself as well as new relationship skills that can improve your current marriage or prepare you for a happier marriage in the future.

Couples helping couples save their marriages

Some couples with troubled marriages find participating in a marriage-enrichment program that involves working with other married couples that are trained to help strengthen marriages helpful. The Association for Couples in Marriage Enrichment (ACME), an international, nonprofit, nonsectarian organization, runs such a program. Go to ACME's Web site (www.better marriages.org) or call ACME at 800-634-8325 to find out more about the organization and its marriage program and to locate a local chapter in your area.

Another option is Marriage Enrichment, Inc., a nonprofit Christian organization, that sponsors workshops intended to improve communication between married couples. The workshops are conducted in cooperation with local churches and other organizations. To find out more about Marriage Enrichment or to contact the organization, go to www.marriageenrichment.org.

Your spouse's unwillingness to attend marriage counseling sessions with you may signal that he or she is no longer committed to your marriage or it may mean that your spouse simply doesn't believe in using counselors to solve problems. Try to talk with your spouse about why he or she won't get counseling and if there are any circumstances under which your spouse would talk with a therapist or religious advisor about your marriage. If your spouse is adamant about not getting counseling and offers no good alternatives, you probably need to face facts and recognize that your marriage is over.

Looking into mediation

Mediation involves a trained mediator who encourages you and your spouse to calmly discuss your problems and helps you work together to identify mutually acceptable solutions. The mediator doesn't take sides, interject opinions, or find a solution for you. In mediation, you and your spouse have an opportunity to give each of your opinions and to explain each side of the issue. When one of you is talking, the other listens without interrupting and remains calm and focused on the subject at hand. If your mediation session (or sessions) is successful, you and your spouse may end up with a written contract that you've negotiated that spells out the new terms of your relationship. (For more on the subject of mediation, turn to Chapter 15.)

Mediation has a couple of other advantages, too. Mediation can be a good way to address very specific problems that play havoc with your marriage. Maybe those problems include arguments over who should do which household chores or how to share child-care responsibilities. But mediation is *not* appropriate if your marriage has a host of problems or if your problems are emotionally complex.

Another important advantage of mediation is its low cost. A mediation session is relatively inexpensive and is considerably cheaper than a divorce.

But mediation isn't a substitute for therapy. In fact, you may need to spend some time in therapy by yourself or with your spouse before you can use mediation successfully. Therapy can help you get a handle on the emotions that can derail mediation and can help you come to terms with the end of your marriage so you can discuss the practical aspects of getting a divorce.

Mediation is about mutual understanding, cooperation, and problem-solving; it's not about winning. But like the tango, mediation takes two. So, if one of you is unwilling to give mediation a try, it's not a viable option for your marriage.

To find a mediator who's experienced in helping couples resolve marriage-related issues, look in the business pages in the phone book under "Mediation" or contact the Association for Conflict Resolution, which can provide you with information about mediating marital problems and refer you to family mediators in your area. You can call the association at 202-464-9700 or go to www.mediate.com/acrfamily to browse its mediator referral list. The names on the list have met the association's standards, which include at least two years of family mediation experience and a minimum of 60 hours of family mediation training.

When Living Apart Is a Better Option

Living together while you try to resolve your marital differences and save your marriage may be an unrealistic option for some people. Instead, you may decide to separate or live apart for a while or you may decide to separate permanently with no intention of divorcing. (Chapter 4 discusses separations in detail, including the legal issues and financial considerations you should bear in mind before you separate.)

Separating can provide you with an opportunity to find out what living in separate residences is really like. Meanwhile, the door is still open for you to get back together. On the other hand, separation can also be a prelude to divorce or a permanent alternative to divorce.

Before you separate for even a relatively short period of time, protect yourself by talking with a family law attorney, especially if you want spousal or child support. In addition, the attorney can warn you about anything that you can do that may jeopardize your standing in a divorce if your marriage ends. For example, dating others while you're separated usually isn't a good idea because you can leave yourself open to charges of adultery.

You can opt for either of two types of separation — an *informal separation* or a *legal separation*.

- ✔ Couples who separate informally simply begin living apart. This option may be appropriate if you and your spouse clearly anticipate that your separation is temporary and that you'll eventually reconcile.

- ✔ If you view your separation as the first step toward a divorce and have no plans for reconciliation or you intend to live apart without any plans to divorce, then a legal separation formalized with a legally binding separation agreement is best. A legal separation can be a court-ordered arrangement or one that you and your spouse agree to in writing.

In some states, if you and your spouse decide to divorce, depending on the grounds for your divorce, you may have to live apart from one another for a certain period of time first, usually from six months to a year.

A legal separation is often preferable for the following financial and legal reasons:

- ✔ You formalize the terms of your separation, including whether or not one of you will help support the other financially while you're living apart; how you will deal with the issues of custody, visitation, and child support if you and your spouse share minor children; and how you will divide up the property that you own together.

- ✔ Having everything spelled out minimizes the potential for conflict while you're separated.

- ✔ If one of you reneges on the terms of your separation agreement, getting the court's help to enforce that issue will be easier.

- ✔ You and your spouse will have fewer issues to decide if you eventually decide to get a divorce.

While you're married and going through a divorce, even if you're separated, you and your spouse can file a joint tax return or individual returns. You and your spouse should talk to a CPA about what's best and what to do about any deductions you may be eligible for.

If divorce isn't an option for you because of religious, financial, or even health insurance considerations, you can opt for a permanent legal separation. A legal separation means that you're still married, but you're no longer living together. If you decide to legally separate, formalizing your new living arrangement with a written separation agreement is important. Like a divorce agreement, a separation agreement addresses the division of your marital property, child custody, child support, and spousal support, as appropriate. The process for preparing such an agreement is similar to what you'd do if you were getting divorced. For example, you and your spouse can work together to negotiate the terms of your separation or you can both hire divorce attorneys to help you negotiate your agreement or to represent you before a judge who will decide the terms of your separation for you.

If you and your spouse work out the terms of your separation together without the help of attorneys, be sure to file an order with the court for the judge to sign. The order will set out all the terms of your separation. Then, if your spouse fails to do what he or she agreed to do in your separation agreement, you can go to court to get the agreement enforced. Court enforcement is especially important if your separation agreement provides you with spousal support and/or child support.

Getting an Annulment

An *annulment* is a court action that voids your marriage and proclaims that it was never legally valid in the first place. It's like the marriage never happened. Annulments were a much more common option when getting divorced had more of a social stigma attached to it.

But legal annulments and religious annulments are two different animals. In some religions, if you divorce and want to remarry, your religion won't recognize your new marriage unless your old marriage is annulled. Religious annulments are most commonly associated with the Roman Catholic faith (see the "Securing a religious annulment" sidebar for more information about the religious annulment process). If you get a religious annulment, you don't have a legal annulment, and vice versa.

Legal annulments are available in most states, but the process for obtaining one varies. To get a legal annulment, you have to go by the criteria established by your state to prove to the court that your marriage is legally invalid. People usually can obtain legal annulments shortly after the start of a marriage.

The most common criteria for a legal annulment include the following:

- Your spouse lied to you or misled you in some way and, had you known the truth, you would not have gotten married. For example, you want a family, but your spouse never told you that he is impotent, or your spouse never told you that he or she had a criminal record or has a sexually transmitted disease.

- Your spouse refused to consummate your marriage.

- At the time of your marriage, your spouse was already married.

- Your spouse was not a legal adult when you got married.

- You were forced into marriage.

- Either or both of you were under the influence of alcohol or drugs at the time of the marriage.

An annulment voids your marriage but, if you have young children from that relationship, an annulment doesn't modify or cancel your parental responsibilities to your children in any way.

Securing a religious annulment

If you're a divorced Catholic and want to remarry in the Catholic Church, you must obtain an annulment. Although the annulment process differs somewhat from church diocese to diocese, here's an overview of the basic process:

✔ First, you must complete an application for an annulment. You can obtain this application at any local parish within your church diocese. The priest or a layperson at the church can help you complete it.

✔ After you complete the application, a marriage tribunal (a church court usually composed of at least three judges assisted by outside experts) meets with you to talk about your personal background, courtship, the problems in your marriage, the reasons for your divorce, and your life after divorce. (Rather than meeting with you, the tribunal may ask you to provide this information by completing a written questionnaire.)

✔ You have to provide the names of witnesses who can talk about your courtship and marriage. The tribunal may interview them about

these things or ask them to complete written questionnaires.

✔ You have to provide the tribunal with certified copies of your marriage license, divorce decree, baptismal certificate, and other documents related to your annulment request.

✔ The tribunal office notifies your former spouse that you're seeking an annulment. He or she has the right to provide proof that no grounds exist for invalidating your marriage.

✔ After reviewing all the evidence, the tribunal determines whether, according to church policy, you have grounds for an annulment. If the tribunal doesn't grant your request, you can appeal its decision. If you lose your appeal, you can take your request to the Vatican in Rome.

An annulment can take anywhere from eight months to several years. Just how long it takes depends on your diocese, the degree to which your witnesses cooperate, and how quickly you provide all the information that the tribunal requests.

Chapter 3

Preparing Financially

- -

In This Chapter

▶ Familiarizing yourself with your family's debts and assets

▶ Getting a financial education

▶ Updating your job skills

▶ Building positive credit in your name

- -

*N*o matter your sex, age, or personal situation, preparing not only for the possibility that your marriage may end in divorce (about 50 percent of them do), but also for the financial consequences that the breakup of your marriage can bring, makes sense. At a minimum, your preparation should include

✔ Familiarizing yourself with your family's finances

✔ Learning how to manage your money

✔ Building and maintaining a positive credit history in your own name

✔ Building and maintaining marketable job skills

If you aren't up to speed on your family's financial situation or if your credit history or job skills are lacking, this chapter can help. If you think that a divorce may be in your future, the sooner you act on the advice in this chapter, the better prepared you'll be, both financially and legally, for life on your own.

Taking care of yourself when it comes to your finances isn't selfish. When you take care of yourself, you gain the confidence and the resources — both inner and financial — to look out for yourself (and your kids) if your marriage ends.

Getting Smart about Your Family's Finances

Relying on your spouse to pay your household bills, to reconcile your checkbook, to make investment decisions, and so forth isn't a good idea. At the very least, you should know

- How much money comes into your household every month and how much goes out
- Who you owe money to and the total amount of each debt
- Your monthly living expenses
- How much money is in your checking and your savings accounts
- What sources of cash are available for you and your spouse in the event of an emergency
- What assets you and your spouse own
- Where your money is invested

If you review this list of financial-ought-to-knows and come up lacking, don't panic. You can find out what you need to know about your family's financial situation in several ways. If you and your spouse have an amicable relationship despite the fact that you are divorcing, ask him or her to sit down and explain your family's finances to you — what you own and what you owe, how your assets are titled, what kind of insurance you have, and so on. Also ask your spouse to show you where key documents and other important records are kept and have him or her answer your questions.

If you and your spouse are no longer on speaking terms, becoming fully informed about your family's finances may be somewhat of a challenge. If you know where your family's financial records are located and you have access to them, make copies of that information. Also, talk with your family's financial advisors if you know who they are. They may include a CPA, a banker, and a financial advisor and/or broker. And don't overlook information stored on your home computer; many families use personal finance software to help manage their money.

If you're able to locate little or none of your family's financial information, you will probably need a divorce attorney to help you obtain it using the discovery process. Chapter 16 describes how this process works.

Taking inventory

Taking inventory of your family's financial situation gives you a good idea of your overall state of financial well-being. You need to find out not only what you own, but also what you owe. The section "And now for a quick lesson in property law," later in this chapter, explains how your assets and debts get divided during a divorce.

What you own

You don't have to be a CPA or a math whiz to figure out your family's financial worth. Use a notebook or your computer to list the following financial information:

✔ Your total household income and the sources of that income.

✔ The checking and savings account numbers that you, your spouse, and the bank(s) use.

✔ Your family's significant assets. An *asset* is a thing of value, such as cash, vehicles, or art. Depending on the type of assets you have, you can use them to purchase something, sell them, or use them as collateral or to secure a loan. To help figure your family's financial worth, estimate the market value of each asset. *Market value* is what an asset is worth now — what you could sell it for, not what you bought it for. Assets can be tangible (like your car and house) or intangible (like stocks and mutual funds) and may include

- Brokerage accounts, including stocks, bonds, and mutual funds

- Business interests

- Cash

- Certificates of deposit (CDs)

- Deferred compensation plans, including IRAs, SEPs, 401ks, stock options, and profit-sharing plans

- Fine art, antiques, and other collectibles

- Fine jewelry

- Household furnishings

- Money market accounts

- The cash value of your life insurance policy

- Vehicles (including recreational vehicles, such as boats, Jet skis, motorcycles, and snowmobiles)

- Your home and other real estate

Joint property and your rights to it

You can own joint assets in a number of ways. How you own your assets affects your legal rights to those assets when your property has to be divided.

- **Joint tenancy with the right of survivorship:** If your spouse dies, his or her share automatically goes to you, no matter what your spouse's will or trust says, and vice versa.

- **Tenancy by the entirety:** This form of ownership is similar to joint tenancy, but only spouses can own property this way. In other words, unlike joint tenancy with the right of survivorship, you and another relative, a friend, and so on cannot own property as *tenants by the entirety.*

- **Tenancy in common:** You have no legal claim to your spouse's share of the asset and vice versa. Therefore, your spouse can do what he or she wants with his or her share of the asset — give it away, sell it, trade it, use it to collateralize or secure a loan, or encumber it with some sort of claim.

- **Community property:** Only certain states permit this kind of joint ownership. In those states, each of you has an undivided ½ interest in the property you acquire and the income you earn during your marriage, no matter whose name is on the ownership papers or who earns the most money.

You should know whether each asset is a *joint asset* — that is, one you and your spouse own together — or an *individual asset*. In addition, know how your joint assets are titled or deeded; they can be joint tenancy with right of survivorship, tenancy by the entirety, tenancy in common, or community property (which we describe in the sidebar "Joint property and your rights to it," later in this chapter).

Usually, any assets owned by you and your spouse are best off being in both your names. However, circumstances may arise when joint ownership may not be a good idea. If you have questions about the best way to own a particular asset, consult your CPA.

To make certain that your inventory list is comprehensive, look through your home safe and bank safe-deposit box for titles to property, deeds, securities, wills, or other documents related to your ownership of property. Also, recent loan applications should also provide much, if not all, of the information that you need about your assets.

What you owe

Your family's financial portrait is only half-finished until you inventory and value your household debts, which may include

- Credit card debts
- Home equity loans or balances on home equity lines of credit

✔ Mortgages

✔ Notes you or your spouse may have cosigned

✔ Other types of personal loans, including car loans, student loans, and business loans for which you or your spouse is personally liable

Next to each debt, note whether it's *secured* or *unsecured.* If a debt is secured, note which asset secures the debt. For example, your home secures your mortgage and your car secures your vehicle loan. When one of your debts is secured, the creditor is entitled to take the asset that secures the debt if you don't pay the debt according to the terms of your loan agreement. For example, if you fall behind on your mortgage, the lender is legally entitled to *foreclose* on your home, or take it from you.

The documents you need

In order to create as complete and as accurate an inventory of your assets and debts as possible, you need to refer to a variety of financial and legal documents in addition to your checking and savings account registers and bank statements. Those documents include

✔ Copies of your tax returns for the past five years

If you don't know where your family's tax returns are filed and your spouse won't tell you, you can obtain copies by writing the IRS, assuming that you filed joint returns. The IRS has a Web site where you can download federal tax forms and publications, check on the status of your tax refund, and find out how to contact the IRS Taxpayer Assistance Center nearest you. Check out www.irs.ustreas.gov. Your family's CPA should also be able to provide you with copies of your tax returns, assuming that he or she prepared your tax returns.

✔ Real estate tax bills

✔ Copies of all life insurance policies that list you or your spouse as the owner or a primary or contingent beneficiary

✔ Account statements for your stocks, bonds, mutual funds, and other investments

✔ Copies of any financial statements you prepared separately or together when you applied for a loan

✔ A copy of your will, your spouse's will, and any other estate-planning documents that you may have prepared, such as a living trust agreement

✔ Profit-and-loss statements and balance sheets for the business that you, your spouse, or both of you own and copies of related partnership agreements or articles of incorporation

✔ Copies of any prenuptial or postnuptial agreements you may have signed

If you hire an attorney to help negotiate your divorce, your attorney needs all this information. The more you and your spouse willingly share with your respective attorneys, the less information the attorneys need to obtain through the formal discovery process — and the more money you save. (We tell you about discovery in Chapters 14 and 16.) Making copies of all the documents you pull together on your own is a good idea, just in case your spouse takes the originals.

Other things you should know about your family's finances

Besides all the financial information this chapter has already indicated that you should have, you still need some other information before you can claim to be fully informed about your family's finances and ready for whatever may happen to your marriage. That other information includes

- ✔ Which bills are regularly paid online and the user name and password for each account.

- ✔ What your Equifax, Experian, and TransUnion credit histories say about you and your spouse. These three national companies dominate the credit-reporting industry in the United States. The "Building a Positive Credit History" section, later in this chapter, tells you how to order copies of your credit histories.

- ✔ The names, street addresses, e-mail addresses, and phone numbers of your family's CPA, banker, attorney, financial advisor, and stockbroker.

- ✔ Where financial and legal documents important to your family are stored, including bank records; tax returns; wills and other estate-planning documents; titles and deeds; loan agreements; insurance policies; documentation pertaining to any IRAs, stocks, bonds, and mutual funds that you or your spouse may own; and the paperwork related to your and your spouse's retirement plans.

And now for a quick lesson in property law

When you get divorced, your state's property laws entitle you and your spouse to a share of the assets that you acquired together or separately during your marriage and to a share of the income that you both earned while you were married. Together those assets and income make up your *marital property*. Exactly how your marital property eventually gets divided depends, in part, on whether you live in an equitable distribution state or a community property state (we distinguish between these two types in the following sections).

Share and share alike

If you live in a *community property* state, each of you owns an undivided ½ interest in the value of your marital property, regardless of whether your income alone purchased most of what you own, whether your spouse made significantly more than you did, or whether your spouse stayed home to care for your young children throughout your marriage. However, in a divorce, a judge can order that you receive more or less than your ½ interest (see the next section "Everything is relative when it comes to fairness"). You and your spouse can agree to something different, too.

Most states are equitable distribution states, except for the following nine, which are community property states:

Arizona	New Mexico
California	Texas
Idaho	Washington
Louisiana	Wisconsin
Nevada	

If you live in a community property state, a creditor has the right to collect from your share of your marital property if your spouse fails to pay on the debts that he or she acquired during your marriage.

Everything is relative when it comes to fairness

Equitable distribution states use the concept of "what is fair" to decide how a couple's marital property and debts should be divided between them when they get divorced. "What is fair" varies from divorce to divorce, although each equitable distribution state uses certain criteria to guide the division. The most-common criteria include

- How much each of you earns and could earn in the future
- Your current standard of living
- The value of the separate property each of you may own and the value of your marital property
- The contribution each of you made to your marriage (by the way, being a full-time homemaker or stay-at-home parent has financial value)
- The employee benefits to which each of you may be entitled
- The length of your marriage
- Your age and health
- Whether or not you have children from your marriage who are *minors* (children under the age of 18 or 21, depending on the state you live in) and your custody arrangements for those children

Factors that may influence the division of your marital property

A variety of factors may come into play when you and your spouse or a judge is deciding what marital property you're entitled to and what property your spouse will get. Whether or not some of these factors apply to your divorce may depend on whether you live in a community property or an equitable distribution state. Here are a few of the factors that may apply to your divorce:

✔ If your divorce is a fault divorce, judges in some states take that fact into consideration when deciding how your marital property and debt will be split between you and your spouse. Those states that do consider fault penalize the spouse at fault.

Judges in community property states may use these same factors in determining whether divorcing spouses should leave their marriage with more or less than their presumptive ½ share of their marital property.

✔ If you and your spouse acquire property while living in a community property state and then move to an equitable distribution state, the property you take with you from the first state to the second is considered community property and is treated as such in your divorce. The opposite is true if you move from an equitable distribution state to a community property state. Obviously, the more often you move among equitable distribution and community property states during your marriage and the more assets you acquire in each of those states, the more complicated negotiating your property settlement agreement is if you divorce.

✔ In some equitable distribution states, a spouse's contribution to the end of a marriage plays a role in determining how a couple's marital property is divided between them. For example, if your marriage ended because you committed adultery, the judge may give you less marital property than you're entitled to according to your state's property law.

✔ Community and equitable distribution states treat inheritances and gifts a spouse received during marriage separate from marital property. Also, any property you bring to your marriage is considered separate property, too. How a court treats a personal injury cash settlement in a divorce depends on the state; some view the money as separate property and others don't.

✔ If you *commingle* property (meaning that you mix your separate property with your spouse's or you mix your separate property with marital property), you can unwittingly convert it to marital property. For example, you and your spouse open a joint bank account and deposit your separate funds into the account. You've now commingled your funds.

Managing your financial future

Many low-cost and even no-cost sources of information and help are available if you want to improve your financial skills and know-how so that you can become a more confident and competent money manager. In this section, we highlight some of those resources.

Money management and personal investment classes are a good resource for increasing your financial skills and knowledge. Your local college or university may offer such classes for little cost. Also, many investment companies and financial advisors offer investment seminars as a way to attract new clients or to develop additional business from their current client base. These seminars are usually free, and you don't have to purchase anything. However, sometimes these advisors assume that their audience has a better-than-average knowledge of investing, not to mention better-than-average money to invest.

Another possible source of financial education is a nonprofit credit counseling office that's affiliated with the National Foundation for Credit Counseling (NFCC), most of which are known as a Consumer Credit Counseling Service (CCCS). These organizations offer low-cost to no-cost money management classes, including classes on how to develop and use a budget. If you don't find a listing for a CCCS office in your local phone directory, go to the NFCC's Web site (www.nfcc.org) or call 800-388-2227 for the name and contact information for the NFCC-affiliated credit counseling agency nearest you.

If you can't find a financial education class that fits your needs, ask your family banker, CPA, broker, or financial advisor for a referral to a class.

Magazines such as *Money* and *Kiplinger's Personal Finance Magazine* offer solid, easy-to-understand financial information and advice on a wide variety of consumer-related subjects. Although you won't become another Warren Buffett just by reading an issue or two, over time, you can increase your consumer IQ about subjects like choosing a bank card, buying stocks and mutual funds, living on a budget, buying a car, purchasing real estate, and avoiding consumer scams.

Bookstores are another financial education resource. Their shelves are overflowing with books about personal finance and investing. Even if you're a financial neophyte, you can find many books written for people just like you. We don't mean to be self-serving, but *Personal Finance For Dummies,* 4th Edition, by Eric Tyson (Wiley) is a darn good book. We also recommend *Talking Money: Everything You Need to Know About Your Finances and Your Future* by Jean Chatzky (Warner Business Books) and *The Savage Truth About Money* by Terry Savage (Wiley).

You can also find a good bit of money-management information and advice on television. For example, every network morning show seems to feature a regular segment on personal finance topics, and CNNfn and CNBC also devote airtime to personal finance and investment topics.

If you prefer getting your financial education by staring at a computer screen instead of a TV, many excellent Web sites offer information on personal finance issues. Here are a few great sites you can check out:

- ✔ Bankrate.com: This site offers a wide variety of information on nearly every aspect of financial management, from choosing a credit card, paying down debt, buying a home, and getting a mortgage to information on insurance, investing, taxes, and much more. Subscribe to Bankrate.com's free online newsletter to discover something new about personal finance every week.

- ✔ CBSMarketwatch.com: If you go to this Web site, click on Personal Finance to discover a wealth of practical, easy-to-understand information on investing, life and money, retirement, and real estate. While you're there, sign up for a free newsletter.

- ✔ MoneyCentral.msn.com: At this site, you can read stories about the main financial news of the day and peruse articles and special reports on money-related topics, among other things.

- ✔ www.finpipe.com: The Financial Pipeline Web site is "dedicated to financial education and understanding." Here you find information about retirement planning, buying and selling real estate, devising an investment strategy, and more.

- ✔ www.consumerworld.org: This public service, noncommercial site offers more than 2,000 useful consumer resources.

- ✔ www.ftc.gov: The Federal Trade Commission (FTC) publishes numerous easy-to-understand publications to help everyday people understand their legal rights on spending money and using credit. You can download text or PDF versions of its publications by going to this Web site.

- ✔ www.gsa.gov/money: The Federal Consumer Information Center is another federal government resource you can check out. It features links to countless brochures and fact sheets on a wide variety of financial topics, including getting and using credit, consumer scams, dealing with financial problems, estate planning, and taxes.

- ✔ www.gfn.com: The Gay Financial Network offers same-sex couples financial and investing advice. Visitors to the site can access its directory to find gay-friendly financial experts in their area.

Educate yourself before you invest in your education

If you're worried about your lack of job skills and are eager to increase your employability by getting additional education, you may decide to attend a trade school in your area or an online university. Although many of these educational opportunities are legitimate, watch out for some bad apples, including

✔ **Trade schools that over-promise the marketability of the job they train you for or the amount of money you can make in the job.** Also be alert for schools that overstate the credentials of their teachers or the quality of their facilities and equipment. For guidance on how to choose a reputable trade school, read the Federal Trade Commission's free brochure, "Choosing a Career or Vocational School," at the FTC's Web site, www.ftc.gov.

✔ **Distance-learning universities that are nothing more than frauds.** Many of these phony "universities" advertise in legitimate publications, have very impressive-looking Web sites, and claim to be accredited. Don't be duped. All that window dressing is calculated to convince you that you're dealing with a legitimate institution of higher learning. However, if you enroll in one of these schools, you get nothing in return or, at best, get an extremely poor education that has a limited value in the work world.

Also steer clear of diploma mills. These businesses sell phony degrees from a bogus university with your name on it. For extra money, you can even purchase a fake diploma stating that

you graduated summa cum laude! However, if you purchase one of these degrees and use it to get a job, you commit a fraud and can be criminally prosecuted if your scheme is found out.

Here are some sure signs that you're dealing with a phony university or diploma mill:

✔ Having a Visa or MasterCard is the only admissions requirement.

✔ The "university" claims to be unaccredited or is accredited not by the Council on Higher Education Accreditation (CHEA) but by some phony accrediting organization. You can find out whether or not a university is CHEA-accredited at www.chea.org.

✔ The university's name is similar to a university you are familiar with, but when you check more carefully, you discover that its name is slightly different from the legitimate educational institution. Many bogus universities choose names that are almost identical to legitimate schools in order to dupe unsuspecting consumers.

✔ You're instructed to fax or e-mail your resume to the university so it can review your experience and issue you a diploma based on that information alone.

✔ You can obtain your degree in just a month or so.

✔ When you visit the Better Business Bureau's Web site (www.bbb.org) you find numerous complaints about the university.

Keeping Your Job Skills Up-to-Date

Even though two-income families have become the norm in today's society, many women and a growing number of men choose to be full-time homemakers and stay-at-home parents for at least some time during their marriage. If you're one of them, be aware that in today's fast-changing work world, your job skills can quickly become rusty or even obsolete. While you're staying at home, you may also lose many of your professional contacts.

If your job skills are rusty or if you've never worked outside the home, as soon as you begin to think that a divorce is in your future, take immediate steps to update your job skills and/or to develop new ones. Trade schools in your area as well as nearby private or community colleges and universities are all potential sources of training and education. (See Chapter 17 for more on these training grounds.)

At the very least, learn how to use a computer, if you aren't already computer literate, and become familiar with the most popular software programs. Although different industry sectors and types of businesses vary in terms of the specific software programs their employees use, some of the most popular ones are Word, Excel, PowerPoint, PhotoShop, and QuickBooks. If you can't make it to computer classes, check out *For Dummies* books on these popular programs.

Getting a part-time job is another option for building new job skills, honing old ones, and building your professional contacts. A part-time job also helps you build a résumé. Plus, the money you earn can fund a checking or savings account in your own name. You may need that money to help pay a divorce attorney and to pay your bills if you and your spouse separate. You may even be able to work part-time from your home.

Beware of work-at-home schemes that promise you the opportunity to earn big bucks. You may have to pay a bundle upfront to purchase the supplies and equipment you need to take advantage of the "opportunity," and you may get nothing in return despite the marketer's promise of training, software, manuals, and so on. Furthermore, it's unlikely that you'll ever recoup your investment. Before you take advantage of any work-at-home offer, get the details about it in writing and get all your questions answered. Also, check out the company that's making the offer with your local Better Business Bureau (www.bbb.org), the consumer protection office of your state attorney general (www.naag.org), and the Federal Trade Commission (877-382-4357 or online at www.ftc.gov).

Being prepared to enter the work world as quickly as possible has assumed greater importance now that lifelong spousal support has virtually become a thing of the past. The more quickly you can land a good job after your divorce and earn a good living, the better off you'll be.

Building a Positive Credit History

Your *credit history* is a record of how you manage the credit accounts that are in your name or that you share with your spouse (called *joint credit*). Credit accounts may include credit cards, bank loans, debit cards, lines of credit, and so on. Having good credit in your own name (not just joint credit) is essential to being prepared for the possibility of divorce. In this section, we tell you why.

Your credit history

Whenever you apply for new or additional credit, a creditor reviews your credit history to make sure you don't have a lot of negative information, such as late payments, accounts turned over to collections, defaults, tax liens, or bankruptcy, in your past. Creditors get this information from the three national credit reporting agencies that probably maintain a credit history on you in their vast computer databases: Equifax, Experian (formerly TRW), and TransUnion. If you have negative information in your credit history or if the creditor believes that you have too much credit relative to your income, the creditor may turn down your application or give you credit at less favorable terms than it would have had your credit history been stellar.

But creditors aren't the only people who check out your credit history. Many employers, landlords, and insurance companies review consumers' credit histories. Here are some of the most important reasons you need to have good credit in your own name:

✔ If you get divorced and have a poor credit history in your name, obtaining a bank loan or a credit card, purchasing a home, renting a place to live, renting a car, and even getting the insurance or job you need is apt to be a challenge. Although you can build your own credit history after your divorce, the process will probably take you about two years.

✔ If, prior to your divorce, you or your spouse closed all your joint accounts and you later tell those creditors that you'd like credit with them in your own name, they can require you to reapply for the credit if your joint accounts were based on your spouse's income. If you don't already have a positive credit history with accounts in your name only, the credit company may turn you down for the credit you want or approve you for it at a high interest rate.

Choosing the right credit card

All credit cards aren't alike. Their terms of credit — that is, their interest rates, grace periods, late fees, and so on — vary. So, when you're in the market for a credit card, shop for one with the terms of credit that best meet your needs, depending on how you intend to use the card. Also, be aware that certain credit card features may seem attractive but, in fact, may cost you more than a card that doesn't have those features. When you're shopping for a good deal on a credit card, follow these guidelines:

✔ If you plan to pay your full credit card balance each month, go for a card that offers you a grace period of at least 25 days. (A *grace period* is the time you have to pay the card balance before the company charges you interest.)

✔ If you expect to carry a balance on your credit card sometimes, look for a card that has a low annual percentage rate (APR). Also pay attention to how the company applies that APR to calculate your monthly balance, because some balance calculation methods cost a lot more than others. Most companies use the *average daily balance including new purchases* method; that method works out better for them than it does for you. The most consumer-friendly balance calculation method is the *adjusted daily balance method* because you end up paying the least money in interest. The *average daily balance not including purchases* method is second best. Steer clear of cards that use the *two-cycle average daily balance method* because they cost you a bundle in finance charges. Credit card companies must include their balance calculation method in their card offers' fine print.

✔ Don't automatically go for the card with the highest credit limit. Using a credit card to pay for a major purchase is an expensive financial alternative. You're better off saving up for what you want to buy or getting a bank loan. Also, having a high credit limit can jeopardize your opportunity to obtain an important loan for other credit in the future.

✔ Don't let credit card offers touting special benefits, such as product rebates, frequent flier miles, and so on, tempt you. To take advantage of these offers, you probably have to charge a lot on the credit card first, and some cards with added benefits tack on high APRs, a short grace period, or other unfavorable terms of credit.

✔ Avoid cards with a high annual fee or an annual fee that escalates after a certain period of time. Also, be aware of what other fees a card may have, including a late fee, an over-your-limit fee, a fee for every time you use your card (called a *transaction fee*), cash advance fees, and so on. The more fees a card has, the more it costs you to use it.

✔ Be cautious of credit card offers with especially low interest rates. The low rates may do nothing more than get you to agree to begin using the card or to transfer the balance on another card to the new card. Frequently, the low rate lasts for only a short period. When that period ends, the credit card company may charge you a much higher rate of interest.

✔ Steer clear of cards that increase the annual rate you pay if you're late with your payment or if you exceed your credit limit.

To obtain up-to-date, unbiased information about the best deals on credit cards, visit CardTrak.com or Bankrate.com.

✔ When you and your spouse share joint credit, both of you are legally responsible for those accounts. That means that if your spouse misman-ages the credit you share, your credit history as well as your spouse's is damaged. However, if you have good credit in your own name, that good credit can help counteract the bad effects of the joint credit your spouse has mismanaged. The more individual credit you have, the better off you are.

Credit scores count

A *credit score* is a number derived from the information in your credit history, and it measures how well you've managed credit in the past and how well you're likely to manage it in the future. Most credit scores range from 300 to 850. The higher your score, the better.

More and more creditors, insurance companies, employers, and landlords are checking consumers' credit scores to make decisions about them rather than reviewing their credit histories. For example, they may review a consumer's credit score to decide whether or not to give him or her new or additional credit, insure the consumer, offer the consumer a new job or promotion, and so on.

The Fair, Isaac, Inc. credit score, also known as the *FICO score,* is the score that financial institutions and other businesses use the most. You can obtain your FICO score by going to the Fair, Isaac Web site at www.myfico.com. The site also offers advice about how you can raise your score.

The three national credit reporting agencies also generate their own con-sumer credit scores. You can order your scores from the agencies at the same time you order your credit history or you can order your scores at another time. Every time you check your credit history with each of the three national credit reporting agencies, ordering your credit scores at the same time is a good idea. Because you won't know whether a creditor, insurance company, employer, or landlord will review your credit history or your credit score to make a decision about you, you should know what your credit score is as well as what your credit history says so you can make certain that they're both accurate and correct any problems.

The cost of your credit score varies depending on whether you purchase it at www.fico.com or from one of the three national credit bureaus. The least you'll pay for your score is probably $5, if you're eligible for your annual free credit report. If you're not eligible for a free report, the least you will probably pay is $9.50. When you purchase your credit reports from the three national credit bureaus, they explain when you're eligible for a free credit report, how to obtain your free credit report, and how to obtain your credit report when you aren't eligible for a free one.

Requesting your credit reports from the three national credit bureaus

The federal Fair and Accurate Credit Transactions Act (FACTA) entitles you to a free annual copy of your credit report from each of the three national credit bureaus. At the time this book was written, consumers' initial eligibility for their free reports was being phased in geographically, from west to east, according to the following schedule:

- Residents of the western states December 1, 2004
- Residents of the Midwestern states March 1, 2005
- Residents of the southern states June 1, 2005
- Residents of the eastern states September 1, 2005

When you become eligible for your free annual reports, you can obtain a credit report from each credit report agency by

- Calling 877-322-8228
- Visiting www.annualcredit report.com
- Writing to the Annual Credit Report Request Service, P.O. Box 105281, Atlanta, GA 30348-5281

If you order your copies by mail, you must request your free credit reports using a special form, which you can print from www.ftc.gov/credit. The form is also available on the back of a new FTC brochure, "Your Access to Free Credit Reports," which explains how the free annual reports work. You can receive this brochure by downloading it from www.ftc.gov/opa/2004/11/041130free creditrpts.htm or by calling 877-382-4357. You can order all three credit reports at once or stagger your orders throughout the year.

If you want to purchase additional copies of your credit reports, the current cost in most states is $9. (You may have to pay sales tax, too.) However, depending on your state, you may be able to obtain one or more additional credit reports each year for free or for less than $9. Those states are Colorado, Georgia, Maine, Maryland, Massachusetts, New Jersey, and Vermont.

To order additional copies of your credit reports, you must contact each of the national credit reporting agencies individually by calling or writing to them, or by visiting their Web sites.

Experian
National Consumer Assistance Center
P.O. Box 2104
Allen, TX 75013
888-397-3742
www.experian.com

TransUnion
Consumer Disclosure Center
P. O. Box 1000
Chester, PA 19022
800-888-4213
www.transunion.com

Equifax
Disclosure Department
P.O. Box 740241
Atlanta, GA 30374
800-685-1111
www.equifax.com

If you've ever been denied credit, employment, or insurance due in whole or in part to information in your credit report or because you've been the victim of identity theft, you're entitled to a free credit report from whichever credit reporting agency provided the information. Use the preceding contact information to find out how to order your free report.

When you compare your FICO score and your three credit reporting scores, you'll probably find that each of them is a slightly different number. The reason is because the credit reporting agencies and Fair, Isaac each give different weights to the various types of credit record information they use to calculate your scores, among other reasons.

Establishing a credit history of your own

Before you begin the credit-history building process, request a copy of your credit report from each of the three national credit reporting agencies (listed in the previous section of this chapter). Review each of your credit reports so that you're familiar with their information and know whether or not the information is accurate. Also, make certain that they include all your credit accounts — any accounts you may have in your own name and any joint credit accounts with positive histories that you and your spouse share.

If you find any problems in your credit reports, correct the problem by initiating an investigation with the credit-reporting agency that produced the report. Information about how to begin an investigation should come with your credit report.

Knowing what's in your spouse's credit report is a good idea, too, if you live in a community property state because your finances and your spouse's are legally intertwined. For example, if your spouse incurs individual debts and does not pay them, your spouse's creditor can come after your share of your marital property to collect money. However, to obtain your spouse's credit report, he or she has to agree to let you order it, and that's unlikely if there is a lot of animosity between the two of you or if your spouse has anything to hide. For example, he or she may be using credit to pay for an asset you know nothing about. However, your credit reports alone provide you with information on most of your joint debts as well as your individual ones. They just don't tell you about your spouse's individual or separate debts.

The Credit Repair Kit, 4th Edition, by John Ventura (Dearborn) and *The Ultimate Credit Handbook*, 2nd Edition, by Geri Detweiler (Plume) are two good resources for understanding how to interpret the information in your credit reports, how to correct credit record problems, how to rebuild your credit history after financial trouble, and how to build a credit history in your name if all your credit is joint credit.

If all your credit is in your spouse's name, request that each of the three national credit bureaus establish a credit history in your own name, too (Susan Smith, not Mrs. Robert Smith, for example). If you live in a community property state, also tell each creditor that you want them to begin reporting the payment history on the credit accounts in your spouse's name that you're contractually liable for to the credit reporting agencies it reports to. Ask the creditors to begin reporting information on these accounts in your name as well as your spouse's. Assuming that these accounts have positive payment histories, having them in your credit file may help you build your own credit history.

If you used to have credit in your maiden name, make sure that this credit is a part of your credit history. If it's not, ask that the credit bureau add that information.

If some of the joint accounts in your credit history show late payments or even defaults due to your spouse's mismanagement of those accounts, try to distance yourself from that negative information by preparing a 100-word statement explaining the reason for the negatives. Send the statement to the three national credit bureaus (see the sidebar "Requesting your credit reports from the three national credit bureaus"). The statement you provide becomes a permanent part of your credit record. However, given that a growing number of creditors, insurance companies, employers, and landlords are making decisions based on your credit score rather than the details of your credit history, make a copy of any written explanation you may add to your credit history. Then, when you apply to one of these businesses, share your written explanation with the business.

Being an *authorized user* on your spouse's accounts will *not* help you build your own credit history. The reason being that an authorized user means you get to use the credit, but you have no legal responsibility for the account.

The federal Equal Credit Opportunity Act (ECOA) says that when creditors report information to credit bureaus about joint accounts that were opened prior to June 1, 1977, the information must be reported in both your names. That way, the information is in your credit history as well as your spouse's.

After you clear up any credit record problems and contact the credit bureaus about reporting certain accounts in your name as well as your spouse's, continue the credit-building process by applying for a small ($1,000, for example) *unsecured* bank loan. If you can't get one, apply for a *cash-secured* loan. (If you're approved for an unsecured loan, the bank's only requirement is that you promise to repay what you borrow according to the terms of the loan. But, if you can obtain only a cash-secured loan, the bank requires you to keep a certain amount of cash in a savings account at the bank or to purchase a certificate of deposit [CD] from the bank. If you don't pay off the loan, the bank can take the money in your savings account or your CD as payment.)

Ordinarily, when a consumer is building a solid credit history in his or her own name, the consumer pays back the loan over a period of 12 months.

However, depending on your marital situation, you may not have too much time. Therefore, let the degree of crisis in your marriage dictate how quickly you pay back what you borrow.

If the bank won't loan you money without a cosigner, don't ask your spouse to cosign the note because you end up linking your credit to your spouse's. Ask a relative or close friend to cosign instead.

After you pay off the loan, take a few more steps to secure a good credit history:

✔ Order a copy of your credit report from each of the three national credit reporting agencies to make sure that your reports reflect your loan payments. If they don't, ask the bank to report your payment history to the credit bureaus it works with. Next, apply for a MasterCard or a Visa card. But don't charge many purchases on the card, and make all your payments on time.

✔ You may have to apply for a second loan that's unsecured or isn't cosigned before you can get a credit card in your own name.

✔ If you don't qualify for a regular Visa or MasterCard, apply for a secured card. With a secured card, you have to collateralize, or secure, the card by opening a savings account or by purchasing a CD from the company issuing the card. If you default on your payments, the company can withdraw the money from your account or take cash from your CD to cover the charges. Make the secured card a stepping stone to an unsecured card by not exceeding your credit limit and by making all your account payments on time.

Chapter 4

Separation: A Healthy Breather or a Prelude to Divorce?

Separation is more than just a matter of living apart from your spouse. It's an important step that has legal, financial, and emotional ramifications, and it requires plenty of advance planning. Separation can be the beginning of the end of your marriage or the start of a better-than-ever union. Either way, don't take the decision to separate casually.

Before you and your spouse separate, you need to fully understand the pros and cons of such a change in your living arrangements. If possible, you and your spouse should also be clear about the direction you anticipate your separation will take you — toward reconciliation or to divorce court. Otherwise, you may be setting yourself up for disappointment and more heartache. But realistically, sometimes the whole reason couples separate is to figure out that decision.

This chapter can help you analyze your reasons for separating and alert you to some potential drawbacks of living apart from your spouse while you're still married. It also explains the steps you must take to protect your legal rights and financial well-being after you separate. If you're using separation as a way to save your marriage, this chapter also provides you with sound advice about how to engineer a successful reconciliation.

Weighing the Pros and Cons of Separating

Separation is the equivalent of marital limbo. You no longer live with your spouse, and you may even feel single again, but you're still married. However, your relationship has changed. When you live apart, you see each other less frequently — maybe not at all — and are less accountable to one another for your comings and goings and what you do and don't do. To help you decide whether or not you should separate from your spouse, the following sections highlight the pros and cons of taking that step.

If you're contemplating a separation, consult with a family law attorney first in order to gain a clear understanding of the pros and cons of separating given the laws of your state and the particulars of your situation. If you and your spouse aren't certain that separating is your best move, a marriage counselor, therapist, or your religious advisor may be able to help you decide.

Arguments for separating from your spouse

In this section, we list some of the most common advantages of separating from your spouse, some of which may or may not apply to you. The more factors that apply to you, the stronger your argument may be for a separation.

- You get to find out what living on your own feels like.

- You have time to assess your commitment to your marriage, away from the day-to-day stress and responsibilities of the relationship.

- You can get your emotions under control and analyze your marriage from a new and different perspective.

- You can send your spouse a strong message that things have to change if you're going to stay married. (For example, your spouse has a drug or alcohol problem and has been unwilling to deal with it.)

- You can give your spouse time to realize that living on his/her own isn't so bad and ease your way into a final break.

- Your spouse may miss you so much while you're living apart that your spouse decides that he/she really doesn't want a divorce.

- You can get a court order for a legal separation quickly to resolve issues such as how child custody, child support, and spousal support will be handled before you and your spouse begin living apart.

Other reasons why you may consider separating include the following:

- The law in your state requires that you and your spouse separate before you get divorced. No separation, no divorce.

✔ Even though you anticipate an amicable divorce, living with your spouse until your divorce is official is emotionally impossible.

✔ You and your spouse are estranged and can no longer live under the same roof.

✔ Your spouse has become physically violent, and you're afraid for your safety or your children's safety.

✔ You have religious objections to divorce.

The drawbacks of separating

Although separating certainly has its pluses, living apart from your spouse can have its drawbacks, too. So before you agree to separate, determine whether any of the following situations apply to you. If any of them do, decide how important those drawbacks are to you. Also, consult with a family law attorney who's experienced in handling divorces and separations.

✔ Your individual living expenses will increase after you and your spouse separate.

✔ If you're the spouse who moves out of the house, your new digs may not be nearly as plush as your former home.

✔ If you view your separation as temporary and anticipate living together again, your children may have a hard time understanding that "Daddy and Mommy are just spending some time apart."

✔ Separating may only be delaying the inevitable. You may be doing nothing more than prolonging the pain of your failed marriage and postponing the process of getting on with your life.

✔ If you don't have your own source of income, you may not have enough money to live comfortably.

✔ In some states, if you separate against your spouse's wishes, you may give your spouse grounds for a fault divorce because you can be accused of abandoning your marriage.

✔ If you separate, you can still be held responsible for your spouse's debts and legal problems, even though you're no longer living together. And, you can still be treated as a married couple with regard to pensions, life insurance, inheritance, and contractual obligations. However, a carefully worded separation agreement written by a family law attorney can help address these issues.

The attorney files the separation agreement with the court and asks the judge to issue a court order requiring both spouses to live up to everything in the agreement. Keep a copy of the agreement and the court's order in your files because you'll need that information if your ex doesn't live up to the terms of the agreement in some way and you have to go back to court to get the agreement enforced.

✔ If you're the one who decides to separate from your spouse, you can be charged with abandoning or deserting your marriage, which can weaken your position in your divorce negotiations and reflect badly on you when you're before a judge. A well-worded separation agreement can effectively deal with this issue, too.

State laws vary greatly on legal separations. In fact, a handful of states don't even recognize legal separations.

✔ If your spouse agrees to pay certain marital debts while you're separated and fails to do so, your creditors may have a legal right to come after both of you for payment if the debts are joint debts, regardless of whether you live in a separate or community property state.

In a community property state, if one spouse agrees to pay certain marital debts and fails to do so, the creditors can try to collect from the other spouse's share of marital property. Furthermore, if you live in a community property state and your spouse gets into debt while you're separated and doesn't pay the debt, the creditors your spouse owes can try to collect from your share of your marital assets, even if you have a written agreement to the contrary. The value of the written agreement is that if you end up paying what your spouse was supposed to pay, you can sue your spouse for reimbursement.

✔ Depending on your state, your separation can affect what is and isn't marital property. If you separate legally as a prelude to divorce, the property and debts you acquire during your separation may be considered yours and yours alone. But if you're not legally separated, the property and debts you acquire during your separation may be considered marital property and debts.

Initiating a Separation

You and your spouse should discuss the reasons for your separation (assuming that you can have a calm and productive conversation) in addition to consulting with a family law attorney before you separate. You should also be clear with your spouse about why you are separating — as a prelude to a divorce, as a last-ditch effort to save your marriage, or to sort things out so you can decide whether or not you want to try to stay married.

You and your spouse also need to decide whether you will have a legal or an informal separation. An *informal separation* is easy — you just begin living apart. This type of separation is probably all that you need if

✔ You and your spouse both earn a good living and can comfortably support yourselves. In other words, you're not asking your spouse to provide you with money or pay any of your bills while you're separated.

✔ You have no minor children from your marriage, so you don't have to worry about child custody or support.

✔ You don't share joint accounts or jointly owe a great deal of money.

✔ You're confident that your separation will be relatively brief and amicable.

An *informal separation* isn't a good idea if you and your spouse have young children or if one of you wants spousal support, wants to remain on your spouse's health insurance, or has some other important financial issues that you want your spouse to help with while you're separated. In these instances, you need a court-ordered *legal separation agreement* instead, which is a formal, written statement of all the terms that you and your spouse will abide by while living apart. That way, if your spouse doesn't abide by the terms of the agreement, you can get the court to help force him or her to do so. (In some states, you can obtain a legal separation *only* as a preliminary step to getting a divorce.)

In many states, a *legal separation* begins exactly the same way as an informal separation does — by writing a separation agreement. In these states, the key difference between an informal and a formal separation is that you file the separation agreement with the court so that the judge can issue a court order requiring each spouse to live up to the terms of the agreement.

However, some states require that a legal separation be initiated by one spouse (or the spouse's attorney) filing a petition for separation with the family court in his/her area. The petition formally asks for a legal separation and states what the spouse wants in terms of child custody, child support, spousal support, marital assets, debts, and so on. The spouse who initiates the legal separation can file the petition himself/herself or hire an attorney to do it. After the couple has negotiated the terms of their separation, the agreement is filed with the court.

Whether or not your state requires filing a petition for a legal separation, you and your spouse may work out the terms of your agreement on your own and hire attorneys to review the agreement before filing it with the court; you may hire attorneys to help negotiate your agreement from start to finish or, if there are sticky issues that you and your spouse simply cannot see eye to eye on, you may try to work them out through mediation or let a judge decide those issues.

A handful of states don't recognize legal separation agreements. Call your local or state bar association or talk to a divorce attorney to find out whether your state is one of them.

But think before you walk. Walking out in a huff definitely makes a strong statement about your feelings toward your spouse and your marriage. But if you stay away from home for an extended period of time (and just what constitutes an "extended" period depends on your state), the court may view your act of bravado as desertion or abandonment, and the spouse you left behind may have the last laugh. If you walk out, you may have put yourself in a legally disadvantageous position for working out the terms of your separation or divorce, especially if a family law judge decides your case. Furthermore, in some states, if you desert your spouse, you forfeit your legal right to your share of marital assets. That's a hefty price to pay for making a dramatic exit.

Traditionally, the spouse who wants the separation is the one who moves out of the couple's home. However, if your spouse is the one who wants a divorce and he or she is the primary caregiver of your young children, you should consider moving out so that the lives of your children are disrupted as little as possible.

Protecting Yourself When You Separate Informally

If you opt for an informal rather than a formal or legal separation, you should still work out all the terms and ground rules for your separation and commit them to paper so that you have a record of what you both agreed to. After you have an agreement, both of you should hire divorce attorneys to review it. The attorneys can make certain that you didn't overlook anything that should be in your agreement and that the agreement doesn't create the potential for problems between you and your spouse down the road. Your final agreement should be dated and you should both sign it. Make sure that each of you gets a copy of your final signed agreement. Having a written informal separation agreement provides you with something to refer to if there's any confusion during your separation about exactly what one of you agreed to do or not to do.

Your written agreement should identify any issues that may disrupt the peacefulness of your time apart and should determine ahead of time the best ways to deal with those potentially disruptive conflicts whenever possible. Working out solutions to possible problems in advance minimizes the potential for disagreements and misunderstandings during your separation. If problems do arise, instead of relying on your individual recollections of who promised to do what in order to resolve your differences, you can refer to your written agreement. Plus, you won't have to hammer out a solution in the heat of the moment if you already have one on paper.

When you and your spouse prepare your informal or legal separation agreement, be sure to ask yourselves the following questions:

- How will you share the money in your joint bank accounts?
- What will you do about your joint credit cards?
- Who, if anyone, can access the line of credit you have with your bank?
- Who will remain in your home?
- How will you pay your pre-existing debts?
- Who will pay the debts either of you may incur while you're separated?
- Will one of you pay maintenance to the other while you're separated? If so, when will the payments be due and how much will they be?

- ✔ How will you share responsibility for the care of your children?
- ✔ When will your children spend time with, and stay with, each of you?
- ✔ Will one of you pay child support to the other and, if so, how much will the payments be and when will they be paid?

If your spouse mismanages your finances while you're separated, your credit history and your credit score, not just your spouse's, may be damaged. For that reason, in your separation agreement, include provisions stating that during your separation, your spouse will *not* include your name on any new financial or banking accounts, will *not* sign your name on any documents whatsoever, especially financial documents, and so on.

Formalizing a Legal Separation Agreement

If you and your spouse decide to legally separate, you won't live together anymore, but you won't be divorced, either. In this section, we tell you when you should separate legally rather than informally and what you should include in your legal separation agreement.

Who should get a legal separation agreement?

A legal separation agreement (called a *temporary court order* in some states) is essential if you're separating permanently as an alternative to divorce, assuming that your state recognizes legal separations (remember, not all states do). To protect yourself, you need everything to be black and white and filed with the court so that if either of you fails to live up to the terms of your agreement, the other spouse can ask the court to help enforce it.

Other instances when a legal separation agreement is essential include when

- ✔ You're separating as a prelude to divorce
- ✔ You're so estranged from your spouse that communication and cooperation are impossible
- ✔ You don't trust your spouse to live up to his or her verbal promises
- ✔ One of you wants spousal support while you're living apart
- ✔ Minor children are involved

The longer you live apart, the greater the chances are that your relationship will deteriorate. As time goes on, you may find cooperating with each other harder to do. For example, your spouse may become involved in a new romantic relationship and abandon your reconciliation plans. At times like these, having a written separation agreement can help prevent a total breakdown of your relationship, even if you anticipate an eventual divorce.

If you and your spouse can't come to a negotiated separation agreement, a family law judge will decide the terms of your separation.

What should be in a legal separation agreement?

A legal separation agreement should address most, if not all, of the same issues that you would cover in a divorce agreement, including how you will handle the custody of your children; how much child support one spouse will pay the other; whether one of the spouses will receive spousal support and, if so, the terms and conditions of the support; and how you will handle your marital assets and debts. If you and/or your children are currently covered on your spouse's insurance policy and that coverage will continue, your separation agreement should address the coverage, too. For an overview of these issues, turn to Chapter 1, and for greater detail, read the chapters in Part III. Although the discussions in these chapters focus on divorce, most of the discussions apply to legal separations, too. In fact, if you separate and then decide to divorce, all or some of what you include in your separation agreement can be converted into your divorce agreement.

Depending on your state, the personal property that's in your possession when you're separated may become the personal property you end up with in your divorce. Therefore, if you move out of the home you share with your spouse and you plan on leaving some of your personal property in that home, you may want to include a provision in your separation agreement stating that the property will be yours if you divorce.

Hang on to your liquid assets

Ideally, your agreement should give you ready access to the *liquid assets* (cash or another kind of asset that you can quickly convert to cash) that you and your spouse own. Certificates of deposit, cash advances on your credit cards, your checking account overdraft, a line of credit, as well as money market accounts and bond funds that allow you to write checks against your investment are all liquid assets. You may need these assets during your separation to help pay bills, to put food on the table, or to cover unexpected expenses, especially if your income is low and you won't be receiving much, if any, direct financial support from your spouse.

Try the art of compromise

When working out the terms of your separation, a give-and-take strategy usually works better than strong-arm tactics. In other words, don't expect to get everything you ask for. You can refuse to compromise in an effort to have everything your way, but that approach is likely to backfire because you may end up in court, where a judge decides the terms of your separation.

Be careful about what you sign

Question anything in a separation agreement that you don't understand. And don't agree to any provision in your agreement because "it's good enough for now" or because you "can live with the arrangement for a while." Separation agreements often become *divorce agreements,* and after something is in a separation agreement, having that provision voided or modified can be difficult, if not impossible, to change, unless you and your spouse agree to the change or the problems it caused were obvious and significant.

Give yourself some room to maneuver by clearly indicating in writing that the separation agreement in no way binds you to the same terms in your final divorce agreement. This statement should be a part of your agreement.

The financial benefits of having a legal separation agreement

Having a legal separation agreement can provide you with some specific financial benefits besides helping to ensure that if your spouse fails to live up to his/her obligation in the agreement, the court will take steps to make your spouse do what he/she agreed to. Here are some of the other benefits of a legal separation:

- ✔ If one spouse pays the other spousal support, the spouse making the payments can claim them as a deduction on his/her federal tax return. The payments must be part of a legal separation agreement or court order.

    If your spouse claims your spousal support payments on his or her tax return, then you have to report that money as income.

- ✔ A legal separation agreement can help limit your liability for any debts that your spouse may rack up during your separation, assuming you live in a separate property state. Spouses who live in community property states do not get this protection.

✔ The agreement can help ensure that certain financial benefits that you currently receive as a spouse continue during your separation. Those benefits could include health insurance and continued access to credit if you and your spouse share joint accounts or if you're an authorized user on your spouse's accounts.

Alimony pendente lite and *separate maintenance* are legal talk for spousal support payments during separation. You may hear your attorney use these terms or hear them in court if you look to a judge to decide some of the terms of your separation agreement.

Other things you should do when you're separating legally

Besides negotiating a legal separation agreement, if you're moving out of the residence you share with your spouse, and especially if your separation isn't amicable or if you don't fully trust your spouse, you should also protect yourself by

✔ Taking your name off your lease if you are renters.

✔ Taking your name off your family's utility, phone, cable, Internet, lawn maintenance, and newspaper delivery accounts and so on, assuming that doing so doesn't cause a hardship for your spouse or your children. If your spouse can maintain these things by himself or herself, taking your name off the accounts is fine, but if your doing so would mean that your spouse and children will lack heat, phone service, and so one, don't do it. Furthermore, under those circumstances, if you end up in court, a judge will not look kindly on what you did.

✔ Contacting all your joint creditors and putting a freeze on those accounts so that your spouse cannot run them up.

✔ Making copies of your family's tax returns for the past six years.

✔ Creating a record of all your joint credit account numbers, bank accounts, insurance policies, investment accounts, and so on. Also create a record of whatever you and your spouse have stored in bank safety-deposit boxes.

✔ Obtaining credit in your own name if all your credit is joint.

✔ Taking any personal property that's important to you and that you fear your spouse may destroy or discard out of anger.

Following Separation Etiquette

If Emily Post wrote rules of proper behavior for separated spouses, they'd have to include the following do's and don'ts. Ignoring these rules of separation etiquette can turn an amicable split into a hostile one, derail any plans for reconciliation, and even weaken your position when the time arrives to negotiate your divorce.

Take heed of these separation don'ts:

- ✔ Don't get involved in a serious relationship, especially if the relationship means that you spend less time with your young children or that you neglect them when you and your new romantic interest are with your children. If your spouse finds out about your love affair, that information is likely to increase the hostility that he or she may already feel toward you. Also, a new main squeeze is likely to put you in a disadvantageous position when you negotiate the terms of your divorce.

- ✔ If you do have a new romantic interest, don't bring him or her home for the night when your children are staying with you.

- ✔ Don't bad-mouth your spouse — ever! If your children hear what you say, they're likely to repeat your comments to your spouse. Plus, nothing short of spousal abuse will send a judge into a tirade more quickly than learning that you've been saying disparaging things about your spouse.

- ✔ Don't do things that you know will be hurtful to your spouse or to your kids. Ultimately, the person you hurt most may be yourself.

- ✔ Avoid having sexual relations with your spouse without first understanding the potential ramifications of doing so according to the laws of your state. In some states, if you have sex with your spouse while separated and if you've already filed for a fault divorce, you may lose your grounds for divorce. Furthermore, you may mislead your spouse into thinking that you want to reconcile.

While you're at it, keep these separation etiquette do's in mind:

- ✔ Do keep the lines of communication open between you and your spouse. As long as your communication is at least civil, being able to talk with one another when necessary makes your separation easier on you and on your kids.

- ✔ If your children are living with you, allow your spouse to spend plenty of time with them (unless your spouse has been abusive, if you suspect that he or she has sexually molested the children, or if you are concerned that your spouse may kidnap your children). If you're legally separated, your agreement states when and where your spouse can see the children.

- ✔ Meet all your obligations to your spouse and children without fail. Besides the fact that it's only fair that you live up to your family obligations, if you don't, you can end up in court and a judge may order you to do whatever you haven't been doing or may decide to take certain rights away from you. For example, if you and your spouse share custody of your children, but you're never available when your turn comes to have your kids live with you, the judge may give your spouse sole custody of your children and let you have visitation rights. In addition, not meeting all your obligations under your separation agreement can minimize your bargaining power if you and your spouse decide to divorce eventually and you're negotiating the terms of your divorce agreement.

If You Kiss and Make Up

Some of you will breathe a huge sigh of relief after you've separated, but others of you may begin to miss certain aspects of married life. If you're the one who moved out and are now living in a smaller place surrounded by rented furniture and just a few items from your home, you may miss the old familiar comforts. If your spouse took care of most of the cooking (and boiling water sums up your culinary skills), you may quickly tire of fast food and scorched meals.

If your children are still young and aren't living with you, you'll miss having them around; if you're the parent with primary responsibility for the children while you're separated, you may feel overwhelmed without your spouse to help out. Or maybe you've determined that you truly love your spouse and are willing to do what's necessary to repair your marriage. For any or all of the reasons we listed, you and your spouse may decide that living together is better than living apart. And, like many couples who reach that conclusion, you will reconcile and end your separation.

Be sure that you're reconciling with your spouse because you really want to, not because you feel guilty, are scared to be alone, are lonely, are tired of doing your own laundry or eating by yourself, are afraid of the future, or for other reasons that may not be the right ones. Initially, after you've reconciled, you may feel a sense of exhilaration and renewed hope for your future as a couple. But sooner or later, the old problems in your relationship are likely to resurface, and you may respond to them in the very ways that contributed to your marital troubles in the first place. Also, you may feel angry with yourself that you returned to your marriage and now have to separate and disrupt your life all over again.

Despite your happiness at being together again, both of you may harbor negative feelings toward one another, such as anger, hurt, doubt, and distrust, as a result of your separation or because of problems that triggered your separation. Although these feelings may be quite natural under the circumstances, they can get in the way of rebuilding your marriage. Therefore, if you and your spouse are really serious about staying together and repairing your marriage, begin seeing a therapist or marriage counselor, if you aren't already doing so.

If you and your spouse get back together, you're more apt to make your marriage work if you begin therapy or counseling while you're still in the honeymoon phase of your reconciliation because you're both more motivated to make it work.

Part II

Moving Forward with Your Divorce

In this part . . .

The chapters in this part provide important information if your marriage is definitely over and you're getting a divorce. Chapter 5 offers advice for breaking the news to your spouse, helping you decide what you want out of your divorce, and providing guidance about what to do if you anticipate that your divorce will be hostile. Chapter 6 suggests how to tell your kids about your divorce and helps you anticipate the tough questions that they may ask. Finally, Chapter 7 provides suggestions on how to cope with the roller coaster of emotions that you may be feeling now that you know your marriage is ending.

Chapter 5

Putting Your Divorce in Motion

• •

In This Chapter

▶ Starting the divorce paperwork

▶ Telling your spouse that you want a divorce

▶ Determining your divorce goals and priorities

▶ Planning a budget for life after divorce

▶ Protecting your assets if you anticipate an ugly divorce

▶ Keeping yourself safe from a violent spouse

• •

*W*hen you realize that you and your spouse are headed for splitsville, you must take certain steps to get the divorce wheels in motion, including filing the proper paperwork and breaking the news to your spouse, assuming that your divorce isn't a mutual decision.

This chapter reviews the legal process that begins every divorce and offers practical advice for how to tell your spouse that you're ending your marriage and words of compassion for those of you who hear your spouse say, "I want a divorce." This chapter also helps you begin working out the details of your divorce agreement, regardless of whether you and your spouse do the negotiating yourselves or hire attorneys to help you (Part IV can help you with both situations). For example, it's never too early to begin thinking about what you want from your spouse in terms of a property settlement, spousal support, child custody, visitation, and child support.

To help you organize your thoughts, this chapter offers suggestions for defining your divorce goals and priorities, advises you on the financial information you should pull together before you begin working out the terms of your divorce, and discusses the importance of working with a post-divorce budget. It also offers special divorce preparation advice for those of you who anticipate that your divorce will be extremely hostile.

As part of your preparation, consider reading through some issues of *Divorce* magazine, which, as its name implies, is devoted entirely to the subject of divorce. It publishes editions for readers in southern California; southern Florida; Illinois; New York/New Jersey; Texas; and Ontario, Canada. For subscription information or to sign up for the magazine's free divorce newsletter, go to `www.divorce.com`. This site also offers a wide variety of information, resources, and products for people going through a divorce.

Initiating the Divorce Proceedings

Every divorce officially begins when one spouse files a petition with the court. That filing marks the legal start of a couple's divorce. Next, the other spouse is officially notified of the filing of the petition for divorce, although, in many marriages, the fact that one spouse filed for divorce comes as no surprise to the other spouse.

Depending on your state and whether you're getting a *fault divorce* (a type of divorce where one spouse alleges that the other spouse has harmed their marriage by committing certain misdeeds such as adultery, mental cruelty, or physical abuse), you may need to live apart from your spouse for a period of time before you can file for divorce.

Filing a petition

No matter which state your divorce takes place in and what sort of divorce you anticipate — friendly or hostile — every divorce starts out the same way: One spouse must file a *complaint* or *petition* with the court, which initiates a divorce civil law suit. The spouse who files becomes the *plaintiff,* or the *petitioner,* in the lawsuit, and the other spouse becomes the *defendant,* or *respondent.*

If you file the petition, you use it to establish the facts and the issues of the divorce as you see them. You file either a *fault* or *no-fault divorce* (see Chapter 1 for a discussion about the different types of divorce) and also indicate want you want from your divorce — spousal support, child support, custody of the children, and so on (see the "Planning for Life after Divorce" section, later in this chapter, to help you make these decisions).

Most couples don't work out the terms of their divorce until after one of them files a divorce petition. However, if getting divorced is a mutual decision for you and your spouse, and you and your spouse decide to negotiate a divorce agreement without the help of attorneys, you may work out the terms of your divorce before one of you files a divorce petition.

Serving the papers

After you file for divorce, your spouse is formally notified of your action. If you hire a divorce attorney, your attorney arranges for service after he or she files your divorce paperwork. If you don't hire an attorney, the clerk in the court where you file your petition can tell you what your particular serving options are.

Although states vary in regard to how this notification can happen and the service requirements can be different depending on whether or not you and your spouse share minor children, service can occur in one of the following ways:

- ✔ **You deliver the paperwork to your spouse yourself.** You would only want to use this method if you believed that your divorce was going to be amicable.

- ✔ **A sheriff or constable formally serves your spouse with the notification by physically delivering it to him or her.** You're most likely to use this method if your divorce is hostile. You have to pay a fee for serving your spouse this way. The amount of the fee varies widely depending on the part of the country you live in, but the fee is unlikely to amount to more than $150.

  If you or the sheriff or constable can't find your spouse — perhaps because your spouse is evading service — you can hire a private process server. Your spouse will have a tougher time eluding this person because private process servers wear street clothes, so they aren't as easy to spot as a constable or sheriff. But hiring a private process server costs more than using a sheriff or constable. Most private process servers charge between $25 and $75 per hour. Therefore, the amount you pay a private process server depends on the server's hourly rate and how much time he or she takes to serve your spouse at home, at work, or wherever he or she can be found.

- ✔ **You mail your spouse the notification.** You may be able to send the notice via regular mail, or you may have to use certified or registered mail. Not all states provide this option.

If your spouse can't be served, either because he or she is hiding or because he or she has moved and you don't know where your spouse currently lives or works, don't worry: You don't have to stay married forever. In most states, you can publish several legal notices in your local newspaper or in the newspaper in the community where your spouse is living if you don't reside in the same town anymore. The published notices inform your spouse that you have filed for divorce and outline your spouse's legal rights. If your spouse fails to respond within a certain period of time after the date of the last notice, you get a default divorce judgment from the court. However, some issues may remain unresolved until you find your spouse — for example, child support or spousal support.

Ordinarily, the court cannot order your spouse to pay temporary spousal or child support until your spouse has been served.

Processing the response

After your spouse is served, he or she has a certain amount of time — usually 20 to 60 days— to file a formal *response* to your lawsuit, also known as an *answer.* An answer is a legal document that states whether your spouse disagrees with anything in your petition, what he or she wants from the divorce, and so on. If your spouse has a divorce attorney, the attorney takes care of preparing the response and filing it with the court.

If your spouse agrees with everything in your petition and you didn't file a fault divorce, he or she probably won't file a response. This situation happens in many divorces. In fact, if your divorce is amicable and, especially if you and your spouse see 100-percent eye to eye regarding the terms of your divorce, your spouse can sign a *waiver of service,* which means that he or she won't be formally served with your divorce paperwork. Under this scenario, your divorce will probably move forward pretty quickly because fewer legal paperwork and administrative procedures will slow it down.

If your spouse doesn't agree with what you included in the divorce petition, your spouse will file a response stating what he or she wants from the divorce. For example, maybe you asked for sole custody of your children in your petition, but your spouse wants joint custody. Also, if you alleged fault in your divorce petition, your spouse may counter by denying that he or she is at fault and/or your spouse may point the finger at you instead. If you and your spouse don't see eye to eye on the facts of your marriage and on how to end it, your divorce is likely to be complicated and expensive unless your attorneys can diffuse the bad feelings between you and your spouse.

If you and your spouse aren't already legally separated but plan on living apart now that your divorce has begun, having a written agreement that details your living and financial arrangements and how you will handle child-related issues during the divorce process is a good idea. (See Chapter 4 for more details on legally separating.)

Discussing Your Decision with Your Spouse

If getting divorced isn't a mutual decision, how you break the news to your spouse can have a big impact on whether your divorce will be amicable or contentious. It can also help set the tone for your post-divorce relationship, an important consideration if you have minor children. Not wanting to be married anymore is no reason to be insensitive to your spouse's feelings.

Breaking the news gently

Most couples in troubled marriages try just about everything to resolve their problems but, at some point, it may become obvious to one or both of them that things are simply not going to work out and that the time has come to call it quits. Hopefully, if only one spouse reaches this conclusion, that spouse can sit down with the other spouse and explain his or her decision. Ideally, if you're the one who's made the decision to divorce, you should have this conversation with your spouse before you file for divorce and your spouse is served.

Your spouse should learn about your divorce plans from you first, not through the rumor mill (from mutual friends, relatives, or even your kids) or from a courier. Getting the news from anyone other than you is a cruel way for your spouse to find out that his or her marriage is ending and is a sure way to make for a bitter divorce. Additionally, you owe your spouse a face-to-face conversation about your divorce plans out of respect for him or her and the relationship you have shared. As difficult as having this conversation may be, it's the kindest way to convey the news. However, if you're afraid that your spouse will harm you physically after hearing the news, meeting face to face isn't a good idea.

The following suggestions may help you ease into such a difficult conversation and help your spouse accept the news as calmly as possible:

✔ Quietly and slowly tell your spouse your reasons for wanting to end your marriage. Review what you consider to be the problems in your marriage, what you have done to try to fix them — together or separately — and why you feel that those efforts haven't worked. Even if you've covered this ground many, many times before, go over it again patiently.

✔ As much as possible, talk in terms of how you feel, not in terms of what your spouse did or didn't do in your marriage. It's harder to argue with someone about his or her feelings and you're less apt to put your spouse on the defensive.

✔ Avoid accusatory or derogatory language and try to steer clear of starting an argument. If your spouse tries to argue with you, calmly reiterate your feelings and intentions — over and over, if necessary.

If a calm conversation is impossible because your spouse is simply too upset about the idea of divorce, don't get mad or act impatient. Give your spouse time to process the news that his/her marriage is ending. Tell your spouse that you would like to talk again later. Your next conversation will probably be a little easier. You may need to have a few conversations concerning your intention to divorce before your spouse finally accepts the news.

If you can't tell your spouse in person or with a phone call, write your spouse a letter. It's best if the letter comes from you, not from your attorney. An attorney's letter is an impersonal way to convey such very personal news. Furthermore, your spouse will probably be hurt and angry that you didn't bother to write it yourself.

Waiting until your spouse is ready to begin negotiating

Don't expect to begin negotiating your divorce agreement as soon as you tell your spouse the news. If the fact that you want a divorce comes as a surprise to your spouse, he or she probably won't respond with an "Okay, let's work out the details and be done with it" attitude. More than likely, your spouse will react with anger, shock, denial, and/or disbelief.

Give your spouse time to let the news sink in, to begin coming to terms with what's happening, and to do some of the upfront divorce-related planning you may have already begun. Realistically, it may take weeks or even months before your negotiations can begin, so be patient and move slowly.

Pushing your spouse to begin working out the details of your divorce may backfire on both of you. For example, feelings of guilt or remorse on your part or feelings of anger or abandonment on your spouse's part may result in bad decisions that you both will regret later. You may concede too much to your spouse or be too willing to compromise. Your spouse may make unreasonable demands out of anger, spite, and hurt feelings. Also, your spouse may panic and immediately hire an attorney, possibly turning your divorce into a hostile battle when it could have been an amicable split if you had been more patient.

But sometimes waiting for the right time to begin working out the terms of your divorce may be impossible or impractical given the particulars of your situation. Therefore, you may not be able to hold off until your spouse is ready. The truth is, if your spouse is adamantly against getting divorced, he or she may *never* be ready. Or maybe you're so estranged from one another that being civil to each other and working cooperatively is impossible.

Assuming that your spouse comes around eventually and is willing to start talking about your divorce, have a general discussion about the issues involved, particularly whether you want to do the negotiating yourselves or hire attorneys to help you work everything out, and try to develop a general timetable for moving forward.

Keeping cool if your spouse initiates the divorce

Even if the writing has been on the wall for months or maybe years, finding out that your spouse wants a divorce can send you into an emotional tailspin of shock and disbelief. As time goes on, you may vacillate between feelings of anger and sadness, or anger and depression.

The sooner you face the facts and move forward, the better off you'll be. Although feeling sorry for yourself is an understandable response to learning that your marriage is ending, especially if you didn't want it to end, painting yourself as a victim and wallowing in self-pity aren't healthy responses to your situation. Obsessing over "the unfairness of it all," how you've "been wronged," and "what could have been" will prevent you from working out a reasonable divorce agreement and moving forward with your life. Also, the "poor me" refrain will eventually drive away most of your friends and family members at the time when you may need them most. Also, don't get hung up on the idea that if you just do or say certain things, your spouse will have a change of heart and you can stay married. That probably won't happen.

As you work through your emotions and begin dealing with the practical realities of your divorce, avoid angry recriminations and don't insult your spouse. Also, don't go out of your way to spend time together or to remain apart; do what makes *you* feel most comfortable.

If you need help understanding and handling the emotions you are feeling, turn to Chapter 7.

Planning for Life after Divorce

Whether ending your marriage is your idea, your spouse's idea, or a mutual decision, getting divorced is a big step that can affect your life for years to come. As difficult as stepping back and considering what you need out of your divorce may be, doing so is important so that when the time comes to work out the details of your divorce settlement, you're clear on what to push for and what to give up.

Evaluating your divorce goals and future financial needs

Before your divorce begins or immediately after, start thinking about what you want your life to be like after your marriage ends, what you need from your divorce to create that life, and how you want to handle issues like spousal support, child custody, and child support. Define your goals for your divorce — what do you *really* need and/or want from your divorce? Also, consider what you're willing to give up to get them. Unless you have a clear idea going into your divorce negotiations of what you want, you're apt to end up with a divorce agreement that doesn't meet your needs and leaves you feeling frustrated and resentful toward your spouse.

When thinking about the financial aspects of your divorce, be realistic. You may wish that your post-divorce life could include a mansion, an expensive car, and a constantly cushy checking account balance, but all those things may be a pie-in-the-sky dream, depending on the current state of your family's finances, your individual and joint assets, your own earning power, and how much your spouse makes. You also don't want to ask for the moon just to hurt or upset your spouse. If you do, you risk setting yourself up for disappointment and making your divorce more difficult than it needs to be. Dealing with the financial matters of your divorce is no time to let your emotions take over. An amicable, cooperative divorce is easiest on your emotions and your pocketbook, and it's always the best kind of divorce when young children are involved. However, to divorce amicably, you and your spouse must behave like reasonable adults, be open to compromise, and not bring your anger and hurt feelings to the negotiation table. For some of you, that may be a tall order.

Another benefit of being clear about your divorce goals is that if you hire an attorney to help work out the terms of your divorce, you'll be better prepared to provide him or her with direction and feedback during the divorce process. Also, you're more likely to hire the right attorney for the job. For example, if you decide that you're willing to fight your spouse on certain issues no matter what, you probably need an attorney who's aggressive and has a lot of experience with litigated divorces. On the other hand, if you want to avoid controversy and conflict at all costs, you want an attorney who's great at negotiating and at creating win-win resolutions to problems. For details on hiring the right attorney and getting the results you want, turn to Chapters 13 and 14.

Ask yourself the following questions to help you begin identifying practical goals for your divorce:

- How much will I need in order to pay my living expenses after I'm divorced? Develop a post-divorce budget that projects the income and expenses you anticipate.

- Will I need spousal support? If so, come up with an idea of how much you'll need and for how long. In most divorces these days, spousal support isn't a permanent thing (see Chapter 9 to find out more details on spousal support). The "Developing a budget for life after divorce" section, later in this chapter, helps you figure out how much support you'll need.

✔ What adjustments should I be prepared to make in my life in order to be able to meet my financial needs?

✔ What skills do I need to get a job in today's market if I will be working outside the home after my divorce for the first time or will be returning to the work force after an absence of several years?

✔ Where can I get the job skills I need? How long will it take to get them and how much will the education cost? Remember to factor in educational expenses other than your tuition (like textbooks and a computer) to your post-divorce budget and any transportation and childcare costs you may incur while you're building your job skills.

✔ Are any certain assets from my marriage really important to me, either financially or emotionally? If so, write them down.

✔ What kind of child-custody arrangement do I want? Am I willing to share custody with my spouse or am I willing to turn my divorce into a hostile battle in order to fight for sole custody? Think in terms of what's best for your children. That's the criteria a judge uses to decide the issue if your divorce ends up in court.

✔ How much child support will I need if I end up with custody of the children?

As you think about your answers to these questions, try to distinguish between your needs and your wants. Think of a *need* as something that's essential to your post-divorce life (or to your children's lives) and a *want* as something that would be nice to have but isn't necessary. During your divorce negotiations, you may end up having to trade a want to satisfy a need. For example, you may decide that you're willing to get fewer assets in your divorce in exchange for getting bigger spousal support payments or in order to receive the payments for a longer period of time.

After you decide on your divorce goals, write them down in order of importance and put the list away in a safe place. After you've had some time to think, take another look at your list. You may find that you want to add, subtract, or reorder a few items.

Pulling together all your financial information

If you haven't already followed the advice in Chapter 3 about gathering the financial and legal documents and other information you need to work out

the terms of your divorce, begin that process right away, even if you anticipate an amicable divorce and totally trust your spouse to treat you fairly.
Complete and accurate financial information is essential to obtaining an equitable divorce settlement. Without it, you may get saddled with more than
your fair share of your marital debts and too little of your marital assets.
Also, you may not receive a reasonable amount of spousal support if you
need it, and you may come up short when asking for child support.

Trying to negotiate a settlement agreement with your spouse when you don't
have all the necessary financial information is like playing poker without
knowing what cards you're holding. In other words, you have a snowball's
chance in hell of coming out a winner because you have to guess about when
to raise the stakes, when to hold, and when to fold. Also, if you hire an attorney to help with your negotiations and you cannot provide him or her with
the necessary information, your attorney will have to obtain it through the
discovery process, which increases the cost of your divorce. Chapter 14
describes the discovery process.

Developing a budget for life after divorce

If you want spousal support and/or child support, knowing exactly how much
money you need will be difficult, if not impossible, if you have no idea how
much your living expenses will be after your divorce. In addition, when the
time comes to divvy up your marital assets and debts, you may not be able to
advocate for yourself and get good results. For these reasons, as soon as
your divorce begins, you should develop a budget for your life after divorce
using the sample form in Table 5-1 in this chapter.

When preparing your budget, you may have to estimate your income and
some of your expenses. Come up with your best guesses, basing them on
your own experience and by reviewing your checkbook register, bank statements, records of your ATM withdrawals and debit purchases, your cash
receipts, and so on. As time goes on and you have more information, you can
adjust your budget appropriately.

Developing a post-divorce budget also helps you determine whether you
should look for a better-paying job, whether you can realistically continue
living in your family's home, whether you need to turn in your gas-guzzling
SUV for something more economical, and so on.

For help developing and using a budget, pick up a copy of *Personal Finance
For Dummies* by Eric Tyson (Wiley) or *The Budget Kit* by Judy Lawrence
(Dearborn Financial Publishing, Inc.).

Savvy budgeting tactics

A spending plan, better known as a budget, is a basic money-management tool. It helps you plan how to spend your household income each month so that you don't come up short when you have to pay your bills and also have enough left over to cover your day-to-day living expenses. A spending plan also helps you allocate income to help pay for things that are important to you and your family, such as a down payment on a home, your children's college education, family vacations, a new car, or your retirement.

Developing a spending plan isn't difficult. It's simply a matter of recording your monthly household expenses, tallying them up, and comparing them to your monthly household income.

To get a comprehensive picture of your monthly expenses, review your checkbook register, your bank statements for automatic debits to your account, your ATM withdrawals, and your cash receipts. Also keep track of what you pay for with your debit card. The best way to do that is to record it in your check register, just as you record the checks you write. (At least we hope you do!) To get a true picture of your expenses, look at several months' worth of information.

Some expenses are *fixed,* whereas others are *variable,* meaning the change monthly. Still other expenses occur *periodically* throughout the year. (To budget for periodic expenses, divide the total annual cost of each periodic item by 12, which gives you a monthly cost to include in your budget.)

Your *total net monthly household income* is the actual amount of money available to spend (gross income minus your expenses, taxes, and other deductions). That income may include wages and salaries, commissions, investment income, and child support.

Try using a form like the one in Table 5-1 in this chapter to record your income and expenses. If the total amount of your monthly expenses exceeds your total household income each month, you need to reduce your spending. Otherwise, you face serious financial trouble in the future.

If your budget shows that you have a surplus of cash at the end of the month, you can pay off your debts more quickly, put more money into savings and investments, or spend some of the money on things that you or your family really want or need. If you have a lot of debt, the wisest thing to do is focus on paying it down and then thinking about putting money in savings, investments, and so on. This advice is particularly important to follow if you have high-interest debt.

One final comment about spending plans: Developing one may not be difficult, but living with one can be really tough if you don't exercise self-control. In the end, a spending plan is only as good and as useful as the discipline you put behind it.

Table 5-1 Sample Form for a Household Spending and Saving Plan

Fixed Monthly Expenses	*Dollar Amount*
Rent or mortgage	_____
Car payments	_____

(continued)

Table 5-1 *(continued)*

Fixed Monthly Expenses	Dollar Amount
Other installment loans	
Insurance	
Children's allowances/activities	
Day care	
Monthly dues	
Cable TV and subscriptions	
Internet service	
Total	$

Variable Monthly Expenses*	Dollar Amount
Groceries	
Utilities	
Telephone	
Gasoline	
Clothing	
Credit card payments	
Out-of-pocket medical/dental	
Magazines and books	
Church or charitable donations	
Haircuts and grooming supplies	
Restaurant meals	
Miscellaneous	
Total	$

Estimate the entire year's expenses and divide by 12 for the monthly amount.

Periodic Expenses*	Dollar Amount
Tuition	
Other educational expenses	
Auto registration and license	

Periodic Expenses*	Dollar Amount
Insurance	_____
Taxes	_____
Household repairs	_____
Birthday and holiday gifts	_____
Entertaining	_____
Subscriptions	_____
Total	$_____

*Estimate the entire year's expenses and divide by 12 for the monthly amount.

Total Monthly Household Expenses (The three previous totals from this table combined.)	$_____
Net Monthly Household Income	$_____
Surplus or Deficit (Net Household Income minus Total Monthly Expenses)	$_____
Surplus Allotted for Savings	$_____
Surplus Allotted for Investments	$_____

Safeguarding Your Money If You Anticipate a Hostile Divorce

If you suspect that your divorce will be a knock-down, drag-out fight or if you're certain that your divorce won't go smoothly, prepare to take the following steps prior to the start of your divorce. Protecting yourself from financial harm and having ready access to the financial resources you may need during your divorce is important.

Open accounts in your own name

If you share a savings account with your spouse, withdraw only some of the money in the account — maybe half, depending on your needs and the amount in the account — and deposit it in a new account in your own name at a different bank. Open your own checking account in the same way.

If you haven't informed your spouse of this financial move, after he or she learns about it, expect some fireworks that'll make your divorce agreement negotiations more difficult. If you withdraw an unreasonable amount of money (and just what constitutes an "unreasonable" amount is something your attorneys have to decide), you may end up getting less in your property settlement.

Also, beware of leaving too little in your checking account to cover your monthly expenses, especially if the checking account you share with your spouse usually contains just enough funds to pay the monthly bills. Bounced check charges and angry creditors are the last things you need right now!

Close your joint accounts

Close any joint credit card accounts you have with your spouse. Also, if you and your spouse have a line of credit with a bank or credit card, cancel or reduce it. Be sure to inform your spouse of what you have done.

If you can't close a joint account because of an outstanding debt that cannot be paid off immediately, write the creditor to explain that you won't be responsible for any additional debts on that account beyond the current outstanding balance.

Individual credit — that is, credit in your own name — is essential to your having a life on your own. But building a credit history in your own name can take time. If you don't have individual credit when you close your joint accounts, you may have to wait several years before you have access to credit at the best terms. (See Chapter 3 for more on building your own credit history.)

Stash your important personal property

If you're concerned that your spouse may try to damage, destroy, or steal any of your personal property in anger or out of a desire for revenge, find a safe place to hide your valuables. That can be a safe-deposit box in your name, the home of a trusted friend or family member, your office file cabinet, or any other place where your spouse can't access it.

If your spouse steals or damages your personal property, you may be able to sue your spouse for theft or destruction of property. Your attorney can use evidence of your spouse's destructive behavior as leverage during your divorce negotiations or divorce trial.

Protect your mutual assets

If your spouse is angry about your divorce or wants to get revenge, he or she may try to use up your joint assets rather than allow you to get a portion of those assets in your divorce. If you're concerned that your spouse may attempt this, consult a family law attorney right away about what steps you can take to safeguard your joint assets. For example, the attorney will probably advise you to avoid maintaining large cash balances in your joint checking accounts or will file a temporary restraining order and request an emergency hearing regarding the property in question.

Identify sources of cash

Protecting your legal rights when you're involved in a hostile divorce takes money, and lots of it. If you anticipate that your divorce will be hostile, start identifying the financial resources you have at your disposal right now. Those resources may include your separate property (such as your savings account, stocks, bonds, or mutual funds), borrowing against your retirement fund, getting a second mortgage on real estate, borrowing money from family members, and anything else along those lines.

Talk with a CPA or your financial advisor about the tax consequences and other implications of selling stocks or mutual funds, borrowing against the funds in your retirement account, or taking a second loan on the real estate you own.

Taking Action If Things Turn Violent

Sometimes when a marriage falls apart, one spouse (usually the man) begins to threaten the other with violence or becomes physically violent. If this happens in your marriage, take the threats or the violence very seriously. Ignoring them literally can be a matter of life or death.

Being prepared if your spouse becomes violent

When there's violence in a marriage, it isn't uncommon for the violence to escalate when a spouse begins to assert herself or talks about a separation or a divorce. If your spouse becomes physically violent with you, do the following:

✔ Call your community's domestic abuse hot line and/or your local police.

✔ Go to the hospital no matter how minor your injury. Get copies of your medical records from the hospital because they can help you if you go to court.

✔ Have a friend or relative take photos of your injuries and create a written record of the date that the injuries took place, what happened, and so on. Keep the photos and the written record in a safe place where your spouse can't find them. For example, you may want a trusted friend or relative to keep them for you.

✔ Join a support group. The people on the other end of the National Domestic Violence Hotline can help you find a group in your area (800-799-7233 or www.ndvh.org/index.html), or you can call your local domestic abuse shelter for information. Joining a group may give you the resolve you need to deal with your situation in a decisive manner.

✔ Testify in court against your spouse if the district attorney in the area where the abuse occurred presses charges against your spouse because your spouse has been physically violent toward you. If no police report exists regarding the incident, you must provide the district attorney with evidence that it happened before he or she will agree to prosecute your spouse. Examples of evidence include photos of what your spouse did to you, medical records related to the injuries you suffered, letters he or she may have written threatening you with abuse, and so on.

What you can do to protect yourself from a violent spouse

If your spouse has been violent in the past or is threatening you with violence for the first time, don't wait for the worst to happen. You can take legal or nonlegal steps to minimize the likelihood that your spouse will harm you.

Get a protective order against your spouse

A *protective order,* sometimes called a *restraining order* or an *injunction,* is a court order that makes it illegal for your spouse to enter or come within a certain distance of your home, your workplace, or your children's school or day care center; to stalk you; harass you; or try to intimidate you; and so on. Call your local police or domestic violence center hot line to find out how to obtain a protective order. A judge, who may or may not be a family law judge, will issue the order after you apply for it.

Keep a certified copy of your protective order with you at all times to help make certain that the police will arrest your spouse if the situation requires it.

Many states have different types of protective orders, and the process for obtaining one differs depending on which type of order you want. Not only can these order options be confusing for the spouse who's seeking a protective order, but the orders can also be confusing for local law enforcement officials as well, which can affect how effectively they enforce orders that are violated.

In most states, a protective order lasts for only a limited amount of time — between one and three years, although some states allow for longer-lasting orders under certain circumstances. All states allow you to apply for an extension of your protective order, but, in some states, you must go to court and face your spouse to get the extension. A few states have authorized permanent protective orders in certain situations.

Be as specific as possible in your protective order about exactly what you do not want your spouse to do. The order will not apply to anything you do not include in it. If you've called the police in the past because of previous incidents of spousal abuse, include that information in the court order, too.

If your spouse violates the terms of your protective order, the penalty involved depends on the laws of your state. Possible sanctions include being charged with a misdemeanor, a felony (a type of crime that's more serious than a misdemeanor), or contempt of court. A few states require anyone who violates a protective order to spend time in jail, whereas others require a violator to pay a fine or to pay a fine and go to jail. In a few states, someone who violates a protective order must receive counseling or be electronically monitored.

All states have *antistalking laws* that can help protect you if your spouse is following you, waiting for you outside your residence or your place of employment, following you in his car, using the phone or e-mail to threaten or harass you, or displaying other behaviors to intimidate and frighten you. Be sure to call the police if you're being stalked.

Reporting every incident of domestic violence, threat of violence, harassment, intimidation, or stalking by your spouse to the police is a good idea because, in some communities, getting a protective order against your spouse is easier when you've filed police reports on past incidents. The reports can also help if you file criminal charges against your spouse.

If you need immediate protection and the courts are closed because it's a weekend, evening, or holiday, your local police can issue a *temporary protective order.* However, it stays in effect for only a few days, so you need to file the appropriate paperwork for a longer-lasting protective order as soon as possible.

Don't let your guard down just because you have a protective order. If your spouse is intent on harming you, he won't care about the order. Therefore, you should consider changing your habits and should develop an emergency plan of action so that you know exactly what to do if your spouse violates the protective order. The "Make yourself more secure with a safety plan" section, later in this chapter, provides advice for what should be a part of your plan.

File criminal charges

If your spouse has already been physically violent toward you, in addition to getting a protective order from the court, you should ask the district attorney in your community to file criminal assault charges against your spouse. However, the district attorney won't file those charges unless you have evidence of an assault. Taking both actions provide you with different and overlapping protections.

Call 911

Domestic violence is a crime in all states, although how each state deals with the problem varies. Even so, if your spouse harms you or threatens to harm you, call 911. One or more police officers will come to talk with you and will prepare a police report. Get a copy of the police report number because it may be very helpful if you end up in court. If you've obviously been abused, the police will probably arrest your spouse on the spot.

A small minority of police officers believes that domestic violence is not a matter for the police to handle; some believe that it's a private matter between a husband and wife. Therefore, if you call the police for help and the responding officers seem reluctant to prepare a police report, calmly request that one be prepared, and get the officers' names and badge numbers. If the officers still refuse to write up a police report, this information will be helpful to have when you contact their superiors.

Head for a crisis shelter

If you're afraid to remain in your home or apartment despite the fact that you have a protective order against your spouse, consider going to your local domestic abuse shelter. You can take your young children with you. If you are in a crisis situation (your spouse has just beaten you or is threatening to) and you can get to a phone, call the shelter's crisis hot line. The person answering the phone can calm you down, advise you on how to handle the situation, and call the police for you. If you don't have the shelter's crisis hot line memorized, dial 911.

If you're in an abusive relationship, the excellent book *Getting Free: You Can End Abuse and Take Back Your Life* by Ginny Nicarthy (Seal Press) can help you break away.

Call the National Domestic Violence Hotline at 800-799-7233 to find out about resources in your area for victims of domestic abuse or if you're afraid that your spouse may become abusive.

Make yourself more secure with a safety plan

In addition to memorizing the phone number of your local domestic abuse shelter, take the time to develop a safety plan for yourself if your spouse has been abusive in the past and you're afraid that he will harm you again or if your spouse is threatening you with violence for the first time. Know exactly what to do if violence does occur and take certain actions ahead of time, just in case. Planning ahead can mean the difference between minor injuries and very serious injuries or even life and death.

Make the following practices part of your safety plan:

- Memorize the phone number of your local domestic abuse shelter.

- Hide an extra set of keys, some money, and some clothes in a safe place in case you need to get out of your home quickly. That safe place may be at a friend's or relative's home, in the locked trunk of your car, at your office, and so on.

- Always have a safe place to go that your spouse doesn't know about. It can be your local women's shelter, a friend's home, and so on.

- If you feel that you can trust one of your neighbors who lives next door, decide on a signal that you can use to let your neighbor know that you need help and that your neighbor should call 911, just in case you're not able to get to a phone. The signal could be turning on a specific inside or outside light, pulling the curtains together on a certain window, and so on.

- If you have children, be sure that they understand what to do if your spouse becomes violent. For example, you may want to tell them that if you say a certain "code word," that's the signal for them to run to a neighbor's house or to call 911.

- Tell everyone you know about your spouse's abuse. Sharing this information with others diminishes the power of some abusers.

Chapter 6

Telling Your Kids

*P*utting your children first when you're getting a divorce can seem like an awfully tall order, especially if the breakup of your marriage is full of conflict. After all, you have your own emotions to cope with! Plus, concerns about how you and your spouse will resolve the financial and legal issues in your divorce and what your future may be like may distract you.

Certainly, you have a lot on your plate. But remember, you're the parent. You have a responsibility to your children to tell them about your divorce in as caring and as sensitive a manner as possible. You also have an obligation to provide them with all the love, attention, and support that they need throughout your divorce so that you can minimize any emotional trauma that they may experience. If you don't, research shows that they may struggle as adults to lead happy, well-adjusted lives.

In this chapter, we offer guidance and advice regarding how and when to tell your kids about your divorce. We also discuss what you should and shouldn't do after you break the news to them, explain the importance of staying attuned to signs that your children may be having emotional problems as a result of your divorce news, and help you anticipate the kinds of questions they may ask you.

Breaking the News with Your Spouse

The best way to handle the situation is for you and your spouse to break the news about your divorce together to your children, even if you have to put your animosity toward each other aside for a while. By explaining your divorce together, you convey to your kids that, although your marriage may be ending, you can cooperate as their parents, that they still have a family — just a different kind of family — and that you both will remain actively involved in their lives. Such behavior is very calming and reassuring to them.

Before you tell your children about your divorce plans, taking the time to decide what you're going to say to them is a good idea. Get your story straight so that you don't contradict one another or send them conflicting messages. If you and your spouse need help deciding what to say to your children, talk things over with your religious advisor or schedule an appointment with a mental health professional.

You should both agree that when you talk with your children neither of you will blame the other for your breakup nor encourage your children to side with one of you against the other. Putting your kids in the middle is unfair to your children and can inflict irreparable emotional harm. Furthermore, when you criticize your spouse, your comments can backfire on you — your children may side with the parent you maligned.

Here are more tips to discuss with your spouse before you break the news to your children:

✔ **Be honest with your children about why you're getting divorced, but keep their ages in mind and avoid sharing the lurid details behind your split.** Tell them as much as they need to know and no more. If you haven't been able to hide the discord in your marriage, you may want to acknowledge what your children already know by saying something like, "We know that you've heard us fighting a lot, and here's why. . . ."

✔ **Don't hide the fact that life is going to be different for everyone in the family because of your divorce.** Prepare your kids for some of the changes to come. Reassure them that your divorce hasn't and will not change your love for them and that you both will continue to be involved in their lives. But don't promise them things you can't deliver. Make sure that your reassurances and promises are more than hot air. Otherwise, your children will become distrustful of you and cynical about your reliability and honesty.

✔ **Be very clear with your children that your divorce has absolutely nothing to do with them.** Otherwise, they may feel somehow responsible for the divorce and assume that if only they had behaved better or gotten higher grades you wouldn't be ending your marriage.

✔ **When you tell your kids about your divorce, avoid angry or irritated facial gestures and body language, and don't argue with your spouse in front of them.** Such behavior contradicts the messages you want your kids to hear from you.

✔ **Try not to get emotional when you tell your children about your divorce.** Watching a parent cry or get very upset can be frightening for children. Don't add to their anxiety with histrionics and overly dramatic behavior. You're likely to make them more concerned about your emotions than their own and, as a result, they may not let you know exactly what they're feeling.

If you and your spouse don't plan on breaking the news about your divorce to your kids together, try to agree about which of you will tell them. This decision may be an easy one for you to make because one of you has no interest in delivering such difficult news to your kids or because one of you is emotionally incapable of doing so. Or, you may both agree that the parent who your children most often turn to for emotional support should talk to them. You and your spouse should also reach a general agreement about what that parent tells your kids. That way, if your children later ask the other parent questions about your divorce, that parent won't tell them something that contradicts what their other parent said. Receiving contradictory information from the two of you can unsettle your children more than they already are after learning about your divorce plans.

If you separate before your divorce is final, your children should visit the parent who moves out as soon as possible so they're assured that they'll continue to have a relationship with both of you. However, if your children refuse to visit their other parent or act reluctant to do so, don't force them to go. Also, make sure that they have their other parent's new address, phone number, cellphone number, and e-mail address.

Finding the Right Time to Talk with Your Children

Most of us tend to put off doing things that are unpleasant or that we're nervous about doing. As a result, you may come up with countless reasons to delay telling your children about your divorce plans. However, make sure that you tell them before anyone else does. They need to hear the news from you in your own words. And, in the same breath, you need to reassure them that you will always love them and take care of them.

The right time to talk with your children about the changes to come depends on their ages and on the circumstances of your divorce. For example, if your spouse announces that he or she has already filed for divorce and is moving out next week, you should tell your children about the split sooner, not later.

Letting your older kids know sooner

Bear in mind that you usually need to tell preteens and teens sooner than very young children (assuming that you have some control over the timing of your conversations with your children), because they're more likely to learn about your divorce plans by overhearing a conversation or by coming across divorce-related papers. Also, they're better at sensing that something's up. Therefore, when you're certain that you will be divorcing and have worked out at least some of the details, especially those that affect your children, have a talk with your preteens and teens as soon as possible.

Be sure to tell your older children not to share your news with their younger siblings if there's a significant age gap between them. For example, say your teenage children have two younger siblings, ages 5 and 7. Explain to your older kids that you want to tell the younger siblings yourself in your own way. But be sure to let your older kids know when you've had that conversation so that they can talk with their younger brothers or sisters about your divorce and be a support to them.

Don't discuss your divorce plans with your older children until you've talked the plans over with your spouse. Making your kids your divorce confidantes and seeking their advice and counsel is unfair and is an inappropriate and unhealthy role for your children to play. If you need advice and counsel, talk to a trusted friend or family member, your religious advisor, or a mental health professional.

Waiting to share the news with your younger ones

If you have toddlers and elementary-age children, avoid telling them about your divorce plans too far ahead of the date that you and your spouse plan to begin living apart. Young children tend to have a different sense of time than adults and older children have. For them, a week can seem like a month, and a month can seem like a year. If you tell your younger children prematurely, you risk intensifying the anxiety they have over knowing that their lives are going to change in ways they don't yet understand.

Regardless of their ages, whenever possible, don't wait until just before you and your spouse begin living apart to break the news to your children. Instead, tell them far enough ahead of the day you plan to separate so that they have time to process your news, ask you questions, spend time with both of you in a relaxed manner, and enjoy your affection. All those things are essential preparation for the changes ahead. A week before the separation begins is probably about the right amount of time for younger children.

Deciding Whether to Tell Your Children Individually or All Together

If your children are close in age and maturity, telling them all together has important benefits:

✔ **It can help foster a "we're all in this together" attitude among your children.** That feeling can be a comfort and a source of strength to them.

✔ **If all your children find out about your divorce at the same time, each of them knows exactly what his or her siblings know.** This may not seem important to you but, if you tell each of your kids separately, they may worry that they don't know what their siblings know or that you're going to treat them differently than everyone else in the family.

If your children have significant disparities in their ages, maturity levels, or emotional needs, talk to your children individually about your divorce so you can tailor an appropriate message for each child and provide him or her with as much support and comfort as he or she may need after hearing your news.

If you meet with your children separately, tell each child that you're having a similar conversation with his or her siblings. Unless your children are very young, they're probably going to talk with one another about what you've told them. Therefore, your message about why you're getting a divorce and what is going to change or stay the same in their lives should be consistent, though you may decide to use different words to convey it. If you tell each child something different, you only add to their anxiety and confusion.

Preparing for Your Children's Responses

You can't possibly predict exactly how your children are going to react to the news of your divorce. Their reactions depend on their ages, maturity levels, personalities, emotional makeup, and the relationships they have with you and your spouse, among other things. In this section, we explain the kinds of emotional reactions your children may have after you tell them about your divorce.

Calming their emotions

Interestingly enough, you may find that their emotions mirror yours. Those emotions may include anger, depression, disbelief, fear, rejection, and sadness.

Practice the art of "active" listening

If you've never practiced *active listening* with your children before, now is the time to start. Active listening requires you to stay attuned to the feelings behind your children's comments and questions and lets them know in a non-judgmental way that you heard what they said.

For example, say that your 10-year-old son tells you, "I'm scared about what's going to happen now that you and Daddy are getting divorced." Rather than telling him not to be scared or that being scared is silly, ask your child, "What are you scared about?" Carefully listen to his answers and reassure him as much as you can.

Active listening doesn't involve interrupting to correct your children, preaching or lecturing, or analysis or problem-solving. Its purpose is to encourage your children to open up to you and to tell you what they think and how they're feeling. Active listening can help you gain information and insights into your children that you can use to help them cope with your divorce.

Active listening promotes a feeling of love and trust between you and your children, which are feelings they need in order to deal with their parents' divorce.

Telling your children about your divorce is apt to trigger a new flood of emotions inside of you, even if you thought that you had them under control. For example, you may feel guilt about the fact that you couldn't make your marriage work and that now your kids are hurting; anger toward your spouse if he or she did something to cause the divorce; sadness because your news made your kids cry; and so on. Be prepared to do whatever you need to do to deal with your own emotions because if you're an emotional basket case, you're not much help to your children and are likely to make them even more scared and worried than they already are. If you need suggestions for how to meet your own emotional needs, turn to Chapter 7.

In some jurisdictions, parents who are getting divorced are required to take parenting classes taught by mental health professionals. In these classes, parents learn about children's reactions to divorce, effective parent-child communication, and resources that can help parents and their children go through a divorce.

Fielding their questions

After you tell your children about your divorce plans, give them an opportunity to ask questions. Your children's initial questions will probably relate in some way to how your divorce will change their lives and what will stay the same. For example, depending on their ages, they may want to know

✔ Where will they live?

✔ Will they still go to the same school?

- Will you and your spouse still live in the same town?
- Will they spend time with each of you?
- Will you continue to coach their soccer or little league team?
- Can they continue their music or dance lessons?
- How will you share parenting responsibilities?
- Can they still go to camp next summer?
- Will there be enough money?
- Where will their dog or cat live?

Answer your children's questions clearly, calmly, and honestly. If they ask you something that you can't answer, admit that you don't know or that it's too soon to tell. When appropriate, tell them that you will give them an answer by a certain date or as soon as you can. If your children don't ask direct questions, you may be able to intuit their thoughts through their behavior and actions or by reading between the lines when they talk to you.

Your younger children may have a hard time grasping the concept of divorce and realizing that you and your spouse will always continue to love them and care for them. They may ask you the same questions over and over, which can really tax your patience. Understand that right now they need constant reassurance.

You can help your younger children deal with your divorce by reading them age-appropriate books that deal with the subject. We recommend the following titles to help your younger children acknowledge and express their fears and worries about your divorce and the changes that are occurring in their lives:

- *Dinosaurs Divorce: A Guide for Changing Families* by Marc Brown and Laurence Krasny Brown (Little, Brown & Co.)
- *Mama and Daddy Bear's Divorce* by Cornelia Spelman (Albert Whitman & Company)
- *I Don't Want to Talk About It: A Story About Divorce for Young Children* by Jeanie Franz Ransom (Magination Press)

And don't be surprised if your children don't ask you many questions at first. Learning that you're getting a divorce may come as quite a shock to them, even if they're aware that you and your spouse were having marital problems and even if they have plenty of friends with divorced parents. They may need to let the news sink in before they're ready to ask you questions. They'll likely come to you with questions after they've shared your news with friends, especially if their friends' parents are divorced and their friends tell them what their parents' divorce was like for them. Let your children know that you're willing and available to talk with them about your divorce and to answer their questions whenever they want. If they seem reluctant to ask you questions, take the initiative by talking with each of them individually about your divorce and asking them whether they have any questions about it.

Pick up a copy of *Difficult Questions Kids Ask and Are Too Afraid to Ask About Divorce* by Meg F. Schneider and Joan Offerman-Zuckerberg (Fireside). We recommend this title if you want advice on how to tell your children the truth without frightening them, how to strengthen your relationship with them, and how to keep and build their trust. Regardless of the age of your children, you should find this book helpful.

Divorce can be particularly difficult for preteens and teens, so you may want to purchase some of the following books for them:

✔ *The Divorce Helpbook by Teens* by Cynthia MacGregor (Impact Publishers): This book talks to teens about divorce; discusses the emotions they're feeling; and addresses many of the difficult issues they may be thinking about, such as how to deal with the sadness and depression they feel, how to tell one parent that they don't want to spend as much time with him or her, and what to do if their parents are trying to make them go-betweens.

✔ *How it Feels When Parents Divorce* by Jill Krementz (Knopf): This book can be helpful to teens as well as younger children. It shares the experiences and feelings of children whose parents have gone through a divorce. The book helps children understand that the emotions they may be feeling are normal and that other children of divorce have had to deal with many of the very same changes that they're facing now.

✔ *My Parents are Divorced, Too: A Book for Kids by Kids* by Jan Blackstone-Ford, Annie Ford, Melanie Ford, and Steven Ford (Magination Press): Written by kids for kids, this book takes on the toughest questions your older kids (ages 8 to 12 year, approximately) may have about your divorce.

If your kids act uninterested in the books when you first bring them home, leave them in a place where they can see them and, when they're ready, they may start reading the books. Also, before you give the books to your children, you may want to read them to gain insight into what your kids feel like right now. That insight can help you do a better job of parenting them during your divorce.

Helping Your Kids Cope Over Time

After you've told your children about your divorce plans, you must act in a way that reflects the promises you made to your children about what life would be like for them in the future.

Watching your own behavior around your children

Monitor your own behavior around your children. What you choose to do (or not do, as the following list will tell you) can help reassure them that things will be okay or can add to their anxiety about the future.

- Don't fight with your spouse when your children are around.

- Don't say negative things about your spouse to your children or to someone else within earshot of your children.

- Avoid sharing your anger or frustration about your spouse with friends and family when your children are around. They may overhear the very information you want to withhold from them, and your tone of voice and body language may upset them.

- Don't get overly emotional around your children about your divorce or about what life will be like for them and you after the divorce. You risk increasing their insecurity and fear about the future.

- Don't use your children as liaisons between you and your spouse. If you have something to convey to your spouse, speak directly to your spouse or through your attorneys.

- Don't interfere in your children's relationship with your spouse by trying to manipulate them into thinking of you as the "good parent" and your spouse as the "bad parent."

- Don't pressure your kids to choose sides.

- Avoid making dramatic changes in their daily routines. As much as possible, keep everything in their lives just as it was. Children generally don't like change, and divorce is change enough.

- Don't attempt to assuage your guilt over how your divorce may affect your children by giving them special gifts or privileges or by relaxing your discipline with them.

✔ Avoid making your children your confidantes. Keep your adult worries and concerns to yourself or share them only with other adults.

✔ Don't expect your children to comfort you. You should be the one comforting them.

✔ Don't expect your child to become "the little man" or "the little woman" of the house. Your kids are kids, not surrogate spouses.

Remaining sensitive to your children's feelings

When you get divorced, you and your spouse aren't the only ones affected by the change in your marital status. Your divorce means the end of family life as your children know it, which is something that has been important to them and they've probably always taken for granted.

Your divorce may also mean that your children must experience a change in economic circumstances or they may have to move out of their home and neighborhood, attend a new school, and make all new friends. Therefore, unless you're aware of what to do and what not to do in regard to your children while keeping an eye on their moods and behaviors, your divorce can be emotionally devastating for them, even if it is a good thing for you.

When parents divorce, children often fear that they will lose one of their parents or that their parents will abandon them and they'll have to fend for themselves. Therefore, both parents need to convey in their words *and* deeds that they will always be there for them. For example, if you promise your children that you'll do something for them, do it. Also let your children know that you love and appreciate them, and make plans with them to do something in the future — maybe a trip to the beach. Also, if your children are nearing college age, start talking with them about which colleges they want to attend and make plans to visit some of those schools with them.

If you don't tend to your children's needs during your divorce (and afterward), you risk making them the innocent victims of your marital breakup. Studies have shown that children whose parents divorce are more likely to have trouble in school and with the law, which means that you may end up spending money later for therapists, tutors, and attorneys' fees.

Research also shows that parents who openly express their hatred, anger, feelings of betrayal, or desire for vengeance — feelings that many couples have toward one another during divorce and sometimes long after — unwittingly program their kids to be unhappy adults with troubled marriages of their own. Parents also harm their children by manipulating them in order to gain the upper hand in custody negotiations or to get back at the other spouse. Couples who use their children as pawns in their divorce games put their children in a terribly difficult position because most children love both of their parents equally.

If your children have gone through a divorce before, don't assume that it's easier for them the second time around. The second divorce may trigger the very same emotions that they experienced during your first divorce. Their lives are again being disrupted by changes in their lifestyle and the discomfort of living with two adults who are preoccupied with the end of their marriage. Furthermore, because they will be older than they were when you got divorced the first time, their emotions may be more intense, and they may experience new emotions and/or respond to your second divorce in ways that they didn't the last time your marriage ended.

To help monitor how well your children are dealing with the news of your divorce, spend some extra time with them (but not in an interfering way). It may simply require being in the same room with them more than you usually are so you can watch their behavior or being more attuned to them when they're in the car with you. The time you spend together gives your kids the opportunity to express their feelings and concerns about their daily lives.

Although your children may appear to be coping well, don't assume that they're not having trouble in school or at play or won't have trouble later on. Watch for any mood swings or changes in behavior that may signal emotional problems. Touch base periodically with their teachers and caregivers to find out whether they've noticed any problems.

What your kids may be fearing (and not telling you)

During and after their parents' divorce, children (especially the younger ones) often become fearful that terrible things will happen to them or believe that they're responsible for the breakup of their parents' marriage. Some of the most common fears and misconceptions kids have about divorce include

✔ The parent I no longer live with will leave me forever.

✔ My parents' divorce is my fault.

✔ If I am really good, my parents will get back together.

✔ I have to choose between my parents. I can't have a relationship with both of them after they're divorced.

✔ My mother's or father's new significant other will replace my real parent.

✔ My stepbrother or stepsister is going to replace me.

Understanding the thoughts that may be going through your children's minds can keep you alert to any signs that your kids are having trouble coping with your divorce.

Being prepared for your children's initial reactions

After your children find out about your divorce plans, they may begin to feel isolated and cut off from their friends. They may feel as though they're the only children whose parents ever got divorced and may be embarrassed about what's happening to them. On the other hand, if you and your spouse fought openly and often during your marriage or if violence or substance abuse colored your relationship, your divorce may be a relief to your children and it may represent a positive change in their lives.

For a sensitive and comprehensive overview of the stresses that children commonly feel when their parents are going through a divorce, and detailed advice on what parents can do to help their kids, head to the University of Missouri Extension Web site at http://muextension.missouri.edu/ xplor/hesguide/humanrel/gh6600.htm.

If your children are having trouble coping with the news of your divorce, all you may need to turn their frowns into smiles is to cuddle them more and give them a little extra attention. But sometimes it's not that simple. When your children need more than what you can give them, consider involving a school counselor, mental health professional, social worker, relative, or another adult who's especially close to your children. Participating in a support group may also be helpful to your older children.

Tell your children's teachers, babysitters, other caregivers, the parents of their close friends, and any other adults who they see regularly about your divorce plans. Your heads-up will help them stay attuned to any significant changes in the ways your children behave. Ask these adults to keep you informed of any changes.

Another option is to contact your state's family law court, your divorce attorney, mental health professional, or a social worker who works with children and families to find out about any public or private resources (such as classes, workshops, and support groups) that may be available in your area to help your kids cope with your divorce. Some of these same resources may also offer counseling for divorcing parents.

For valuable resources that can help your children cope with your divorce, check out

- **The Divorce Kids Web site** (`http://www.divorce-kids.com`): This Web site reassures kids that they're not the first kids to go through a divorce and helps them adjust to the changes in their lives. It also helps kids cope with stepparents and stepsiblings. This site also helps parents understand what their children may be going through and offers advice on how to help them.

- **A Kid's Guide to Divorce** (`www.kidshealth.org/kid/feeling/home_family/divorce.html`): This site provides caring explanations of divorce and why it happens, discusses the feelings kids may experience when they learn that their parents are breaking up, and suggests things kids can do to cope.

- **KidsTurnCentral** (`www.kidsturncentral.com/topics/issues/divorce`): This Web site is just for kids. It features a variety of information and other resources for kids of all ages, like links to Web sites to help them cope with divorce, a Web site for posting their divorce-related drawings, personal stories from kids who have gone through divorce, and a chat group where kids can talk to one another about how they're feeling and what they're experiencing, a children of divorce bill of rights, and much more.

- *The Truth About Children and Divorce: Dealing with the Emotions So You and Your Children Can Thrive* by **Robert E Emery (Viking Books):** Written by a therapist and mediator, this book helps parents help their children as well as themselves get through divorce and rebuild their lives after divorce.

- *Helping Your Kids Cope with Divorce the Sandcastles Way* by **M. Gary Neuman (Random House):** This book is based on the Sandcastles workshop concept, a workshop for children ages 6 to 17 that helps them deal with their feelings about your divorce through activities, such as drawing, poetry, role playing, and so on.

Chapter 7

Surviving Your Emotional Ups and Downs

In This Chapter

▶ Understanding the six stages of grief

▶ Keeping your emotions from taking over

▶ Handling responses from your friends and family

For better or worse, your marriage is an important part of your life. So, if you're like most people, ending it won't be easy — whether you initiate the divorce, it's a mutual decision, or your spouse is the one who calls it quits.

As the reality of your divorce sinks in, clear and rational thinking may become difficult, if not impossible. While one part of your brain may know that divorce is for the best (or at least inevitable), the other part may be a jumbled and confused mess of emotions. Focusing on your day-to-day activities and getting a good night's sleep may become increasingly difficult to do. You may find yourself distracted by questions such as, "Will I have enough money to survive?"; "Where will I live?"; "How will my divorce affect my children?"; and "Will I ever marry again?" Because divorce is a highly personal experience, you can't predict exactly how you'll respond to it. Nevertheless, you'll likely find yourself experiencing a wide range of powerful emotions.

Getting divorced can be like taking a ride on an emotional roller coaster. One day you feel angry, sad, depressed, and guilty, and the next you feel hopeful about the future and confident in your ability to handle whatever comes your way. Your feelings may even change from morning to afternoon or hour to hour. They'll probably be most intense at first and, gradually, will lessen over time. You may also experience the same sorts of emotions when you separate. Little things may trigger your mood swings: You may hear a song that you and your spouse used to enjoy; you may go to a party by yourself and feel awkward trying to make conversation; you may run across photos of happier times; or your child may ask you a question that you find especially painful.

If you did not initiate your divorce, and especially if your spouse's desire to split up took you totally by surprise, you'll probably experience more intense emotions than your spouse will. Whatever your situation, this chapter helps you understand the emotions that you're likely to feel and provides you with suggestions for how to keep them under control. The more you understand your feelings, the better you'll be able to put them in perspective, to handle your emotions in a positive way, and to prevent them from derailing your divorce.

Understanding the Stages of Grief

Elisabeth Kubler-Ross, MD, wrote an important book about grief and loss called *On Death and Dying* (Scribner, reprint edition). In it, she explains that when someone loses a close loved one, that person must progress through a series of stages in order to get over the loss and heal emotionally. Those stages, which follow, have been found to apply to the loss of anything that is especially important in life, including the loss of a marriage.

- ✔ Shock and denial
- ✔ Anger
- ✔ Depression
- ✔ Bargaining
- ✔ Sorrow
- ✔ Understanding and acceptance

Understanding each of the stages you must pass through in order to recover from a divorce won't make your pain go away. In fact, as you experience some of the earlier stages of grief, you may feel like you're going crazy or that life will never be normal again. However, knowing what to expect, realizing that what you're feeling is normal, and finding out that countless other people in your situation have gone on to find happiness in life can be very reassuring.

Because your judgment may be somewhat impaired during the early stages of the healing process, avoid making important decisions related to your divorce and to your life in general as much as possible until you've reached the understanding and acceptance stage. If important decisions must be made, seek some objective input from a trusted friend or family member.

How long it takes to get through the grieving process is different for everyone. Some people take only a few months, whereas others take a year or more. Furthermore, even after you think you've stopped grieving, something can happen to trigger your emotions all over again. Receiving your final divorce papers, seeing your former spouse with someone new, or the advent of a special holiday are apt to dredge up feelings you thought you'd put behind you. When that happens, think about what helped you cope with your emotions when you were in the early stages of the grieving process and try those same things again.

Shock and denial

Even if you knew that your marriage had problems and that your spouse was unhappy, the news that he or she wants a divorce can be gut wrenching. *Divorce?* That's something that happens to other people, not to you! If the decision to divorce is a mutual one, you may still find comprehending the idea that your marriage is actually ending difficult.

During this stage, you may waver between thinking that it's all just a silly misunderstanding and that you and your spouse can work things out. You may also find yourself questioning your judgment (were you too naïve?) and the assumptions you made about your marriage and your spouse (were you too trusting?). You may also feel anxious about all the changes about to take place in your life and feel unprepared to deal with them.

Anger

Anger commonly follows shock (although not with everyone). Anger is a normal response to the demise of your marriage, especially if your spouse initiates the divorce. In addition to being angry with your spouse, you may be angry with yourself for the things you could have done but didn't do during your marriage or for all the sacrifices you made on behalf of your spouse and your relationship.

Expressing your anger is actually a healthy response that can help relieve some of the pressure you feel. Keeping all that anger bottled up can lead to depression. Of course, you can get *too* angry. If you let your anger get the best of you, you may find yourself lashing out at your children, experiencing problems at work, and making your divorce far more difficult and ugly than it needs to be.

If you get angry every time you talk with your spouse or even think about him or her, try to figure out why. Doing so may take professional help. What buttons does he or she push for you and vice versa? The sooner you can answer that question, the quicker you can get off the emotional roller coaster ride you're on.

When you feel angry, write down the reasons why you feel that way or write down all the things you would like to say to your spouse. Sometimes just putting your feelings on paper can help you clarify your emotions and take away their intensity so that you can deal with them better. You may also want to check out the anger tool kit available at `www.angermgmt.com`. It can help you dissect your angry feelings so you can deal with them constructively and move beyond them.

You may also want to talk to a close friend or relative about the anger you feel. Ideally, this person will just listen to you blow off steam and won't tell you how to think, argue with you, or take your spouse's side. Avoid sharing your feelings with someone who will reinforce your anger and convince you that feeling angry all the time is okay. Feeling some anger for a little while is okay, but harboring too much anger for too long is dangerous and destructive. It's important to move beyond it.

When you can't seem to shake your anger, especially if you've become confrontational or violent, seek the help of a mental health professional immediately. Confiding in someone who can help you put your feelings in perspective is imperative.

Depression

Depression is another perfectly normal response to a difficult life situation. However, if your depression doesn't go away or grows worse, if you begin drinking too much or doing drugs to numb your feelings, or if you begin having thoughts of suicide, immediately seek help from a mental health professional. You may need some ongoing therapy sessions or medication to help you get through the tough times and out of your depression.

If you're crying a lot, having difficulty sleeping or sleeping too much, gaining or losing weight, or ignoring your physical appearance, you may benefit from antidepressant medication. If your doctor prescribes an antidepressant (in combination with therapy, if necessary), it doesn't mean that you're crazy; it simply means that you need some help to get through the trauma of your divorce in the safest way possible.

A correlation exists between divorce and suicide. In fact, some studies indicate that the rate of suicide among divorcing couples is three times higher than among married couples.

Right now you may not believe that you will ever feel happy again, but take heart. Over time, your negative emotions will subside and, eventually, you'll feel like smiling again.

Bargaining

At times during the healing process, you may respond to your divorce by trying to strike bargains with your spouse. In desperation, you promise to do just about anything to keep your marriage together and to make the pain go away.

Avoid making such deals. If your spouse accepts your offer and you stop your divorce proceedings, you're only postponing the inevitable. The promises you make may be impossible for you to keep, and you may find that you're more miserable than ever in your marriage. If you're tempted to promise your spouse the world in order to save your marriage, talk to a trusted friend or therapist first to get an objective outsider's viewpoint.

Sorrow

Feeling sad is yet another normal response to the end of your marriage. You may cry over what your relationship used to be or over the realization that all the dreams and hopes you had for your marriage won't be realized. You may mourn the loss of your role as a spouse and greatly miss the lifestyle you enjoyed as a married person.

You may also feel remorse over what your divorce may do to your children. Your kids may have to move into a smaller house or apartment and leave behind their neighborhood, best friends, and favorite teachers. If your children will live with your spouse, you won't be as much a part of their lives, and that aspect of your divorce can be very difficult for you and your kids to deal with.

The realization that you're losing the wife or husband role that you greatly value may also trigger feelings of sorrow. You may feel sad about the upcoming lifestyle changes — living apart from your children, moving into a smaller home, living in a less comfortable neighborhood, or giving up club memberships or hobbies that you can no longer afford.

If you're feeling sad about what divorce is taking from your life, realize that no situation lasts forever. In the future, you may experience a more loving and more successful relationship, make more money, and even have more children. Use what you learned in this last relationship to make your married life better the next time around.

Understanding and acceptance

If you're like most people, eventually you will begin to accept the fact of your divorce. Ideally, you should reach this stage before you begin negotiating your divorce agreement with your spouse, but many people cannot resolve their emotional conflicts until after their divorce is over. When you reach this stage, you finally begin to experience some peace in your life.

Although you may still feel some anger toward your spouse or depression over the changes that have occurred in your life, those emotions will gradually dissipate. Your energy level will climb, and your enthusiasm for life will return. Laughter will come easier to you, you'll be ready to begin dating again, and you'll feel ready to take on new challenges.

Sometimes it's good for a trusted friend who knows you and your spouse well to play devil's advocate when you're talking about what went wrong with your marriage, especially if you're expressing a lot of anger toward your spouse and feeling particularly wronged by him or her. By doing so, your friend may be able to help you gain a balanced perspective about your marriage and why it ended.

If you begin dating, keep it casual. Studies show that rebound marriages — marriages that occur just a short time after a couple's divorce is finalized — have a high failure rate. Divorced spouses need time to gain a perspective on why their marriages failed and how to increase their chances of marital success the next time around.

Preventing Your Emotions from Taking Over

How you handle your emotions can mean the difference between creating a fulfilling life for yourself as a single person and remaining stuck in the past. It can also mean the difference between helping your children cope with the situation and jeopardizing your children's happiness now and in the future. You can end up bitter, angry, and defeated, or you can emerge from your divorce a stronger and more self-confident person.

It's important to recognize the possible negative effects of not dealing with the emotions you're feeling. Letting your emotions go unchecked can

- Impede your ability to make sound decisions
- Sap your energy at the time you need it most
- Prevent you from recognizing and acknowledging how you may have contributed to the demise of your marriage

✔ Make you more apt to acquiesce in your divorce negotiations, especially if you feel wracked with guilt and remorse

✔ Drive away your friends and family

You can take some steps to help yourself move through the emotional healing process as quickly as possible.

✔ **Give yourself permission to cry.** Crying is not a sign of weakness. A good cry can be a great way to release emotion. Plus, crying releases natural antidepressant chemicals in your brain. However, if you cry all the time, you probably need to see a therapist. You may be depressed.

✔ **Reach out to close friends and family members.** Sometimes just talking with people who are close to you, sharing a meal with them, or letting them pamper you a little will make you feel a whole lot better.

✔ **Join a divorce support group.** A support group is a particularly good idea if you're not comfortable talking with friends and family, if you feel that you may be wearing out your welcome with them, or if you don't feel that they're giving you the support that you need.

✔ **Keep a journal.** Sometimes the process of recording your thoughts and feelings on paper can have a calming effect and can help you gain a new perspective on your life.

✔ **Begin an exercise program or start exercising more.** Exercise makes you feel better about yourself, which is something you may really need if your spouse initiated your divorce. Additionally, science has shown that exercise helps release those wonderful endorphins, which help lift your spirits naturally and ease depression.

✔ **Be kind to yourself and enjoy focusing on your own needs instead of on your spouse or on your marriage problems.** Renew your interest in a sport you used to enjoy, pick up a new book by your favorite author, or take up a new hobby.

✔ **Enroll in a class, just for the fun of it, or with an eye toward future employment or a new career.** You can explore and develop new talents while making new friends.

✔ **Do something you've always wanted to do.** Plan a trip with a friend, take a hot air balloon ride, or sign up for ballroom dancing classes.

✔ **Volunteer.** Getting involved in a cause that you care about can boost your self-esteem and take your mind off your own problems. If you have trouble getting motivated to do anything other than sleep and eat, the more you can structure your life, the better. Volunteer work is one way to do that.

✔ **Get reacquainted with friends you lost touch with after your marriage began failing.** Renewing friendships with people you used to enjoy may be just what you need to put a little spark back in your life.

✔ **Focus on your career.** However, don't let your work consume your entire life. Withdrawing into your job won't make the unpleasantness of your current situation disappear.

✔ **Spend more time with your children.** Making your children an even more important part of your life than they already are helps reassure them that your divorce in no way diminishes your love for them and that you will continue to be a part of their lives, no matter what.

✔ **Appreciate nature.** The beauty of nature can help heal a wounded spirit. Go for walks in the park or along a waterfront, pause to take in the sunrise and sunset, listen to the birds, or smell the air after a hard rain.

✔ **Make a point of taking a break from your troubles.** Go for a bike ride or a drive in the country, go to a movie, enroll in a class, or take a short vacation if you can afford it and if the time away doesn't interfere with your divorce proceedings.

✔ **Explore your spirituality.** Become more involved in your church, temple, or synagogue. Begin meditating or studying yoga. To get started, try the video *Yoga Workouts For Dummies* or pick up a copy of *Meditation For Dummies* by Stephan Bodian or *Power Yoga For Dummies* by Doug Swenson (all published by Wiley).

✔ **Seek out the friends and family members who have a positive influence on your life.** Doing things together and sharing your thoughts with people you like and trust can take your mind off your troubles and help you gain a healthy perspective about your life changes.

✔ **Schedule time with your religious advisor or a mental health professional.** Counseling can help you put your marriage in perspective and assess what went wrong. Then you can think more clearly about what the future may hold.

If you've tried the suggestions we just listed and you're still feeling blue, figure out what's missing in your life and identify safe and healthy ways to fulfill those needs. For example, if you miss the physical contact you had with your spouse, a massage or hugs from your friends may help you feel better. If you enjoy restaurant meals, ask a friend to split a two-for-one meal coupon.

Use your creativity. You may discover inexpensive activities that are just as enjoyable — and maybe even more enjoyable — than some of your more costly pre-divorce pastimes.

Dealing with the Response of Friends and Family

No doubt most of you will share the news that you're getting divorced with your friends and family soon after you've made your decision. You may even discuss the pros and cons of divorce with your very closest friends and family members before you decide to end your marriage.

Your decision to divorce shouldn't affect your close personal relationships; your true friends will remain friendly no matter what your marital status may be. But be ready for those friends and family members who may view the divorced you a little differently than the married you.

If your friends give you the brush off

Almost inevitably, some of the friends and acquaintances you and your spouse shared as a couple will stop calling you after your divorce becomes common knowledge. Others may act aloof and distant when you cross paths. That sort of behavior can be very hurtful, especially if you already feel rejected.

Some friends may behave as they do because, for whatever reason, they decided to side with your spouse and reject you. Some of these friends may have business or social reasons for doing so, or they may feel some loyalty toward your spouse because they knew him or her before they knew you. Try not to dwell on their behavior. Some of those friends may come around over time, but others never will.

Some friends who act uncomfortable around you may do so because your situation reminds them of their own marital troubles. Others may feel awkward because they're uncertain how to behave around you. They may be wondering whether they should tell you that they're sorry about your divorce or ignore the subject until you bring it up.

If certain friends are important to you, consider making the first move — invite them over for coffee, ask them if they want to play tennis or go shopping, or invite their children to come play with yours.

If your family disapproves of your divorce

You may also notice your relationship with some of your family members becoming chilled now that you're getting a divorce. They may disapprove of your divorce plans, perhaps because your divorce is your family's first, your family's religion frowns upon divorce, or because they're fond of your spouse.

Your family (and your in-laws, if you were close) may begin to resent that you're relying on them for help with childcare more now than you did before. Maybe they're uncomfortable with your asking to borrow money from them, or have grown tired of complaints about your ex-spouse.

Although you should expect your family to support you through tough times, don't take their support or patience for granted. If they help you out, let them know that you appreciate their generosity and stay alert for ways that you can return their favors. Also, try to be sensitive to just how much you can lean on them — everyone has his or her limits — and avoid crossing that line.

If your kids enjoy a loving relationship with your in-laws

If your children have always had good relationships with your in-laws, don't let any negative emotions you may be feeling about your spouse poison your children's relationship with their grandparents. In fact, difficult as it may be, you should do everything you can to let that relationship continue, even if you know that your in-laws are upset about your divorce and maybe even angry with you about it. The grandparent/grandchild relationship is a special kind of relationship, and your children are lucky to have it. So, encourage and support the relationship; don't interfere with it.

Part III
Decisions, Decisions

The 5th Wave   By Rich Tennant

"I'm well aware that the court has requested a lot
from you during the property division hearing in
your divorce, Mr. Harvey. However, I don't
remember sarcasm being on that list."

In this part . . .

Many of the decisions you may have to make during your divorce are likely to be some of the most difficult ones of your entire life. You have to decide how to divide up your marital property and debt, how to handle the custody of your minor children, and what factors to consider when you're planning for your children's financial support. You may also have to make decisions about spousal support. In this part of the book, we provide you with information and guidance on making each of these important decisions, whether you and your spouse make them together in consultation with your attorneys or you rely on your attorneys to do all the negotiating for you.

Chapter 8

Yours, Mine, or Ours? Deciding Who Gets What

. . . .

In This Chapter

▶ Identifying which assets are yours and which ones you own with your spouse

▶ Figuring out the value of the assets from your marriage

▶ Dividing up the assets from your marriage

▶ Deciding what to do about your home, retirement benefits, and other joint business

▶ Determining who will pay your marital debts

. . . .

*I*f your marriage has been a relatively lengthy one, and if you've enjoyed a reasonably comfortable standard of living, you may be surprised when you realize just how much stuff you've managed to collect over the years and just how much it's all worth. Dividing up your property requires thought and deliberation and possibly the advice and assistance of outside experts. Why? Because what you divvy up during your divorce and how you decide to divide it has short-term and long-term financial implications for you and your spouse.

This chapter focuses on what to do about the big stuff from your marriage when you and your spouse are deciding how to divide everything up. The "big stuff" includes your home, the retirement benefits you may have earned during your marriage, and your financial investments — as well as some of the smaller items. We also give you some suggestions for what to do with your marital debts — the debts that you and your spouse acquired during your marriage. For guidance and advice on negotiating the terms of your divorce with your spouse, including how to divide up your assets and debts, see Chapter 12.

Categorizing Your Property

During your marriage, you may have bought a home, furniture, vehicles, expensive computer equipment, or maybe even fine art. No doubt you also own other less-valuable items, too, like kitchen equipment, bedding, a TV set, a DVD player, books, and bikes. And, don't forget that pile of wedding gifts you've had stashed in the attic for years! Now that you're getting divorced, you have to do something with that stuff, too.

You can divide up the less-valuable stuff you own rather informally. This division is usually a matter of making sure that each of you gets your fair share of what you need to set up new households and, also, that you get to take at least some of the items that may have special meaning to you. Chapter 12, which covers some of the divorce matters you can handle without the help of professionals, suggests some ways of accomplishing this division.

Distinguishing between tangible property and intangible property

When you divide up your property, you and your spouse must also take into account your *intangible property,* such as retirement benefits, stocks, and bonds. (An *intangible asset* is an asset that has no intrinsic or marketable value but instead represents value.) On the other hand, your car and your home are *tangible property,* which means that they have a marketable value by themselves.

Identifying separate property versus marital property

Before you can divide up the value of your property, you and your spouse must first determine which assets you own together — which you must divide between you — and which ones are yours to keep. In other words, you must figure out what is and isn't *marital property.* Marital property consists of the assets that you and your spouse own together. (A closely held business or business interest may also be marital property.) You're each legally entitled to a share of the value of your marital property. If you haven't already done so, inventory and categorize your assets. (Chapter 3 gives you some advice on how best to do so.)

Any property that's not marital property is *separate property.* Separate property belongs to you or your spouse but not to both of you. You don't have to share it with one another in your divorce.

The property laws of your state ordinarily determine which assets are marital assets and which ones are not. But if you and your spouse signed a valid prenuptial or postnuptial agreement, you may have already decided how you intend to divide up your property in the event of a split. (See Chapter 19 for more information on prenuptial and postnuptial agreements.)

Commingling and the confusion it can create

In the course of your marriage, you and your spouse may have mixed together your separate property or may have mixed your separate property with marital property. For example, you may have used some of your separate property to improve the rental property that you and your spouse own, or both of you may have deposited your separate money into a joint account. Blending together different kinds of property is called *commingling*.

Unless both of you have kept detailed records of exactly what you did with your assets, you will have a difficult, if not impossible, time distinguishing between marital property and separate property.

If you and your spouse try to decide which portion of your commingled assets you should treat as separate property and who owns that separate property, your decisions will probably be based on your "best guess." But if a judge decides, the standard he or she will apply depends on your state.

You can use accountants to "trace" the commingled assets, but that can cost you more than what your attorneys may charge!

If you want to avoid commingling assets in your next marriage, follow these suggestions:

- ✔ Keep your spouse's name off any deeds or other ownership documents that relate to your separate property.
- ✔ Don't add your spouse's name to your separate accounts.
- ✔ Don't deposit your separate property into a joint account.
- ✔ Don't use your separate money to purchase marital property or to pay for marital expenses.
- ✔ Use a prenuptial or postnuptial agreement to define what is and isn't separate and marital property.
- ✔ Consult an attorney familiar with the property laws of your state if you're concerned that a financial transaction you're considering may have the effect of changing your separate property into marital property.

Interest earned on separate property assets during your marriage can become marital property. For example, if you have a separate bank account and you roll over the interest income into your joint account each month, that income can be considered marital property. Therefore, you'd be commingling separate property with marital property.

Assessing the Value of Your Assets

After you determine what out of everything you own constitutes marital property, you need to assign a dollar value to each marital asset. Ordinarily, that dollar figure is the item's *fair market value*, or the amount that you could reasonably expect to sell the item for (assuming that you didn't have to sell it and that you had a willing buyer).

Although you can probably value many of your marital assets yourselves, you may need the help of outside experts, such as appraisers and CPAs, to determine the worth of particularly valuable or complex assets, such as real estate, certain types of retirement benefits, fine antiques, a closely held business, and so on. An outside expert's services can also be helpful if you and your spouse can't agree on how to value an important asset.

After you value your marital assets, you have to divide up the value of those assets, either by applying the property law concepts and guidelines a judge in your state would use if your divorce went to trial or by applying some other criteria that you and your spouse both agree to.

When deciding which property to take from your marriage, keep in mind your personal goals for your life after divorce, the separate property you already own, and your post-divorce financial needs.

Placing a value on the vehicles you own

Determining the value of the vehicles you and your spouse jointly own is relatively easy and inexpensive. You can

✔ **Look up their values in the "Blue Book":** The easiest way to get this information is to go to the Web site for the *Kelley Blue Book* at www.kbb.com. Your local library should have a hard copy of this trusted resource.

✔ **Ask local car dealers what they would give you for your vehicles:** Because used car dealers tend to make low-ball offers, you and your spouse may want to adjust the offers upward a bit.

✔ **Read the auto ads in the classified section of your local paper for vehicles comparable to yours:** The asking prices of vehicles similar to yours provide a local reference for determining the values of your vehicles.

Divvying It Up

If you don't have a lot of complicated assets — retirement plans, investments, and business interests, for example — or a lot of debt, you and your spouse may be able to divide up your assets and debts by yourselves. The information in this section provides general advice for how to do that and explains the criteria you should consider when you're doing the dividing.

Doing the dividing yourself

If you do your own dividing, your individual judgments about what is and isn't fair and your ability to compromise will certainly influence how you end up allocating the value of your marital property. (See Chapter 12 for details on how to negotiate your marital property.)

Bear in mind that if you and your spouse end up in court after your divorce is final because one of you wants your property division agreement overturned, the judge will assess the fairness of your agreement in light of your state's property laws and property division guidelines. Therefore, even when you divide your marital property yourself, keep your state's laws and guidelines in mind:

- If you live in an *equitable distribution* state (see Chapter 3 to find out what type of state you live in), you're entitled to your *fair share* of the marital property that you and your spouse own. Your "fair share" is whatever the judge decides you're entitled to based on the guidelines that your state uses to divide up marital property or whatever your lawyer negotiates for you.

- If you live in a *community property* state (see Chapter 3 to find out what type of state you live in), the general presumption is that you and your spouse are each entitled to half the value of your marital property. But, in reality, your state probably allows a judge to divide up your marital property on an equitable basis rather than a strict 50/50 split. The judge takes into consideration many of the criteria that a judge in an equitable distribution state uses (see the next section to find out the typical criteria that judges use to determine division of marital property).

- Mississippi law says that who gets what property depends on how the assets are titled. Therefore, if you and your spouse both have legal title to a particular asset, you both own it, and you must divide it between you equitably. For example, you both are on the title to your family's SUV, which means that you're both entitled to half of its value. However, if your spouse is the legal owner of a particular asset, he or she owns it and is entitled to it in your divorce, even if you helped pay for it and used it. Mississippi is the only state that uses this criteria to divide up property in divorce.

If you and your spouse are handling your own property division negotiations, and especially if the total value of what you own together is substantial, you should consult a certified divorce planner, a qualified CPA, or a financial planner before you start dividing up what you own and what you owe. Financial service professionals can use computer models to help you test various scenarios for dividing up what you own and what you owe so that you can make strategically wise decisions. In essence, they can do a cost-benefit analysis of different property-division schemes. Some financial services professionals specialize in providing pre-divorce money management advice. They can help analyze the best way to deal with not only the division of property but also child support and spousal support.

You and your spouse can share the cost of hiring the same financial professional or you can each hire your own. If you share one, don't hire a professional who is related to either of you, is a friend of either of yours, or is a professional associate of yours or your spouse's. If you do, the spouse who doesn't have the relationship with the financial professional may view with suspect whatever conclusions the professional reaches.

Leaving the decisions to the legal experts

If you involve attorneys in your property division negotiations or if you look to a judge to decide who gets what, your state's property laws and property division guidelines take center stage. The judge's prejudices and preferences and the persuasiveness of your attorneys can also be big factors.

Although property division guidelines vary from state to state, they usually take the following factors into consideration:

- ✔ **How much you and your spouse each earn now and can be expected to earn in the future:** Often a judge awards a relatively larger share of marital property to the spouse who earns less money and who has the lower-earnings potential. In evaluating your earnings potential, the judge may consider your education level, physical and mental health, and other factors that may have a bearing on your ability to earn a good living.

- ✔ **Your current standard of living:** A judge tries to allocate the value of your marital property between you and your spouse so that neither of you suffers a dramatic reversal in your lifestyle after you're divorced. But in reality, your lifestyle may change (probably for the worse, especially if you're a woman).

- ✔ **The value of the separate property that each of you may own:** If one of you has considerably more separate property than the other, the wealthier spouse may end up with less marital property.

- ✔ **Your individual contributions to your marriage:** These days, most states recognize that paying the family's bills is only one way that a spouse can contribute to a marriage. In recent years, the courts have started recognizing that being a full-time parent, helping your spouse advance his or her career, and making other contributions to the marriage all have financial value.

If you worked so that your spouse could obtain a college degree or professional license, your state may view that degree or license as a marital asset, and you may be entitled to a share of its value. In other states, you may be reimbursed for your contribution to your spouse's education.

✔ **How long you were married:** The longer you were married, the more likely the court will view you as equal partners. At the very least, a long marriage often entitles the spouse with less separate property or the lower earnings potential to a greater share of the marital property.

✔ **Your age and health:** Older spouses and spouses who are in poor health often receive a greater share of their marital property than younger or healthier spouses.

✔ **Whether either of you squandered marital property:** If one of you wasted your joint funds by gambling or repeatedly making bad business investments or risky personal loans, for example, that spouse may end up with less marital property.

✔ **Other factors:** A judge may consider other factors, too, such as whether either of you has a lot of debt from a previous marriage, is likely to come into a significant inheritance, or helped increase the value of the other's separate property during your marriage, and so on. Also, In some states, the only factor a judge considers when dividing up a couple's property is the value of that property, with each spouse getting approximately half of that value.

Fault can be the single-most important factor in the eyes of some courts in states where judges can consider fault when dividing up a couple's marital property and debts.

Accounting for the decrease in women's standard of living

After a divorce, a woman's standard of living tends to decline, whereas, on average, a man's rises. One explanation for this difference is that men usually earn more than women, so they tend to be able to afford better divorce lawyers and have more financial resources to fall back on after their divorce. Another explanation is that women are more apt to get custody of the children and, although they may receive child support, in most divorces, the amount of the support doesn't allow the average woman to maintain her pre-divorce lifestyle. Of course, a significant number of women with custody of their children don't receive their court-ordered child support or receive it only occasionally.

(continued)

(continued)

If you find yourself in a tough financial position, the following books can help you get by on the money you have and deal with any money troubles that may develop:

✔ *Good Advice for a Bad Economy* by John Ventura and Mary Reed (Berkley Books)

✔ *The Budget Kit: The Common Cents Money Management Workbook* by Judy Lawrence (Dearborn)

✔ *The 9 Steps to Financial Freedom* by Suze Orman (Three Rivers Press)

Deciding What to Do with Your Home

When everything around you is changing, you may be tempted to hold on to your home at all costs. You probably feel comfortable living there and, perhaps spent a great deal of time and energy decorating it and gardening. Also, if you have young children and you're going to be their primary caregiver after your divorce, you may want to stay in your own home to bolster their sense of emotional security.

But when the matter of your home comes up, try to put your emotions aside and to approach the decision about whether or not to keep it from a purely financial perspective. When you do, you may decide that keeping your home after you divorce is neither wise nor financially realistic. On the other hand, with some savvy financial planning, you may find a way to keep your home.

Here's the bottom line: Whatever you do about your home should be a financial decision, not an emotional one. If you let your emotions rule, you may end up losing your home because you can't afford to keep up with the payments, the property taxes, or the cost of maintaining the home. Don't forget that maintenance costs, such as interior and exterior painting, repair and servicing of the heating and AC systems, roof repair, lawn mowing, and snow plowing, add up.

Finding out how much it's worth

You can determine the value of your home in a couple of inexpensive ways. The traditional way is to ask a real estate agent for some recent selling prices of comparable houses in your neighborhood and how much you may be able to get for your house. However, whatever figure a real estate agent gives you only represents an approximation of your home's value.

A better method, albeit a more expensive one, is for you and your spouse to hire a real estate appraiser to value your home. Using an appraiser is better than relying on a real estate agent's estimation because the appraiser's value tends to be more accurate. You and your spouse can hire an appraiser together as long as you select one who you both feel will give you an objective value. For example, you may not want to use an appraiser who's a friend, relative, or professional associate of your spouse. (If your divorce goes to trial, you and your spouse would each have to obtain an independent appraisal by a real estate appraiser.)

Real estate appraisals tend to be imprecise because, in the end, how much a house is worth is somewhat subjective. For this reason, if you and your spouse both get your own appraisals, the results can be quite different. In this case, you and your spouse would either have to agree about which value was more accurate or hire a third appraiser and agree to accept whatever dollar value he or she assigns to your home.

Don't value your home based on its tax appraisal. Tax appraisals are always considerably less than your home's actual value.

Evaluating your options

Most divorcing couples resolve the problem of "what to do about the house" in one of the following ways: by selling it, keeping it, or retaining an interest in it. Read on to find out more details about each of these options.

Selling it

When your home is the only marital asset of real value that you own, you may have to sell it so that you can both leave your marriage with some money in your pockets. You and your spouse may also decide to sell the house because it holds too many unhappy memories for both of you, because it's too big for you to live in and maintain by yourself, or because you can't afford to keep it.

If you decide to sell, remember that the selling price probably won't represent the actual amount of money you and your spouse will split between you. Most likely, you'll have a mortgage to pay off, selling costs, and possibly property taxes to deduct. If you use a real estate broker to sell your home, you'll have to pay the broker a percentage of your home's gross sale price (that is, a *broker's fee*). After all is said and done, when you subtract those costs from your home's anticipated sale price, selling your house may not appear to be a very attractive option, but may, nevertheless, be the best one.

Don't overlook the federal tax implications of selling your home, either, when you're deciding what to do with your house. To understand how a sale may affect your federal taxes, talk to your CPA and read the IRS publication *Tax Information on Selling Your Home,* Number 523. You can order this publication by calling the IRS at 800-829-1040 or you can read it online at www.irs.gov. You may also want to pick up a copy of *House Selling For Dummies* by Eric Tyson and Ray Brown (Wiley).

Keeping it

Taking the house in your property settlement may be an option if you have enough other marital property that your spouse can take another asset of comparable value. However, this option isn't viable for many couples; instead, they may work out a buy-sell agreement in which one spouse buys out the other's interest over time. We describe this option in the next section of this chapter.

If your spouse gives you his or her interest in the home that you owned together, you receive a special warranty deed from your spouse. In turn, you give your spouse a deed of trust to secure your assumption of the mortgage loan.

If you want to take the house, you'll probably get the mortgage that goes with it as well. Therefore, review the household budget you projected for your life after divorce to make certain that you can really afford to take over the monthly mortgage payments as well as the cost of upkeep on your home. Don't forget about property taxes, either, unless your monthly mortgage payments include them. If you take over responsibility for paying all these expenses without making certain that you can afford them, you may have to sell your home eventually or you may even lose it in a foreclosure. If you haven't already developed a household budget for yourself, Chapter 3 tells you how.

If your spouse keeps the home, takes over the mortgage, and then defaults on the loan, the mortgage holder can look to you for payment, no matter what your divorce agreement may say. Therefore, consider adding a *hold harmless provision* to the agreement, which gives you the right to sue your former spouse for the money you may end up paying. However, you have to go to court to enforce it and, even if you get a judgment against your spouse, you have no guarantee that you can actually collect what he or she owes you.

A *deed of trust to secure assumption* gives you the right (in the event that your spouse defaults on the mortgage after your divorce) to dispossess him or her, to put a tenant in the house, or to sell the house in order to eliminate your financial and legal exposure on the home. However, to accomplish that, you have to stay up-to-date on the status of your former spouse's mortgage payments, which may be difficult, if not impossible to do, especially if you and your ex live in different towns and/or have little or no communication with one another.

Retain an interest in it

You and your spouse may want to sell your home but, for practical reasons, decide to delay the sale. For example, you may want your children to be able to live in your home until they complete high school. In this case, the spouse with primary responsibility for raising the children stays in the home with the kids. Your property agreement would then give you and your spouse an interest in that property.

If you opt for this sort of arrangement, be sure that your agreement addresses the following questions:

- ✔ How much of an interest do each of you have in the home?
- ✔ At what point must you put your house up for sale?
- ✔ Who will put the house up for sale?
- ✔ How will you determine the asking price?
- ✔ How will you and your spouse pay all sale-related expenses?
- ✔ How will you and your spouse divide up the sale proceeds?

If you want to give each other the option of buying out the other spouse's interest in your home, you and you spouse should clearly define the *buyout* terms in your divorce agreement.

If you'll still owe money on the mortgage after the buyout, your agreement should also address the following questions:

- ✔ How will you and your spouse pay the mortgage each month?
- ✔ How will you and your spouse pay the home owner's insurance and property taxes?
- ✔ Who will be responsible for the cost of minor repairs and major ones, such as a new roof?

Your agreement should also specify the regular upkeep that your home requires in order to protect your investment in the property. You should specify who's responsible for doing the maintenance and how often. Enforcing this provision, however, may be tough.

Good news about the capital gains tax

It used to be that if a single person or a couple sold their home for more than what they paid for it, they'd either have to purchase a new home within two years or they'd have to pay Uncle Sam a substantial tax on their *capital gain*. A capital gain is the difference between your home's purchase price and its sale price minus the cost of any capital improvements you may have made to it; for example, adding an addition to your home. But now, as a result of a change that President Clinton signed into law in 1997, single people get a capital gains tax exclusion of up to $250,000 when they sell their homes, which means that they don't get taxed on the first $250,000 of gain or profit they may realize from the sale. Married couples who file a joint tax return will get an exclusion of $500,000. But married or single, to qualify for the exclusion, you must have lived in your home for at least two of the five years prior to its sale.

(continued)

(continued)

If you move a great deal, you'll be pleased to know that the capital gains tax exclusion is no longer a one-time thing. You can use it every two years for an unlimited number of times. In addition, to benefit from the exclusion, you used to have to purchase a new home of equal or greater value than the home you sold, but that provision was also eliminated in 1997. This is good news if you get your home in your divorce

and decide to sell it because you cannot afford the mortgage payments or the upkeep.

If you and your spouse are above the 15 percent income tax bracket, you will be taxed at 15 percent. If you're at or below that tax bracket, you'll be taxed at 5 percent. If you don't know what tax bracket you're in, speak to your CPA.

Dividing Up Your Retirement Benefits

In most states, the retirement benefits you or your spouse have earned during your marriage are treated as marital assets and should be included among the assets you have to divide up. Such benefits may include defined contribution plans such as 401(k)s, Individual Retirement Accounts (IRAs), stock-option plans, profit-sharing plans, Keoghs, Simplified Employee Pension Plans (SEPs), and old-fashioned pensions, also known as "defined benefit retirement plans." Most people earn their retirement benefits by working for an employer who either makes a retirement plan available to them as an optional benefit or provides it to them as an automatic perk of their job.

If you've worked for several employers during your professional career, you may have earned a retirement benefit from each. Be sure that your asset inventory reflects all those benefits.

Defined benefit or defined contribution: Which is which?

Retirement benefits fall into one of two categories: defined benefit plans or defined contribution plans.

The *defined benefit plan* is the kind of retirement plan that employees used to receive along with the proverbial gold watch after years of loyal service to an employer. Today, however, that plan is pretty much a thing of the past for the vast majority of employees, namely because it's too expensive for most companies. Typically,

defined benefit plans are available only to people in the highest levels of management.

A defined benefit plan comes as an automatic job benefit — you don't choose whether or not to participate in it. The plan represents a promise from your employer that, when you retire, you will receive either a predetermined amount of income each month or a monthly income determined through a formula. The formula takes into account how long you worked for your employer, your salary, your age, and other factors.

You usually don't have access to the money in your defined benefit plan until you've retired. Therefore, if your spouse wants to share in your retirement benefits, he or she has to wait for that money, just like you.

A *defined contribution plan* is the type of retirement benefit that most employees are offered these days. Participation in a defined contribution plan isn't automatic; if your employer offers one and you want to participate, you have to enroll in it. If you do enroll, you, your employer, or both of you, contribute money to your plan. For example, your employer may agree to match your contributions 100 percent, 80 percent, or at some other level.

In this type of play, your employer doesn't offer any guarantees as to how much income your defined contribution plan will provide you when you retire. That amount depends on how much you and/or your employer contribute to your plan and on what kind of return you get from investing the money that is in your plan.

You can take money out of this type of retirement plan before you retire, although you have to pay an early withdrawal penalty and you may have to treat the withdrawal as taxable income. When you're ready to retire, you can receive all your retirement dollars in a lump sum or you can receive payments over time.

Visit the Web site of the federal Department of Labor's Employee Benefits Administration (www.dol.gov/ebs) for additional information on pensions in general and on the pension rights of spouses and former spouses in particular. You may also want to read an online version of "What You Should Know About Your Pension Rights," a Department of Labor publication that offers a lot of useful information on employer-sponsored pension plans. You can also order a free copy of the publication by calling 800-998-7542. Yet another pension-related resource is the Pension Rights Center, which you can access by going online at www.pensionrights.org or by calling 202-296-3776.

Vesting and your rights

Depending on the type of retirement plan you participate in, if you leave your job, you may have to be *vested* in the plan in order to be entitled to the money that your employer contributed to it. However, you're entitled at any time to receive the money *you* have contributed, whether you're vested or not. To be vested, you have to work for your employer a certain number of years.

Depending on your state, if you're not vested in your employer's retirement plan when you get divorced, the money in your retirement plan may not be considered marital property. Even if you're vested, if your marriage didn't last for at least a year, your spouse is *not* entitled to any of your retirement benefits.

Valuing a defined contribution plan

Assessing the value of a *defined contribution plan* is fairly easy (see the sidebar "Defined benefit or defined contribution: Which is which?" for a definition of this type of plan). In most cases, the value is simply the amount of money that's in the plan at any given time.

To find out how much is in your defined contribution plan, contact the plan administrator or review the plan's most recent summary statement. The federal Employment Retirement Security Act (ERISA) says that any private-sector employer who offers a retirement plan to its employees must also provide a summary annual report that tells employees the value of their plan.

If your participation in the plan predates your marriage, all your retirement dollars aren't marital property. By reviewing the plan reports you received over the years and doing some careful calculation, you should be able to figure out for yourself what portion of it is marital property. If numbers intimidate you or if the total value of your plan is substantial, you may want to hire a CPA or pension consultant to do the figuring for you.

If you participate in a stock-ownership plan, the value of the plan is equivalent to the number of shares you own multiplied by the current dollar value of a share. If the company you work for is *closely held* (one whose stock isn't publicly traded), the company can tell you how much a share of its stock is worth. If the stock is publicly traded, you can find the current per-share value by going to the financial pages of your local newspaper. Or, you can ask your stockbroker or financial advisor for that information.

Valuing a defined benefit plan

Valuing a defined benefit plan and determining how much of that value is marital property can be a rather complicated process. (See the sidebar "Defined benefit or defined contribution: Which is which?" for a definition of this type of plan.) Therefore, if you want it done right, you should hire a pension expert. Ask your accountant to recommend one.

Do not assume that the value shown on your plan summary statement is the actual worth of your defined benefit plan — it may not be.

Parceling out those dollars

This section presents three alternatives for dealing with retirement benefits. When you're considering which alternative may be best for you, you must take into account the following:

✔ The value of the benefits

✔ The value of your share of the benefits

✔ The value of your other marital assets

✔ The value of your separate property

✔ How much money you need now, not later

✔ How close you are to retirement age

✔ The likely tax impact of each option

If you need help analyzing your options in light of these factors, talk with a qualified CPA, your financial advisor, or a family law attorney.

Here are the three ways you can divide up your retirement benefits:

✔ **Let whichever spouse who's earning the retirement benefits retain all rights to them, and let the other spouse take an appropriate amount of other marital assets:** This option is usually the cheapest way to deal with retirement benefits and also tends to be the way most judges prefer to deal with these benefits. For this option to work for you and your spouse, you need other marital property comparable in value to the value of the retirement benefits.

✔ **Share the benefits:** This option provides each of you with regular income after the spouse who's earning the retirement benefits is eligible to receive them. If you choose this option, you will probably need a *Qualified Domestic Relations Order,* or QDRO, to make it work. (See the following sidebar " A crash course on QDROs.")

✔ **Give the spouse who's not earning the benefits a lump-sum payment now as his or her share:** Use this option in lieu of sharing the retirement benefits later. If you go this route, make sure to transfer the money to the spouse who's receiving the lump sum so that the other spouse doesn't have to claim the transfer as taxable income. But, remember, this option doesn't work for every type of retirement benefit. In addition, talk with a qualified CPA before you agree to a lump-sum payment so that you understand the tax consequences. Otherwise, you may face a sizable tax liability.

If you take your share of the retirement benefits in a lump sum, the amount you receive is based on the present cash value of the plan, not its future value. Therefore, you may receive more or less than what you would have received if you had waited to take the money later.

A crash course on QDROs

A *Qualified Domestic Relations Order (QDRO)* is a special type of court order that directs a retirement plan administrator to disperse benefits in accordance with the terms of your divorce agreement or in accordance with a judge's decision. You need a separate QDRO for every retirement plan that you and your ex-spouse share. A QDRO can also collect alimony or child support payments from a pension plan.

If you decide to share military or government retirement benefits (such as U.S. Civil Service Retirement benefits or state retirement benefits) with your ex-spouse, you need to use different kinds of court orders for these types of benefits to accomplish what a QDRO does.

QDROs are complicated legal documents, so don't try to cut corners by drafting one on your own. Hire a qualified attorney to do the job for you because a poorly executed QDRO can jeopardize the tax-deferred status of the benefits and also result in the plan administrator not dispersing the funds in the plan according to your divorce agreement.

If you delay getting a QDRO, you may lose some or all of the benefits you have a right to according to your divorce agreement. Among other reasons, this can happen if your former spouse retires, becomes disabled, or dies before you've obtained a QDRO.

Social security benefits you're owed as a former spouse

Based on your former spouse's work history, if you meet certain criteria when you reach a certain age, you may be entitled to collect social security benefits, including retirement and survivor benefits. Whether you're entitled to these benefits is a matter that's between you and the Social Security Administration, not between you and your former spouse. Your benefits don't depend on what your divorce agreement says.

You may be entitled to retirement benefits if

- ✔ Your former spouse paid into the Social Security Trust Fund.
- ✔ You and your ex-spouse were married for at least ten years and have been divorced for at least two years.
- ✔ You and your former spouse are at least 62 years old.
- ✔ You haven't remarried when you apply for benefits.
- ✔ You're not already receiving social security, spousal, or survivor benefits based on someone else's employment history.

If you meet these criteria, you can either collect the social security benefits you have earned in your own name or you can collect dependents' benefits. The dependents' benefits equal ½ of the benefits that your former spouse is entitled to, even if your spouse hasn't yet begun collecting social security. However, if you're entitled to social security benefits based on your own work history, and those benefits are greater than the dependents' benefits, you will receive the bigger monthly benefits — the ones you earned.

Ordinarily, if you remarry after you've been collecting dependents' benefits, you cannot continue collecting those benefits. However, you can resume collecting them if your new marriage ends in a divorce or an annulment or if your new spouse dies.

If you collect benefits based on your former spouse's work history, the amount of benefits that your spouse can collect is not affected. Also, your ex will never know that you're receiving them.

To establish your eligibility for benefits, visit the social security office closest to you at least three months before you turn 62. Bring proof of

- ✔ **Your identity:** Your driver's license or state ID, for example
- ✔ **Your age and the age of your former spouse:** Birth certificates for the both of you
- ✔ **Your marriage:** Your marriage license proves your marriage
- ✔ **Your divorce:** A copy of your divorce decree, which you received from the court when your divorce was final

If you cannot find all the information you need, go to the Social Security Administration office anyway. The staff there can help you locate what you're missing.

To find out more about the social security benefits you are entitled to, steer your mouse to the Social Security Administration's Web site at `www.ssa.gov`.

Social security survivor benefits

If your former spouse dies and you were married to him or her for at least ten years, you may also be eligible to receive social security survivor benefits, assuming that your former spouse would have been eligible to collect social security benefits at retirement age or was already doing so. However, in most instances, you cannot receive them if you remarry before you turn 60 unless that marriage ends with a divorce or annulment or your new spouse dies. If you remarry after 60 (or after 50, if you're disabled), you can continue receiving survivors' benefits.

By and large, the eligibility criteria for social security survivor benefits mirror the criteria for retirement benefits, except that you can begin receiving reduced survivor benefits when you turn 60 or full survivor benefits when you turn 65. If you're caring for a child who's under the age of 16 or is disabled, and you are eligible to receive benefits based on the work history of your deceased spouse, you may be able to begin collecting survivor benefits when you reach age 50.

If you want to receive an estimate of your survivor benefits, call the Social Security Administration at 800-772-1213 and ask for a Request for Earnings and Benefits Estimate Statement. But be aware that the eligibility rules and benefit amounts for social security benefits are always subject to change, especially because Congress keeps trying to figure out how to accommodate retiring baby boomers. For that reason, the actual amount of the benefits you receive may be less than the estimate.

If you remarry before you turn 60, you're not eligible for survivor benefits; if your new marriage occurs after your 60th birthday, your eligibility is unaffected. However, your new marriage cannot take place within two years of your former spouse's death.

Getting Down to Business: What to Do with Your Joint Enterprise

If either of you owns a closely held business or has a share in one, or if you and your spouse own a business together, some portion of its value is ordinarily considered marital property unless you agreed to a different arrangement through a legally valid prenuptial or postnuptial agreement. (Chapter 19 explains how those agreements work.)

If you and your spouse have both been actively involved in your business, deciding what to do with it can be especially difficult. The idea that you may have to leave the business, shut it down, or sell it can be tough to accept when your marriage is ending. On the other hand, making plans for a new career may be just what you need to get over the loss of your marriage.

Your options in a nutshell

To help you deal with the difficult decision of what to do with the business you and your spouse own, we offer you a number of options that have worked for other couples:

> ✔ **One spouse keeps the business and the other gets marital assets equal in value to his or her interest in the business:** Usually, the spouse who takes the business is the one who's been most actively involved in it or whose skills and knowledge are most essential to its continued success.

For financial reasons or because sufficient other marital property may not exist, the spouse who keeps the business may buy out the interest of the other spouse over time. You need to formalize the buyout in a written agreement. Also, to help secure your spouse's payments to you, placing a lien on his or her real estate, on the assets of the business, or on some other assets, if there are any, is a good idea.

When you let your spouse buy you out over time, you assume certain risks because your ex may be slow to pay you, may stop paying you entirely, or may even bankrupt the business. Unfortunately, you may not be able to avoid assuming these risks, despite the steps you may take to secure his or her payments.

✔ **You divide up the business and each of you takes a part of it:** This arrangement is practical only when you have a logical way to divide up your business and if you can divide it without jeopardizing the financial integrity of each part.

✔ **You sell the business and split the proceeds:** Selling your business may be your only option if all your marital assets are tied up in your business. However, if the continued success of the business depends on your skills and know-how, the business may not have much worth on the open market unless it includes significant assets that would be of value to a new owner.

✔ **Liquidate the business:** If neither of you is interested in continuing the business and you cannot sell it, liquidating it is a reasonable alternative. However, to take advantage of this alternative, your business's assets must have market value. *Marketable assets* can include machinery, equipment, inventory, real estate, or accounts receivables. Depending on the type and value of the assets you are selling, you may want to sell them yourself, hire a liquidator to sell them for you (you'll have to pay the liquidator a part of the proceeds), or auction off the assets.

✔ **Keep operating your business together:** For obvious reasons, only a relatively small number of divorcing spouses who are also business partners choose this option. Most divorced spouses do not want to continue such an important and mutually dependent relationship. In fact, doing so may actually be harmful to the business.

If you worked in your spouse's separate-property business without compensation, your contribution to the business may be a factor in your property settlement.

Assigning a market value to the business

To implement any of the options described in the previous section (except for liquidation), you have to assign a fair market value to your business. If you want to make that determination yourself, you need the following data:

✔ Profit and loss statements for the past three years

✔ Balance sheets for the past three years

✔ Records of accounts receivable

✔ Records of accounts payable

✔ Statements of cash flows for the past three years

✔ Tax returns for the past three years

✔ Contracts for future business

✔ Recent good-faith offers to buy the business, if any exist

✔ Information about the purchase price of businesses comparable to yours

Be aware that valuing a business isn't easy. So, if you and your spouse intend to do the valuation yourself, find out as much information as you can about the process. For example, you can find excellent how-to information at the Divorceinfo Web site (www.divorceinfo.com/businessvalue). Better yet, assuming you can afford it, you and your spouse can each hire outside experts — independent CPAs or business valuation professionals — to determine the market value of your business. From there, you can average their estimates. If you do, be sure to get help from an outside expert who's familiar with your particular type of business, particularly if your business is large, valuable, or complex. Be forewarned that the help of such experts doesn't come cheap. To find a qualified business valuation expert, contact the National Association of Certified Valuation Analysts. It can refer you to one or more trained, certified experts. You can reach the association at 801-486-0600.

When valuing your joint business, don't overlook its *goodwill value.* Goodwill consists of your business's reputation, name recognition, track record in pleasing its customers, role in the local community, and other factors that make it a respected enterprise.

If you're going to leave the business you've shared with your spouse, don't leave it up to him or her to determine its market value. Either take an active role in valuing it or hire an independent CPA or business valuation expert to do it for you. As much as you may trust your spouse, it's in his or her best interest to assign your business as low a market value as possible. That way, either your spouse has to pay you less if he or she buys you out over time or you end up entitled to less of the other marital property.

When you and your spouse began your business, if you had other co-owners, you may have negotiated an upfront agreement regarding what your individual shares of the business would be worth if one of you decided to exit the business. That agreement determines what your share of the enterprise is worth, and that decision isn't one that you and your spouse can make.

Last but Not Least: Dealing with Your Debts

In our credit-oriented society, if you have a lot of debt, you're like countless other divorcing couples. So, unfortunately, your divorce may be more about dividing up your debts than your assets. And sadly, although you can leave your marriage behind, you can't do the same with your debts. Divorced or not, you and your spouse must decide how to pay your debts.

Some of that debt may be *secured debt,* such as your mortgage or car loan. Secured debt is debt that you have collateralized with an asset, which means that if you don't pay the debt, the creditor can take the collateral. You probably also have *unsecured debt,* such as credit card debt, for example.

Unsecured debt has the potential to create a great deal of discord in a divorce because, unlike a secured debt, it's usually not associated with an asset of any significant value. For example, unsecured debts are typically associated with the purchase of clothing, gas for your car, entertainment, vacations, and so on. Therefore, you have nothing of real value to show for having incurred that debt. Although, in many divorces, if you agree to assume responsibility for a secured debt, you get the asset that the debt is financing as well, whereas if you take responsibility for paying some of the unsecured debt from your marriage, you probably have no assets of true value to take that are associated with those unsecured debts.

Tips for avoiding trouble

Because figuring out how to deal with the debts from your marriage is probably one of the least-pleasant aspects of getting divorced — especially if you have a whole lot of debt and a lot fewer assets of any true value — here are some suggestions for resolving that issue:

- **Pay off all your marital debt as part of your divorce.** This solution is usually the best way to deal with marital debt, assuming that you and your spouse have sufficient cash and/or other liquid assets and you don't need those assets to begin your lives as single consumers. The key advantage of paying off all your marital debts is that you both get to begin your post-divorce lives unencumbered by financial obligations from your marriage. Paying off your debts also means that neither of you has to worry about how you will be affected if your ex-spouse doesn't pay the debts he or she agreed to pay. Remember, creditors can look to you for payment of any debts that you and your spouse incurred together, no matter what your divorce agreement may say.

✔ **Trade debt for assets.** If you can't wipe out all your marital debt, you may agree to take more than your share in exchange for getting more of the marital assets — the financial equivalent of taking a spoonful of sugar to make the medicine go down — because you can afford to pay more of the debts than your spouse can.

✔ **Take your fair share.** If you and your spouse own little, if anything, of real value, dividing up your debts may simply mean that each of you takes your fair share of the debt. For example, you may agree to pay off the balance on a credit card that was in both your names but that you, not your spouse, used regularly.

✔ **Pay off your debts together after your divorce.** Avoid this arrangement. It requires too much cooperation and communication between you and your former spouse. However, if this is your best or only option, securing your spouse's obligation to pay his or her share of your unsecured debt (your credit card debt, for example) by placing a lien on one or more of your spouse's separate assets is highly recommended. Also, if you and your spouse agree to pay off your debts together after your marriage, make the details of the arrangement part of your divorce agreement. That way, you can refer to the agreement if one of you does not live up to it and you can ask the court for help getting the arrangement enforced.

If you separate before you divorce, just who's legally responsible for the debts you or your spouse may incur depends on your state. Most states presume that you have joint debts unless you or your spouse can prove otherwise. However, some states treat such debt as individual debt, whereas others consider what the debt financed. For example, if it helped pay for essentials, such as food, clothing, and shelter, it may be treated as joint debt, but it probably would not be considered joint debt if it financed a vacation or a shopping spree.

Where the law stands on your debts

When deciding the best way to deal with the money you owe, bear in mind that a judge considers the same property laws and guidelines that he or she would apply to the division of your assets. (For an in-depth discussion of those laws and guidelines, turn to Chapter 3.)

✔ Any money you owed before you got married is treated as your individual debt.

✔ Your joint debts are "equitably" divided up if you live in an equitable distribution state.

✔ You and your spouse may be held equally liable for the debts you acquired during your marriage if you live in a community property state. When dividing up your debts, a judge considers your individual abilities to pay on the debts and what the debts financed, among other things.

Uncle Sam wants his piece, too

Ordinarily you don't have to pay taxes when a *capital asset* (such as a home, other real estate, retirement benefits, and so forth) is transferred to you in a divorce. But if you sell a capital asset later, you may have to pay taxes on its appreciated value. Also, depending on how you transfer a *tax-deferred asset,* you may incur penalties. (A tax-deferred asset is an asset that allows you to defer or delay paying taxes on the income it generates until you sell it or begin collecting the income on it.) IRAs, 401(k) plans, and Simplified Employee Pension Plans (SEPs) are all examples of tax-deferred assets.

When you and your spouse are deciding how to divide up your marital property, your tax-minimization strategies may depend on the types of assets you're dividing up, the value of those assets, and your individual financial situations. Without appropriate planning, the taxes and penalties you end up paying have the effect of reducing the amount of marital property you both end up with.

Talk with your CPA or a trusted financial advisor about how to minimize taxes and penalties in your property settlement.

Usually, if you secured or collateralized a debt with your separate property during your marriage, the court regards the debt as your individual debt.

Chapter 9

Spousal Support: Determining If, When, and How Much Is Paid

*D*epending on your circumstances, you may want your spouse to pay you *spousal support* (it used to be referred to as *alimony*) after you are divorced. However, even if your spouse agrees to pay it, the two of you may not see eye to eye regarding how much spousal support you should receive and how long the support payments should last. Of course, if getting divorced was your idea, your soon-to-be-ex may bristle at the suggestion that he or she pay you any spousal support at all, regardless of the reasonableness of the amount of support you're requesting in light of your post-divorce earnings potential, the assets you're likely to take away from your marriage, and other considerations. Or maybe, because you're angry and hurt by the fact that your spouse wants a divorce, you decide to retaliate by demanding spousal support, and a lot of it! You figure that paying you the money is the least your spouse should do for you, given what he or she is doing to your life!

Obviously, spousal support can be an especially emotional issue in a divorce. To help you deal with it as dispassionately as possible so you and your spouse can make decisions on the matter that are fair to both of you, this chapter explains what factors to consider when negotiating spousal support. It also addresses the pros and cons of a lump-sum support payment and highlights tax issues related to spousal support.

If you and your spouse have a prenuptial agreement (see Chapter 19), be sure you review it before you discuss spousal support. It may discuss whether one of you pays in the event of your divorce, and it may address the terms of any spousal support payments. Because it is a legal document, there may be little or no room for negotiating. If you have any questions about your prenuptial agreement, review it with your divorce attorney.

If you turn the issue of spousal support over to a judge, the laws of your state will limit what he or she can order. For example, the judge will be restricted in regard to how much support he or she can require one spouse to pay the other and, depending on your state, the judge may not be allowed to require one spouse to purchase life insurance for the benefit of the other spouse or to pay spousal support in a lump sum. However, if you and your spouse negotiate your own spousal support agreement, you won't face such limitations.

The Times They Are a-Changing

Spousal support is the monetary payments that one spouse makes to the other after a couple is divorced. If a couple separates before their divorce is final, one spouse may pay the other temporary support.

It used to be that unless a man continued to support his ex-wife after their divorce, she had no way to provide for herself financially because most wives didn't work outside the home, so they had few, if any, job skills. Furthermore, most well-paying jobs weren't available to women. And, because most ex-wives ended up with the kids, a couple's children would also suffer if their father didn't financially support his ex.

Assuming that he could afford it, an ex-husband paid his ex-wife *permanent spousal support,* usually by sending her a monthly check for a set amount of money. But, in reality, those payments didn't really last forever because most divorce agreements stated that the support checks would stop if the woman remarried or if the ex-husband died.

Since the 1970s, permanent spousal support has pretty much gone the way of the typewriter, eight-track tape, and rotary phone. Even so, permanent spousal support is still a part of some divorces — most often divorces that involve wealthy couples or older couples who are ending lengthy marriages. But today, permanent spousal support agreements frequently state that the payments will stop if the ex-spouse who's receiving them begins a serious live-in relationship and shares living expenses with a new love interest.

Attitudes toward spousal support continue to change as men and women's roles evolve in society. Women used to be the ones who received spousal support 99.9 percent of the time, but today, if the wife is the primary breadwinner in a marriage, she may have to pay spousal support to her ex-husband. In fact, the spousal support laws in all states are now gender-neutral, which means that, in the eyes of the law, men and women are equally entitled to receive spousal support. Despite the evolving attitudes and standards in our society regarding the roles of men and women in marriage and divorce, women are still far more likely to receive spousal support than men.

In terms of dollars and cents, divorce is still harder on women than men, despite the large number of women who work outside the home. Most women — even those who receive spousal support — experience a drop in their standard of living after their marriage ends. However, some divorced men experience the same financial consequences.

Another change related to the payment of spousal support is that it's more likely to be *rehabilitative support,* not permanent support, and it's most likely paid to stay-at-home parents and full-time homemakers. Rehabilitative support is paid for a relatively short period of time in order to help a former spouse get on his or her feet. The support payments also may include money to help an ex-spouse get the training or education necessary to earn a good living.

Readying yourself for the work world with rehabilitative support

These days, if you receive support payments from your ex, it will probably be rehabilitative support rather than permanent support. Rehabilitative support is based on the idea that most ex-spouses, regardless of their gender, can and should earn their own livings after their divorce. This kind of support also recognizes that a spouse (either a woman or a man) may have put her or his own career on the back burner to raise the children or to support the other spouse's career and needs time to become self-supporting after a divorce. For example, he or she may need time to develop new job skills, get a college education, and develop professional connections that will help him or her find a good job. Also, he or she probably needs time to find a job after he or she is ready to begin looking. Rehabilitative spousal support is intended to help a spouse do those things.

Don't summarily dismiss the idea of receiving spousal support out of pride or a desire to be 100 percent free of your spouse. If you believe that you need time to become competitive in today's job market, your wisest course of action may be to swallow your pride and ask your spouse for financial help. Remember, having financial help from your former spouse while preparing yourself for a job and/or looking for one can mean the difference between having enough money to provide yourself and your children with what you need and barely scraping by.

In many divorces, unfortunately, the amount and duration of the rehabilitation support checks inadequately cover the needs of the spouse who is receiving them. This is particularly true when a divorced couple is of modest means and, particularly, when the former spouse who is receiving the payments is an older woman who has never worked outside the home or hasn't done so in many years. Most likely, she has no job skills (or her job skills are totally out of date), and once she gets them up to speed, she's apt to have a very hard time finding a good job because of her age, especially when the job market is tight.

Stay-at-home moms and dads who view raising their children as a full-time job face a difficult dilemma. If they begin preparing themselves for the possibility of divorce by getting the education and training that they need to be employable should their marriage end, they not only take time away from their primary job (child-rearing), but they're also likely to receive less spousal support if they do divorce. On the other hand, if they don't prepare themselves for the job market while they're still married, they may receive more spousal support than if they had, but they may not be as prepared to support themselves when the support payments end.

Making a Case for Support

If you're wondering whether or not support is relevant in your divorce, you don't have a lot of legal precedents to go by because spousal support decisions are relatively subjective and are decided on a case-by-case basis. Technically, divorced spouses have no legal obligation to support one another. Therefore, spousal support isn't as much of a guarantee as child support is in divorces that involve minor children.

If your divorce ends in a trial, the judge will determine if, when, and how much spousal support you or your spouse will receive. If you and your spouse agree to negotiate the terms of your divorce on your own or with the help of your attorneys, spousal support is one of the issues you'll consider. To help guide your spousal support decision-making, the following is a list of factors that judges consider when deciding spousal support. (If you're the spouse who wants to receive support, the greater the number of factors that apply to your marriage, the stronger your argument for getting spousal support is.)

Texas, not very supportive of spousal support

Not a lot of state guidelines exist for determining whether or not an ex-spouse should pay spousal support, how long those payments should last, and the size of those payments. For example, until 1995, Texas had *no* provision for spousal support other than temporary support that would end when a divorce became final. Even now, although Texas law provides for spousal support, the terms under which a court will order it are very limited. For example, a spouse can receive spousal support only if his or her marriage lasted at least ten years and if the spouse is unable to provide for his/her basic needs. The court will also award spousal support to a spouse if the other spouse has been convicted of family violence within two years of the divorce filing or while the divorce was pending. Ordinarily, in both instances, the court-ordered support lasts for a maximum of only three years.

If you're the spouse who may have to pay spousal support, the fewer factors that apply to your situation, the better your chances are for not having to pay spousal support. However, in the end, whether or not one of you has to pay spousal support boils down to need and ability to pay.)

- ✔ **How long you've been married:** If you and your spouse have been married for a long time (and you won't find a legal definition of "long time"), you're more likely to receive spousal support. But if your marriage is fewer than ten years old, a judge probably won't treat it as a long-term marriage — although it may feel like an eternity to you! Typically, the longer the marriage, the larger the support payments will be.

- ✔ **Whether your spouse makes significantly more money than you do and is expected to continue doing so, at least for the immediate future:** When one spouse makes a lot more than the other, the court is apt to have the higher-earning spouse to share some of that income with the lower-earning spouse.

- ✔ **Your age or health status makes earning a good living nearly impossible:** A spouse who cannot work full time, who can't work at all for health reasons, or who's older and did not work during his or her marriage or only worked part-time is more likely to receive spousal support. (The definition of "older" varies from judge to judge, but most judges view a worker in his or her late 50s and beyond as an older worker.) The age of a spouse is a factor because, although employers aren't supposed to discriminate based on age, anecdotal evidence indicates that such discrimination happens more often than we may think. Therefore, an older worker can have a very difficult time finding a job that pays well. Also, older workers are apt to have physical limitations that don't suit them for certain kinds of work. As a result, they don't have the range of job options that younger workers tend to have.

- ✔ **The significant contributions you made to your marriage and/or to your spouse's career:** For example, maybe you gave up your career to be a stay-at-home parent, continued to work throughout your marriage and let your career take a back seat to your spouse's so that you could help him or her advance professionally, or helped build your spouse's business.

- ✔ **Your educational background and employment history:** Judges consider whether or not your education and/or your employment history puts you at a disadvantage in the job market. For example, if you didn't work or you worked at part-time jobs during your marriage so you could be home with your children. Therefore, finding a job to support yourself after you are divorced can be difficult, if not impossible, because your job skills are probably outdated and you don't have much work experience to put on a résumé or job application.

✔ **Whether you will be your children's primary caregiver after your divorce:** If you plan to take care of your children full time, pursuing a full-time career is nearly impossible.

✔ **Whether you have any nonemployment sources of regular income, such as income from trusts, real estate, or investments:** Receiving income from other sources can make it less likely that you'll receive spousal support or you may not receive as much as you would have if you didn't have the income.

✔ **Whether you're exiting your marriage with relatively little marital property:** If you exit your marriage with little or no assets, you have nothing to borrow against or sell in order to help pay your bills and pay for the education you may need in order to qualify for a good job.

✔ **Whether you will have sole custody of your children and one or more of them has special needs:** Having sole custody of a child with special needs can preclude you from working or allow you to work on only a part-time basis.

A judge can also take other relevant factors into account if you look to the court to decide whether spousal support will be paid and, if so, how much the payments will be and how long they will last. However, a judge may consider other factors that are things you'd prefer the judge to overlook, like the fact that your spouse filed a fault divorce because he or she found out you had been having an affair or had done something else that was harmful to your marriage.

States that permit fault divorces may allow a judge to take the issue of fault into consideration when deciding spousal support. When a judge does consider fault, he or she is more likely to punish the spouse who's at fault for his or her behavior (adultery, physical abuse, and so on). For instance, the judge may order that spouse to pay more than the usual amount of support. Or if the spouse at fault is the one who will be receiving support, the judge may award him or her less support than what the spouse would have been awarded otherwise.

About half the states allow judges to consider fault in negotiations related to the division of a couple's marital property.

If you and your spouse are working out the terms of your spousal support agreement together, you can take other factors into account, too, like your religious beliefs, your personal values, and so on.

Of course, if your spouse doesn't make much money, the court may not expect him or her to pay you anything, or probably not as much as you may want or need.

Agreeing on an Amount

Deciding how much support one spouse should pay the other can be a challenge because the spouse who's going to receive the support will probably want as much as possible, and the spouse who's paying the support will probably want to minimize the amount of the payments. Furthermore, most states don't have strict guidelines for determining the minimum amount of support that a former spouse is entitled to. So, how much support gets paid is a judgment call usually based on what's fair given the needs of the spouse who wants support and the finances of the spouse who would be paying the support.

Deciding what's your fair share

When deciding how much support one spouse must pay another, judges ideally would like the payments to be large enough to allow the spouse who's receiving them to be able to maintain his or her marital lifestyle. But, in reality, judges know that most ex-spouses don't make enough money to support two households equally well, not even for a short period of time.

In most divorces, how much a spouse receives in spousal support boils down to financial realities — how much money the spouse paying the support can actually afford to pay and the living expenses of the spouse who's receiving the support. Assuming that the spouse who's paying the support is earning more than enough to just get by, the factors we discuss in the earlier section, "Making a Case for Support," can be taken into account when spouses are deciding what is a fair amount of spouse support. To come up with an actual amount of support, spouses should gather up their budgets and other financial information and sit down with a certified divorce planner (CDP), a certified public accountant (CPA), or their divorce attorneys.

If your spouse wants to make the amount of spousal support you receive or its duration contingent upon you doing or not doing certain things, do not agree with the deal unless you feel completely comfortable with it. Some spouses go to almost any length to try to control their partners, even after divorce. For example, your spouse may try to make your receipt of spousal support contingent on you not dating a particular person, on sending your children to a particular school, or on raising your children in a certain religion. If you have any questions about whether your spouse's spousal support offer is fair, consult with a family law attorney.

If you're the spouse who will be paying spousal support, you may want to negotiate an arrangement that gives your spouse more of your marital assets in exchange for making smaller spousal support payments than you would otherwise given your income and other factors or for an earlier than normal end to the payments. You may find such an arrangement attractive because you know that it will be a struggle to pay a set amount of spousal support from month to month — maybe because you're self-employed or work on commission and your income varies from month to month — or because you want as little connection to your ex as possible after your divorce. Or you may want to get your spouse to agree to a lump-sum payment rather than a series of spousal support payments over time (see the reasons why in the section "Getting your support in a lump sum," later in this chapter). Talk to your divorce attorney, CPA, or CDP about which option is best for you.

If you're the spouse receiving support, be wary of agreeing to take more marital property in exchange for less spousal support. Unless the extra property you receive provides you with a regular flow of income after your divorce, you may end up on the short end of the financial stick.

Changing the amount later

Under certain circumstances, the amount of spousal support you receive may increase or decrease after your divorce is final.

- ✔ The amount can change if you and your former spouse both agree to the change.
- ✔ The amount can change if a judge orders it as a result of a request from you or your former spouse.

But in some states, a court loses its ability to change spousal support arrangements as soon as a couple's divorce decree is final.

For a judge to order a change, you or your ex-spouse has to convince the court that you have a good reason for it. By the way, a judge is unlikely to view your desire to share in the hefty salary increase that your former spouse just received as a good reason, or your wish to benefit from his or her share of lottery winnings. But the judge may be more agreeable to allowing your spouse to make smaller payments if your ex just lost his or her job or has become too ill or injured to work and can prove to the court that without a reduction, he or she will quickly land in the poorhouse. On the other hand, the judge may go along with a request to increase spousal support if you can prove that you have a legitimate need for it; for example, you were seriously injured in a car accident and can't work. In both scenarios, however, the adjustments would probably be temporary.

Agreeing on a Payment Plan

When you're negotiating spousal support, one of the issues you must consider is how the support will be paid. Generally, the spouse who's obligated to provide support to the other does so by making a series of fixed payments over a specified period of time. Other times, couples agree (or a judge orders) that one spouse will pay the other a lump-sum amount of spousal support instead.

Receiving support over time

Most spousal support is paid in set amounts on a set schedule. This arrangement has its pros and cons. For example, if you're the one who's receiving spousal support, the payments can provide a steady stream of much-needed income for you while you're building a new life for yourself after your divorce. However, this arrangement can be problematic if your former spouse is constantly late with his or her payments or doesn't make them at all sometimes. Not only can this situation cause money problems for you, but it can also create a considerable amount of tension and anger between you and your ex and cause you to constantly relive the emotions of your divorce.

If you're not far from retirement age and you're going to pay spousal support, stopping your payments when you retire may be appropriate, especially if part of your divorce agreement says that you and your spouse will share substantial retirement benefits.

Getting your support in a lump sum

Some divorced spouses receive their spousal support in a lump sum rather than in a series of payments over time. A lump-sum payment is an attractive option if you don't trust your ex to live up to an agreement that requires making payments over time, if you're concerned that your spouse's financial situation may deteriorate after you're divorced, or that the payments will become erratic or stop all together.

Be sure the lump sum that your spouse offers you is adequate. Although the amount may sound like a lot of money and a fair amount for you to receive, it may not be enough, especially if your spouse wants you to take the lump sum in lieu of receiving any marital property. Talk with a family law attorney, a CDP, or your CPA before you sign any paperwork related to a lump-sum payment of support so that you can be sure that it's in your best interest.

Consider the tax consequences of taking a lump-sum payment of spousal support and what you can do to mitigate those consequences before you agree to accept the payment. You may be able to shelter some of the money using a trust, but this strategy is a subject to discuss with your CDP, CPA, or an estate-planning attorney.

The larger the lump sum, the more important having a plan for investing the money is. Ideally, your plan should maximize the interest you earn on the lump sum and give you ready access to at least a portion of the money. If you simply put the lump-sum payment you receive into your checking account, you may spend it very quickly and have nothing for the future.

If you're giving your spouse a lump-sum support payment, get the help of an attorney or CPA. Your agreement regarding support must be worded so that the IRS will view your payment as spousal support, which you can claim as a tax deduction, and not as a property settlement, which you can't deduct. (You can find out more about taxes and spousal support in the section "Some Important Advice about Taxes," later in this chapter.)

Ensuring that the Payments Arrive

After your divorce is final, your ex-spouse may not make the spousal support payments he or she agreed to make. This may occur because your ex is angry about the divorce, resents having to send you money, experiences financially tough times, or maybe even remarries and is pressured by his or her new spouse not to make them. Whatever the reason, not receiving the money you anticipate can have a devastating effect on your life. Here are some steps you can take before your divorce is final to help ensure that the support arrives:

- ✔ **Get a court order for spousal support.** If you're not working with a divorce attorney, you need one to file your spousal support agreement with the court and argue its reasonableness to the judge so that he or she will approve it and make it an official part of your divorce. If you're the one who's entitled to spousal support and you don't go through this process, and if your ex reneges on your agreement, you will have no legal recourse for collecting the spousal support you are entitled to.

- ✔ **Try to enforce the court order by asking the court to hold your spouse in contempt of court.** Assuming that your state allows you to take this step when your ex doesn't pay your spousal support, a court order puts legal pressure on your ex to pay your support. In fact, your ex-spouse can go to jail for ignoring his or her support obligation.

  In states where you cannot accuse your spouse of contempt for failing to pay you spousal support, you're in the same position as any other creditor that your former spouse hasn't paid. In this situation, whether or not you can collect from him or her depends on the debtor protection laws of your state, which may make all, or most, of your ex-spouse's property exempt from the debt-collection process. If that's the case, your past-due spousal support is uncollectible.

- ✔ **Secure your payments by placing a lien on one or more of the assets that your spouse will exit the marriage with.** (A *lien* is a legal right to someone else's property until the owner of that property fulfills his/her legal obligation to the lien holder. For example, if you have a mortgage on your home, your mortgage lender has a lien on your home, which means that it can take the home if you don't make your mortgage payments according to your mortgage agreement.) If your ex fails to live up to your spousal support agreement, you can ask the court for permission to take the asset with a lien on it as payment for what you're owed. However, if the asset is your ex-spouse's home, you may not be able to get your money until the home is sold. Also, if you have a lien on your ex's retirement account, you may not be able to collect the money you're entitled to until he or she retires or your ex quits or gets fired.

✔ **Use disability insurance to ensure an unbroken stream of spousal support in the event that your ex becomes ill or injured and is unable to work for a period of time.** The court is likely to let your former spouse pay you less during the period of his or her disability, so the disability insurance provides you with a financial safety net.

✔ **Get your spouse to have your spousal support payments automatically deducted from his or her paychecks.** That way, after your divorce is final, you don't have to wonder whether your ex remembered to mail you a support check each month, whether your ex will send you some but not all of what you are entitled to, or whether your ex isn't going to send you any money at all. With automatic deductions, the court issues an order telling your former spouse's employer to deduct a certain amount of money from his or her paychecks and send it to the court, which sends you a check. In other words, your former spouse never sees that money.

Preparing for Life After Spousal Support

Your spousal support may end sooner than you expect, regardless of whether you're receiving rehabilitative support or your spouse agreed to pay you permanent spousal support. Your ex spouse may die, and the payments will end upon his or her death, and you won't have a legal right to his or her estate unless your ex provided otherwise. Therefore, if your spousal support payments are an important source of your income and you have no way of compensating for that loss, the death of your ex-spouse is likely to be financially devastating for you.

Although death can come unexpectedly to people of any age, this issue is of particular concern to individuals who are ending marriages to spouses who are elderly or in poor health. One way to address the problem is to require, as a term of your divorce, that your spouse purchase a life insurance policy and name you as its beneficiary, assuming that your spouse isn't so old or in such poor health that he can't qualify for such insurance. While you're working out the terms of your divorce, talk to a CDP, CPA, or divorce planner about this and other options that may help you protect yourself from the sudden loss of spousal support.

If you're worried that your ex may purchase a life insurance policy and make you its beneficiary, but then let the policy lapse, you may want to purchase the policy yourself, assuming that you can afford the expense. That way, you're assured that the policy stays in effect.

The insurance premium payments your ex-spouse makes on a policy that makes you the beneficiary are tax deductible as spousal support. However, if he or she dies and you begin receiving the insurance benefits, you must claim them as taxable income.

Some Important Advice about Taxes

If you receive spousal support, you must claim the money as income on your tax return. If you pay spousal support, perhaps one of the few benefits is that you can deduct the payments on your federal tax return. Like everything else that has to do with the IRS, to qualify for the deductions, you must comply with certain IRS rules, such as:

✔ You must formalize your spousal support agreement in a divorce decree or in a separate written agreement.

✔ You must make your payments with a check or money order. Ordinarily, property or services in lieu of cash don't qualify as tax-deductible support.

Paying your spousal support in cash is a bad idea because you won't have a record of your payments. Your lack of documentation can be a problem if any questions arise concerning how much you paid your former spouse or exactly when you made a particular spousal support payment.

✔ While paying spousal support, you cannot be living under the same roof with your former spouse. No living on separate floors of the same home or in different parts of your home, either!

✔ You cannot tie your spousal support payments to circumstances or milestones in your children's lives. For example, your agreement cannot provide that when your child turns a certain age you'll reduce the amount of support that you pay to your ex-spouse or stop the payments entirely. If the IRS learns that you've done so, it may reclassify the payments you made as child support and, because child support payments aren't tax-deductible, you may end up owing extra taxes to Uncle Sam.

✔ On a related note, you cannot stop paying spousal support or change the amount that you've been paying your ex-spouse six months before or after the date that one of your children becomes a legal adult — age 18 in most states. Again, if the IRS finds out that you stopped paying spousal support prematurely, it may reclassify some of the payments you made in the past as child support, which can have tax implications for you.

✔ You must file your federal taxes using IRS Form 1040, not Form 1040A or Form 1040EZ.

Don't front-load your spousal support payments. *Front-loading* is paying your ex-spouse excess money during the first two years that you're making the support payments. If you're audited, the IRS views the excess money you paid as a property settlement, not spousal support, which means that those payments aren't tax deductible. Front-loading may apply only if you paid out more than $15,000 in spousal support during each of the first two years that you made those payments and only if you claimed the full amount of the payments as tax deductions.

If an attorney, a CDP, or a CPA helps you work out the terms of your spousal support agreement, you can deduct his or her fees on your taxes. Also, if you pay the medical insurance, college tuition, mortgage, or rent payments of your former spouse as part of the agreement, you may be able to claim them as tax deductions, too.

If you earn considerably more than your ex-spouse and you intend to pay him or her more than your state's minimum in child support, you may want to pay that additional money as spousal support instead because it's tax deductible and child support isn't. However, although doing so increases your tax deductions, it may also increase the tax liability of your ex-spouse. How to deal with this issue is something that you and your spouse should discuss with your CDP or CPA before either of you agrees to such an arrangement.

Chapter 10

Custody: Deciding What's Best for Your Children

. . . .

In This Chapter

▶ Making your own custody decisions

▶ Considering your custody options

▶ Asking your kids what kind of custody arrangement they want

▶ Constructing a shared custody arrangement

▶ Knowing when split custody makes sense

▶ Making primary custody work

▶ Formulating a parenting plan

▶ Preparing for a custody battle in court

▶ Determining visitation

. . . .

Deciding how to handle the custody of your minor children can consume every ounce of your patience and resolve. In fact, this issue is very likely the most difficult one that you and your spouse grapple with during your divorce, and, if one of you isn't happy with the outcome, it can create problems for you and your children after your divorce is final.

If negotiating your own custody arrangement seems about as likely as winning the lottery, take heart! Estimates show that 95 percent of all divorcing parents negotiate their own custody arrangements — either by themselves, with the help of a mediator, or with their attorneys' assistance — and chances are you will, too.

This chapter prepares you to make your own custody decisions by informing you of your options (and their pros and cons) and suggesting ways that you can make your custody arrangement work to benefit everyone, your kids especially. We also cover issues regarding visitation, including each spouse's rights and limitations. If you and your spouse can't come to an agreement on your own, this chapter also explains what can happen if you ask a judge to decide the custody matters in your divorce.

Avoiding the Courtroom: The Benefits of Negotiating Your Child Custody

If you and your spouse can decide one thing and one thing only in your divorce, make it the issue of how you handle the custody of your children. The following list offers just a few of the reasons why *you,* and not a family court judge, should make that decision. (You can find more information on negotiating your own divorce terms without the aid of a court of law in Chapter 12.)

✔ If you go to court, you have no guarantee that the judge will give you the custody arrangement you want, even if it's available under your state's laws.

✔ No matter how well-intentioned the judge may be, because of the case-loads of most family court judges, the judge who hears your case won't be able to devote much time to considering how to handle the custody of your children. Don't your children deserve more attention than that?

✔ Most judges rely on the input of outside experts, such as social workers and psychologists, to help them make custody decisions. Therefore, a bunch of strangers may end up having a great deal of say in where your children will live and your role in their lives after your divorce.

✔ A court custody battle can be extremely costly and time-consuming. One reason is because a variety of experts (who may include your children's teachers, the director of your children's day-care center, the personnel at your pediatrician's office, and so on) will probably testify. And you are expected to pay for their time.

✔ Because the proceedings related to the custody of your children are open to the public, you risk having all your private "dirty laundry" aired in the courtroom for all to see and hear.

✔ Members of your extended family, friends, associates, people in your children's lives, your neighbors — and maybe even your children — may have to go to court to testify.

✔ After the judge decides what to do about the custody of your kids, you and your spouse may not be able to put your differences aside for the sake of your children, especially if the custody hearing was very acrimonious. Worst-case scenario, you and your ex could continue battling each other for years to come, which could take a long-lasting emotional toll on your children and add a lot of stress to your own life.

Not only can a custody battle be extremely expensive, but it can also cause your children long-lasting emotional damage. If you're considering fighting with your spouse over the custody of your kids, try to analyze why you're thinking about it; if necessary, seek the guidance of a mental health professional to help you figure things out. After some serious reflection, you may decide that you're confusing your own wants and needs with what's in the best interests of your children, or that you want to do battle over your children's custody in order to express animosity toward your spouse and/or to hurt your spouse.

Want to talk to other divorcing parents who are dealing with the same custody questions you are? Share ideas and concerns with one another at this interactive child custody forum on the Web: www.divorcesource.com/cgi-bin/divorce/netforum/custody/a/1. Also, some states require divorcing parents to attend parenting classes to learn how to help their children adjust to divorce and to become familiar with some of the issues they're likely to face as divorced parents. Even if your state doesn't require that you attend such a class, you may want to ask your attorney or a mental health professional whether there is one in your area that you could attend. If so, let your spouse know about the class, too.

Your Custody Options in Brief

Every custody arrangement requires you to make two basic, interrelated decisions: how you and your spouse will share the legal custody of your children and how you will share their physical custody.

Legal custody refers to a parent's right and obligation to make decisions on behalf of his or her children after a divorce — including decisions concerning their education, medical care, religious education, and other important matters. *Physical custody* refers to the amount of time the children live with each parent after the divorce.

In most cases, the children spend time with each parent in proportion to how involved each parent was in their lives before the divorce — that is, to whatever degree each parent functioned as the children's caregiver, life planner, and source of emotional support. In addition, each parent has decision-making authority in proportion to the amount of time that the children live with that parent. For example, if your children live with you half the time, then you make decisions on their behalf half the time unless you and your spouse agree to some other arrangement. For example, you may decide that certain types of decisions must be made jointly, such as whether your high-school senior can go to Mexico over spring break or whether your preteen can get her ears pierced.

If one parent has been more involved in his or her children's lives before the divorce, that parent often gets *primary* (or *sole*) *custody* of the kids. (We talk more about this type of custody in the section, "Understanding the Ins and Outs of Primary Custody," later in this chapter.) Primary custody means that the couple's children spend most of their time with that parent and the parent assumes more decision-making responsibilities for the couple's children. The parent with primary custody may make all decisions for the children, or the couple may agree that they will share important decisions related to their kids.

Parents who have been equally involved in their children's lives before divorce normally get nearly equal, if not completely equal, decision-making authority and time with the children after divorce. Those parents are said to have a *shared* (or *joint*) *custody* arrangement. (You can find more on this type of custody in the section "Taking a Closer Look at Shared Custody," later in this chapter.)

Split custody is another option, although few parents use it. With split custody, some or all of your children live with each of you for a part of the year or some of your children live with one of you all the time and the rest of your children live with your former spouse all the time (read more about this custody option in the section "Considering Split Custody," later in this chapter).

Because an increasing number of today's fathers are actively involved in their children's day-to-day care and nurturing, many couples are sharing both the legal and the physical custody of their children. Among the reasons for this relatively new trend in custody arrangements is that more women work outside the home, whether due to choice or financial necessity, and the changing definition of what it means to be a dad.

The laws in most states assume that each parent has an equal legal right to custody of his or her children. In reality, however, the mother usually ends up with primary custody of the kids when the court gets involved. This decision is based on the fact that, in most families, the woman is the children's primary caregiver and the parent who's most involved in their lives (despite the increased caregiving role that many fathers have assumed). However, if the father is the primary caregiver, the courts are more apt to award him primary custody of the children. This case is especially true if the couple lives in an urban area where judges tend to be more progressive and where more precedent-setting rulings are made.

Whatever custody arrangement you decide on, be sure that you and your spouse are happy with it before it becomes a formal part of your divorce agreement. Although you can change the arrangement later, if you and your ex don't see eye to eye on a proposed change, a judge will decide if it's merited, and most family court judges don't like to alter a custody arrangement unless the change is clearly in the children's best interests.

Consulting Your Kids

If your children are old enough and mature enough to know their own minds, especially if you and your spouse want to share custody, you may want to consider their preferences regarding how much time they want to spend living with each of you. They may have already let you know what they would like, directly or indirectly, but if they haven't and you would like to know what they're thinking, have a conversation with them, either with your spouse or separately. Make the conversation a casual chat, and don't pressure your children to decide one way or the other. Also be prepared for the possibility that some of your children will want to live with you, and some will want to live with your ex.

Don't bribe your children into spending more time with you by making fantastic promises about what their lives will be like if they do, and avoid "guilting" your kids by telling them how sad and lonely you'll be if they don't choose to be with you more often.

If you got divorced when your children were young but now they're adolescents, you may want to give them the option of changing their living arrangement if they have not already broached the subject with you. At this age, they may prefer living with you or your ex most of the time. Not only does living in one place give your kids ready access to all their belongings, but it also means that their friends always know where to find them.

Your children very much want your approval, which means you may not be able to take their "preferences" at face value. For example, your children may tell you what they *think* you want to hear, not what they really feel, and for that same reason, they may tell your spouse the exact opposite of what they tell you. Therefore, not asking your children what they want until they're old enough and mature enough to honestly assess their needs and desires when it comes to their living arrangements is a good idea. Even then, talking with them about their preferences may not be a good idea if they don't feel comfortable communicating honestly with you.

Most states have laws authorizing the courts to consider a child's preferences if the child is of a certain age (typically 10 or older). However, the judge has the ultimate decision.

Taking a Closer Look at Shared Custody

When parents share custody of their children, they're both responsible for all or some aspects of their children's lives depending on the terms of their custody agreement. A key benefit of shared custody is that it allows both parents to be full participants in their children's lives after their divorce and let's them have equal responsibility for their children's emotional and physical well-being. Shared custody also helps facilitate a continuation of the relationship that the parents and children may have enjoyed prior to the divorce.

Generally, compared to a custody arrangement that gives one parent primary physical custody of a couple's children in a divorce, when parents share physical custody of their children, they're more apt to share the cost of their children's financial support, too. However, child-support arrangements are always decided on a case-by-case basis and depend on a variety of factors. (For the full scoop on child support, turn to Chapter 11.)

All states recognize shared custody as an option, and 35 of them and the District of Columbia have laws that either presume shared custody or explicitly cite it as the preferred custody arrangement. In most of these states, a judge can even order shared custody if one of the parents objects. Other states permit shared custody by agreement only.

Living arrangements

You and your spouse can structure a shared custody arrangement in several ways:

✔ **Have your children live with both of you in your individual homes on a 50/50 basis, a 60/40 basis, an 80/20 basis — whatever seems best for you and your former spouse and your kids.** If you opt for this sort of arrangement, you'll probably parent your children much the way you did during your marriage. The only difference is that now you and your spouse are living under two separate roofs, not one.

✔ **One parent gets sole or primary physical custody of the kids, and the other parent gets liberal visitation rights:** (We discuss liberal visitation rights later in this chapter.) This arrangement lets both parents share responsibility for making the important decisions in your children's lives. This arrangement has its advantages when one parent is out of town a lot, is regularly on call or works night shifts, or when the demands regularly take a parent away from the home for extended periods of time.

If you choose this custody option, you may want to consider adding a provision to your custody agreement that the parent with legal custody must involve the other parent in all important decisions about the welfare of the kids, but that when you and your spouse cannot agree, the parent with legal custody has tie-breaking rights. To avoid confusion and conflict, spell out examples of types of "important decisions" because what may seem important to you may not seem particularly significant to your ex.

If you and your spouse decide to share decision-making authority about some things but not others, avoid conflict and misunderstanding after your divorce by clearly spelling out the areas of shared decision-making in your custody agreement. For example, you may agree that you will both make decisions about your children's nonemergency medical or dental care when the treatment involves invasive procedures, or you will both decide what sort of mental healthcare your children may need, where they will go to summer camp, and so on.

Your state's child-custody laws may specify certain rights and duties that you and your spouse must share at all times after your divorce, the rights and duties that you can share if you want, and the rights and duties that each of you retains whenever your children are in your care. Your attorney can fill you in on what your state's laws say.

Benefits and pitfalls

The benefits of sharing physical and legal custody of your children with your former spouse are obvious: Your children get to maintain their relationships with both of you, and you and your ex are able to stay actively involved in their lives. Nevertheless, shared physical and legal custody have some potentially serious drawbacks, including the following:

- ✔ Shared custody is relatively expensive. For example, unless you opt for bird nesting (see the "Bird nesting: An option that may work" sidebar in this chapter), both you and your former spouse must provide your children with a place to sleep and a place to store their clothes and other belongings when they're at each of your homes (unless you want them living out of suitcases and boxes). Plus, you each have to provide your children with separate sets of clothing, toys, and other items that they use regularly unless you expect them to cart those things back and forth from your home to your former spouse's.

- ✔ For shared custody to work, you and your former spouse must communicate and cooperate with one another much more than you would have to with other custody arrangements.

- ✔ Shuffling back and forth between your home and your ex-spouse's home can be hard on some children, particularly very young children, because they may feel constantly unsettled. Also, moving from house to house can also be hard on your kids if there's a big disparity between you and your former spouse's economic lifestyles.

- ✔ When children live with each parent part-time, their education can suffer unless both parents have the same attitude about homework, getting to school on time, school behavior, and doing well in their studies.

Bird nesting: An option that may work

A relatively new shared custody arrangement is for the children to stay in your family's home and for you and your spouse to take turns living there whenever your time comes to be with the kids. A popular name for this arrangement is "bird nesting." The key advantage of this arrangement is that your children get to live in their own home full time rather than having to constantly shuffle back and forth between your home and your ex's. Plus, your kids can keep all their belongings in one place. As a result, their schedules are less likely to be disrupted, and they enjoy a greater sense of continuity in their lives day to day.

But to make this arrangement work, you and your spouse must be able to afford the expense of three separate residences or must be willing to live in a hotel/motel or some other temporary location when it's not your turn to live with your children. Also, if you and your former spouse were in constant conflict in your marriage over the cleaning and maintenance of your home, inside and out, this arrangement could be fraught with problems because it requires a lot of cooperation on the part of ex-spouses if it's going to work. Also, tempers could flare if one of you begins living with someone or remarries and that new special someone is moving in and out of your family home. Given the potential problems associated with bird nesting, many couples use this arrangement on a temporary basis only — while their kids finish out their school year, while they're trying to sell their family home, until the real estate market in their area picks up, and so on.

If you and your spouse decide to bird nest, minimize the potential for acrimony between you and your former spouse by spelling out in writing exactly how the arrangement will work, the responsibilities of each former spouse when living in the family home, under what conditions a new "significant other" can stay overnight at the home, and so on.

Making shared custody work

To have a successful shared-custody arrangement, you and your spouse must do something you may have had a hard time doing while you were married — get along with each other! To determine whether you and your spouse have what it takes to manage a shared-custody arrangement, read the following shared-custody guidelines:

- **Avoid post-divorce warfare.** Arguing in front of your children, especially about matters relating to them, can be emotionally devastating for both you and the kids. When you and your ex disagree about your kids, have a calm discussion about your differences. Don't shout at your spouse or use insulting language, especially when your children are within earshot.

- **Don't use your children to try to get back at your former spouse.** Your marriage is over — it's time to move on. If you can't forgive and forget, you have no business sharing custody.

✔ **Respect your ex's parenting ability and style of parenting.** Sure, you may not like the way he or she parents your children, but unless your former spouse puts them in danger or unless you have good reason to believe that he or she is harming their emotional, scholastic, or sexual development, how your ex parents is really none of your business. Plus, if you critique his or her parenting abilities, you can expect your ex to do the same to you. With that said, however, for the sake of your children, you and your spouse should agree on certain basic values or standards for your children — for instance, that they go to bed at a certain time on school nights, that they get their homework done each night, that your older children be home by a certain hour, and so on. You can make these kinds of agreements part of a parenting plan, which is something we discuss in "Going the Extra Mile with a Parenting Plan," later in this chapter.

✔ **Support one another's efforts to learn new parenting skills.** Even if you and your former spouse were both active, involved parents, each of you probably had primary responsibility for certain things — one of you may have gotten the kids dressed in the morning and prepared their lunches while the other helped with their school projects and got them ready for bed. Now, you may have to learn new skills so that you can do all those things you both used to share.

✔ **Agree on a schedule for when the children will live with each of you and stick to it.** Children depend on predictability. At the same time, don't be inflexible with your ex.

✔ **Mind your own business when your children are with their other parent.** Don't check up to find out what time your ex-spouse got the kids to bed, what they ate for dinner, or to tell your ex what the kids should wear to school the next day. Your former spouse is in charge of your kids when they're at his or her home.

✔ **Support one another as parents.** Don't let your children play one of you against the other in order to get what they want, and don't criticize your ex-spouse in front of your children. If you need some advice about what to do and what not to do if this situation is happening, you, or ideally you and your ex, should consider getting some advice from a child therapist.

Considering Split Custody

A split-custody arrangement, where some or all of your children live with each of you for a part of the year, or some of your children live with one of you all the time and the rest of your children live with your former spouse all of the time, can make sense when

- One of your children has special educational or medical needs.
- One or more of your children refuses to spend time with you or with your spouse.
- One parent has special problems or limitations. For example, the parent's finances are very limited or the parent has a serious health condition.

This arrangement can also be a good option if one of your children is involved in a gang, has an alcohol or drug abuse problem, is getting into trouble with the law, and you're concerned about his or her influence on your other children. If you or your ex will spend less time with your children after your divorce because of work, travel, or education demands, you may be especially concerned that a delinquent older child may have more opportunity to influence the younger ones.

But in most instances, a split-custody arrangement isn't in the best interests of your children. For most kids, not living with both parents in the same house after a divorce is hard enough, but separating siblings from each other can be downright cruel.

Understanding the Ins and Outs of Primary Custody

If you get primary custody of your children, they'll probably live with you *most* of the time after you're divorced. More than likely, you will have day-to-day responsibility for them as well as the legal right and obligation to make all major life decisions on their behalf. However, you and your ex-spouse may decide that a somewhat different primary custody arrangement better suits your individual situations and the needs of your kids. As long as you and your spouse stay in control of your own divorce, exactly how you structure your primary custody arrangement is up to you.

If the court decides how to handle custody in your divorce, a judge isn't likely to give you or your spouse primary custody of your children, because the courts in most states prefer that parents share custody. Judges usually believe that shared custody is in the best interests of kids. However, if one spouse has serious emotional problems, has abused his or her children in the past, or has a long criminal history, and so on, the judge will probably give the other spouse primary custody of the children.

Surprise, child-support payments aren't tax deductible (but spousal support payments are). If you have primary custody of your children, you may want to consider working out a win-win arrangement with your spouse that gives you more child support in exchange for him or her taking the child-related tax exemptions and deductions.

If you moved out of your family home, left your children with your spouse, and a family court judge must now decide how to handle custody of your children because you and your spouse don't see eye to eye on that issue, the court will probably award him or her primary custody of your children. If you had moved out with your kids and immediately asked the court to grant you temporary custody, you'd be more likely to get shared custody if that is what you wanted.

Visitation rights

When you have primary custody, your former spouse — the *noncustodial parent* — usually has *visitation rights,* or the right to spend time with your kids according to a predetermined, fixed schedule. Also, in most primary custody arrangements, the noncustodial parent pays the custodial parent child support and provides health insurance for the children.

Visitation for most noncustodial parents usually means that they have the children every other weekend, one day midweek each week (the kids may or may not stay overnight), on certain holidays, on birthdays, and maybe during part of their summer vacations. However, if you and your spouse work out your own visitation schedule, you can agree to anything you want. For more on visitation, see the section "Making Visitation Arrangements," later in this chapter.

Primary custody drawbacks

Having the children live with you all or most of the time and being responsible for making all the decisions about their lives makes sense if your spouse doesn't want to be or can't be actively involved with your children after you're divorced or if your spouse has problems that could put your children at risk. However, a primary custody arrangement can be fraught with problems, especially if your spouse ends up with very limited visitation rights but would prefer to spend more time with his or her children.

 ✔ In primary custody arrangements, noncustodial parents often feel excluded from their children's lives.

✔ Many noncustodial parents slowly drift away from their children, especially if the parents remarry and start new families. When that happens, the divorced couple's children no longer have the benefit of a relationship with two biological parents.

✔ Studies show that noncustodial parents who don't get to spend an adequate amount of time with their children are less apt to meet their child-support obligations.

Then again, the custodial parent's situation isn't necessarily a bed of roses. Consider the following:

✔ As most single parents can tell you, shouldering all or most of the day-to-day responsibilities of raising children can be a tremendous burden, physically and emotionally, particularly if you're working full time or even going to school as well. Juggling child care, work, and school, not to mention housekeeping and yard work, all on your own, can leave you feeling completely spent at the end of each day.

✔ You may have little quality time to spend with your kids, much less any time for yourself.

✔ Your children may spend more time in day care, after-school care, or at home by themselves than they did when you were married and your spouse was around to help out. In such situations, children of divorce frequently end up doing more of the cooking and housework and playing parent to their younger siblings.

Most states have expanded the limited legal rights of noncustodial parents by allowing them to make emergency medical decisions for their children and by giving them access to their children's medical and educational records. For example, most noncustodial parents can request that their children's school send them copies of their kids' report cards.

If you find having most of the responsibility for your children to be a difficult and even an isolating experience, you may want to socialize with other parents in your same situation. One such group is the Single Parents Association (SPA), a nonprofit organization with the mission of providing education, resources, friendship, and fun to single parents and their kids. It has chapters in various communities around the country. Check your local phone listings to find a chapter near you. Another group you may want to check out is Parents Without Partners. You can get in touch with the organization by calling 561-391-883 or by visiting its Web site at www.parentswithoutpartners.org.

Making primary custody work

Primary custody can be hard on everyone, but it can be the best option when parents can't put aside the negative feelings they have about the other and can't work together for the benefit of their kids. If you and your ex aren't able do this, your children are likely to experience long-lasting emotional, developmental, and personal damage. On the other hand, study after study shows that kids do best when they receive love and attention from both parents. Therefore, if you have primary custody of your children, for their benefit, do what you can to ensure that they have an opportunity to maintain a strong relationship with their other parent, even if you don't like your ex or feel a lot of anger toward him or her. Terrible spouses can still make great parents.

Here are some suggestions for how you can help your children maintain a relationship with your ex when you're the parent with primary custody:

- Don't place needless restrictions on their time together. Agree on a visitation schedule that's as generous as possible. Also, let your children have some control over when they spend time with their other parent.

- Encourage your children to call their other parent to share their good news and their concerns, and to get advice and/or help from that parent with homework. However, don't make calling a chore or a duty. Also, let your ex know that he or she can call the kids whenever they're at your house.

- Share report cards, homework assignments, school art projects, special awards, and so on with your former spouse.

- Encourage your former spouse to attend parent-teacher conferences.

- When you take photos of your children, get extra copies made for your ex-spouse.

- Let your ex-spouse know the dates and times of your children's recitals, school plays, athletic events, and other extracurricular activities.

- Invite your ex to your children's birthday parties, to go trick-or-treating at Halloween, and to share other important dates with you and your kids.

- Let your ex-spouse know well ahead of time when you will be taking the kids out of town, and don't balk when your spouse wants to take the kids on an out-of-town trip unless you're concerned that the trip is really a ruse to kidnap them. For information about childnapping, read the "Worse than a bad dream: The kidnapping parent" sidebar in this chapter and see Chapter 18 as well.

- Keep your ex-spouse informed of your children's medical problems.

- Consult your former spouse about the important decisions in your children's lives. However, if an issue comes up, politely remind your former spouse that you're not legally obligated to act on his or her wishes or even consider them. Also, be sure that your children understand that consulting their other parent about important decisions they may be making — where to go to college, for example — is okay.

- Don't forbid your children to spend time with your ex's new girlfriend, boyfriend, or spouse. If you do, you force your ex to do things without your children, which can add to the stress they may already be feeling.

Moving and custody don't always mix

A growing number of divorced parents are waging battles with each other over whether one of them should be able to move to a new state with the couple's children or to a location that's far away from where the other parent lives. Typically, these battles are triggered when a woman with primary custody of a couple's children wants to move, maybe because her new spouse has been offered a job out of state, because she has been offered the opportunity to make more money but it means moving away from the area where she and her ex both live, or because she wants to live closer to her aging parents, among other reasons. However, parents with shared custody also end up in conflict over this issue.

This conflict usually has no easy or obvious answer because both parties have valid arguments for and against one parent moving with the kids. For example, fathers may oppose the move because they want to stay involved in their kids' lives and recognize that long-distance parenting makes that difficult, if not impossible. On the other hand, mothers want the freedom to move with their children, to pursue opportunities in life, or to respond to changes in their lives, especially if they believe that those opportunities/changes can improve their kids' lives as well as their own. Although a judge has no say over whether or not a custodial parent can move, a judge may rule that a parent isn't free to move with his or her kids. In fact, judges have made such a ruling.

In recent years, the highest courts in at least seven states have ruled on this issue. In the future, you can expect family courts in many states to deal with a growing number of cases involving moving and custody and for additional higher courts to rule on this issue as well.

Custody Decisions and Their Tax Implications

Don't overlook the tax implications of various child-custody arrangements when you and your spouse are deciding which arrangement is best for you, because depending on the arrangement you negotiate, you could lose your eligibility for certain child-related tax benefits. The following items briefly explain how different custody arrangements can affect your eligibility. However, if you work with a tax CPA, he or she may be able to find ways to get certain tax benefits for you that you wouldn't ordinarily be entitled to. Depending on your income bracket, taking advantage of those benefits can provide you with significant tax savings.

✔ **Filing as head of the household:** You can file your federal taxes as *head of the household* if you meet certain conditions. You must have been unmarried on December 31 of the tax year (meaning you were legally separated by that date or your spouse didn't live in your home during the last six months of the year for which you are filing taxes; one or more of your children must have lived with you more than half of that year; and you must have contributed more than half the cost of maintaining your home during that year). If you and your spouse share physical custody exactly 50/50, neither of you can file as head of the household.

✔ **Exemptions for your children:** According to the IRS, the spouse who has custody of a couple's children gets the tax exemptions for them. However, you and your ex can get around this by filing Form 8332 with the IRS. This form lets you trade the exemptions back and forth with one another. If you have any questions about how to trade or about whether one of you should always take the exemptions, talk to a tax CPA. When you claim a child as an exemption, you also get other tax benefits, including the right to the child credit for each child you exempt as well as the Hope Scholarship and Lifetime Learning credit.

✔ **Childcare tax credit:** You're entitled to this credit only if you are the custodial parent, you have one or more children under the age of 13, and your children attend day care while you're at work.

✔ **Deductions for medical expenses:** You and your spouse can each deduct your out-of-pocket child-related medical expenses, assuming the total amount of those expenses exceeds a certain percentage of your adjusted gross income.

✔ **Earned income tax credit:** This tax benefit is for the spouse who has physical custody of the children and works full time or part time but who earns low or moderate income. If you qualify, you can reduce your federal taxes and receive a refund. To qualify, you must meet certain requirements and file a tax return, even if you're not otherwise required to file. The credit you receive can help pay your bills. However, this tax credit is quite complicated, so you should speak to your CPA to determine if you or your spouse will be eligible for it and exactly how to maximize its benefits.

Going the Extra Mile with a Parenting Plan

A growing number of divorcing parents are preparing written *parenting plans* in addition to, or instead of, having traditional custody agreements. A parenting plan is a highly detailed description of how both parents will be involved in the lives of their children after their divorce. These plans are helpful whether you and your spouse will share custody of your children or one of you will have custody and the other will have visitation rights.

The key difference between a parenting plan and a traditional custody agreement is that a parenting plan is more detailed and specific. Parenting plans spell out in great detail how each parent will be involved in his or her children's lives after a divorce and lists their rights and responsibilities related to their children.

Here are the types of things you may want to include in a parenting plan:

- Exactly how you will share the routine day-to-day care of your children; that is, who will be responsible for what
- How you will share decision-making related to your children
- How you will share your children's time on holidays, vacations, and birthdays
- Each parent's access to their children's medical records, report cards, teachers, and so on
- Who will take off work to care for a sick child
- Who will care for the children when one parent is out of town overnight for business or pleasure
- Exactly how you will share decision-making about your children's religious upbringing, medical care and treatment, education, and day care
- How you will deal with issues related to an older child's dating, curfews, sexuality, or what to do if that child develops a substance abuse problem
- How you will respond to your children's changing needs as they get older
- How you and your former spouse will resolve conflicts/disagreements that you can't work out through a friendly discussion

The State of Minnesota has a parenting plan worksheet that can be useful to parents in any state who are negotiating the terms of their parenting plan. You can download a copy of this worksheet by going to `webdev.extension. umn.edu/Parents Forever/Parenting_Plans.html`.

Having a parenting plan has several advantages. For example, through the process of developing the plan, parents must grapple with issues related to their kids and come up with solutions before the issues become problems. The plan also provides parents with a detailed map or framework that helps define their relationship with one another and with their children after their divorce. Developing a plan can help reduce the potential for post-divorce conflict and power struggles over the kids.

Also, states differ dramatically in the comprehensiveness and level of detail of their custody provisions, but, in those states where the provisions are very general, parents can help minimize future problems by negotiating a parenting plan. Some states, in fact, require that a parenting plan be included as an integral part of a custody agreement or a judge's custody order.

Parenting plans also can help make any custody arrangement work better by

✔ Helping both parents be more realistic about the amount of time and energy required to parent your children on a day-to-day basis as single parents.

✔ Encouraging you to get all your post-divorce parenting issues out on the table. (Acknowledging those issues and resolving them together, before your divorce is final, is better than doing so after you have a custody agreement in place.)

✔ Minimizing the potential for post-divorce strife by helping you anticipate and resolve potential areas of conflict before they develop, by spelling out on paper, before you are divorced, every detail that could make or break your custody agreement.

✔ Letting you establish mutually agreed upon procedures for resolving any post-divorce conflicts that develop related to your kids.

✔ Allowing you and your ex-spouse to express your long-term goals for your children in qualitative terms. For example, your parenting plan can state the following goals: "Our goal is to support our children to the fullest extent possible in their scholastic and extracurricular activities" or "Our goal is to limit the amount of time our children spend watching TV and playing computer games, and to encourage outdoor activities, reading, and conversation to the fullest extent possible."

If you and your spouse negotiate a parenting plan, avoid making it so rigid and inflexible that your plan cannot bend and change over time to meet the changing needs of your children. Remember that what your children need from each of you evolves over time, depending on their personalities and their ages, and that inevitably, issues and problems will arise as time goes on that you didn't anticipate when you were preparing your plan. Your plan should also be flexible enough to respond to the changing circumstances in your own lives. That flexibility may include changing when or how often your children spend the night at your home and assuming more of or giving up some of your decision-making responsibilities. These and other plan adjustments may be necessary because of changes in your professional lives, a serious illness or accident, changes in your living situation or finances, or changes in your children's needs.

When You and Your Spouse Can't Agree: Taking Your Case to Court

The possibility always exists that you and your spouse will end up at loggerheads over how to handle the custody of your children and/or the details of your parenting plan. After all, any number of issues and concerns can complicate your decision-making, including

✔ Fear that you may be squeezed out of your children's lives if you don't participate equally in all ways on decisions regarding your kids

✔ Guilt over how your divorce will affect your children

✔ Anger at your spouse

✔ Concern that if you don't see your children every day, your influence in their lives may diminish or that they won't be well-cared for

✔ Worry that over the coming years you'll miss out on the special moments in your children's lives

✔ Fear that if a new man or a new woman comes into your spouse's life, that person will try to take your place when you're not around

✔ Worry that the political, religious, socioeconomic, or cultural views of your spouse or your spouse's family may have a serious impact on your children's personal development after your divorce

If you and your spouse simply can't see eye to eye on these or other issues, consider talking with your religious advisor, meeting with a mental health professional, or trying mediation rather than asking the court for help. In fact, if you take your case to court, you may be required to try to work out your differences through mediation before the court will agree to give you a court date. (See Chapter 15 to find out how mediation works.) Other courts require couples who cannot agree on a custody arrangement to view special educational videos on the subject before the courts will get involved.

Preparing for the judge's questions

If you take your custody battle to court, the judge who hears your case will probably consider most, if not all, of the following issues when deciding what custody arrangement is in your children's best interests:

✔ Where your children are living now.

✔ The age and gender of your children.

✔ How you and your spouse have shared parenting responsibilities in your marriage.

Whether both of you were actively involved in your children's lives — bathing and dressing them, feeding them, helping them with their home-work, playing with them, helping them resolve their personal problems, addressing their emotional needs, taking them to and from day care or school, attending parent-teacher conferences, taking them to their doctor and dentist appointments, handling their emergencies, and so on.

Whether one of you is a stay-at-home parent, who arranges for your chil-dren to play with their friends, buys their clothes and school supplies, organizes their birthday parties, arranges for babysitters, stays home when one of your children is sick or when your children are on vacation from school (assuming one of you is not a full-time homemaker), and how you and your spouse each discipline your children.

✔ Whether any of your children have special educational or health/mental health needs and how you and your spouse deal with them now.

✔ The kind of relationship your children have with each of you and which parent they turn to for emotional support or help when they have problems.

✔ The hours each of you works, whether either or both of you have to travel for your jobs, and whether you expect that your work and travel schedules will remain the same after your divorce.

✔ Your ability to cooperate with one another on behalf of your children after your divorce.

✔ Where each of you intends to live after your divorce and the kind of home life you can offer your children.

✔ The stability of your finances.

✔ Your physical health.

✔ Your personal habits, for example, whether either of you abuses alcohol, drugs, parties excessively, is sexually promiscuous, and so on.

✔ Your moral characters and religious beliefs.

✔ Whether either of you has ever attempted suicide or been hospitalized for an emotional or psychiatric disorder.

✔ Whether you or your spouse has a criminal history.

✔ Whether your children have an especially close relationship with either or both sets of grandparents.

Before you decide to wage a custody battle in court, compare yourself as a parent with your state's custody criteria. How do you measure up? If you fall short, think twice (and maybe three or four times) about whether a court battle is *really* worth the expense and stress it will create for you and your children. Maybe you need to resolve things with your spouse out of court.

Arming yourself for a custody battle

For many reasons — both good and bad — some parents want to limit the time that their former spouses can spend with their children after a divorce. Others attempt to strip the other parent of the right to make decisions about their children or seek a custody arrangement that isn't merited by the roles they've played in the lives of their children so far. They may seek such an arrangement as a way to reduce the amount of child support they have to pay.

If you're concerned that your spouse may try to limit your right to continue playing a meaningful role in your children's lives after you divorce or if you want to limit your spouse's involvement in your kids' lives after your marriage has ended, you may be headed for a custody battle. If that seems likely, you should take the following actions sooner rather than later to improve your legal standing in such a battle:

- ✔ **Educate yourself about the general guidelines that judges in your state use to make custody decisions.** See how your situation stacks up against those guidelines.

  You should be able to get a copy of the guidelines by calling the family court in your area or a local family law attorney if you're not already working with one. If an attorney asks you to pay for the guidelines, the price should be nominal — little more than the cost to copy them. Two other ways to find out about your state's custody guidelines is to buy an hour of a family law attorney's time, especially if you want an opportunity to discuss the guidelines and get your questions answered, and research the guidelines on the Internet.

- ✔ **Stay involved in all aspects of your children's lives.** That includes participating in parent-teacher conferences, taking your kids to the doctor, dropping them off or picking them up from day care, being home at night to feed and bathe them and get them to bed, and helping them with their homework.

  When child custody becomes an issue in a divorce, most judges look to see which parent has been the children's *primary caregiver,* the parent who has been most involved in their day-to-day lives. One of the best ways to prove that you are integrally involved in your children's lives is to bring objective witnesses into the courtroom who can testify that you were there for your children in the years prior to your divorce and that you appeared to enjoy an ongoing and meaningful relationship with them.

- ✔ **Be there for your children so that they view you as a "go-to" parent.** As your children grow up, their parents should be available to provide them with ongoing emotional, physical, and psychological support and general caregiving.

The tips we just listed may sound somewhat cold and calculating, but you can win close custody battles by presenting this kind of evidence. This advice should serve as a wake-up call for those of you who think that a divorce may be in your future and have been spending too much time at the office, have been using up all your free time honing your golf or tennis game and devoting too little time to your kids, or who have always left most aspects of child-rearing to your spouse. Now may be the time to get your priorities straight. Besides, your life will be richer for playing a more active role in the lives of your children, and you're less likely to have regrets later about your role as a parent.

STATE BY STATE

Custody and same-sex parents

Although society's attitude toward gay and lesbian parents is evolving, the laws are slow to address those changes. For example, the laws in a handful of states — Alaska, California, New Jersey, New Mexico, and Pennsylvania — as well as the District of Columbia state that a parent cannot be denied custody or visitation because of their sexual orientation. Nevertheless, a judge has considerable discretion in deciding custody and visitation matters, and he or she may be influenced by his or her own prejudices or the standards of his or her community when deciding what is in a child's best interest. Other states allow the courts to deny custody or visitation rights to a divorced parent just because of the parent's sexual orientation.

Realizing neither of you may get the kids

In only a very small number of custody cases, neither spouse gets custody of the children. For instance, if both spouses have a history of child neglect or child abuse, substance abuse, emotional problems, or other negative behaviors, a family law judge may decide that neither parent should be awarded child custody. However, a judge doesn't consider making such a decision unless a third party raises the issue or unless it is undeniably obvious to the judge that neither spouse is fit to parent his or her children.

In such cases, the judge appoints a *guardian ad litem* (someone with master's degree–level training or the equivalent in psychology, counseling, or social work) to represent the children in court and to help the court determine where the children should live. Often, a grandparent or another adult relative assumes temporary custody of the children under a court-ordered guardianship until a permanent living arrangement can be established.

Making Visitation Arrangements

Earlier in this chapter, we introduce the concept of visitation — the right of a noncustodial parent to spend time with his or her children. When you and your spouse negotiate your custody agreement, you can decide on the terms of visitation — when your former spouse will have the children, how long the kids will stay with him or her, and other terms. If a judge decides how custody of your children will be handled and he or she awards you primary custody of them, the judge sets the terms of your spouse's visitation rights. By the way, no law requires the parent with visitation rights to exercise those rights. In other words, a noncustodial parent cannot be forced to spend time with his or her children. Fortunately, most parents want to be a part of their children's lives.

Making visitation an issue for the court

When bad feelings between ex-spouses run deep, visitation can become a hotly contested issue, even if the court clearly spells out the rules of visitation. For example, to get back at his or her ex-spouse, the noncustodial spouse may deliberately return the children to the custodial parent later than scheduled, pick them up late, cancel plans to spend time with the kids, or withhold child support. Or the problem may be with the custodial parent. For example, he or she may refuse to allow the other parent to see the children or place unreasonable restrictions on visitation. Often the only way this emotionally charged duel can end is if one parent takes the other to court.

When one parent has primary custody, a judge may order either "reasonable visitation" or "generous visitation" rights for the noncustodial parent and let the parents work out what that means. Or the judge may spell things out more specifically.

To help protect the best interests of the children and to protect the visitation rights of noncustodial parents, too, most states have guidelines that spell out the minimum amount of time that a noncustodial parent can spend with his or her children.

Burying the hatchet for the sake of your kids

When you and your spouse use visitation as a vehicle for expressing your negative feelings for each other, you're likely to do serious emotional damage to your children. Children hate to see their parents fighting, and, more important, they often blame themselves for the discord. Those feelings can create many problems for your children that can follow them throughout their lives, including low self-esteem, emotional distress, problems with intimacy, and even marital troubles of their own. Is this the kind of legacy you want to leave your children?

Your children deserve the opportunity to have both parents in their lives. Remember, a bad spouse doesn't necessarily equal a bad parent. Using your children to get back at your ex-spouse punishes your children as well as your ex. Don't do it! For the sake of your kids, you and your former spouse must act like mature adults and put them, not your hurt and angry feelings, first. If you can't work things out through mediation, you should seek help from a mental health professional — together or separately — so you can get beyond whatever issues are in the way of being able to cooperate with one another for your kids.

Worse than a bad dream: The kidnapping parent

Although not a frequent occurrence (and we're glad of that), parental "childnapping" does happen. Some parents kidnap their children because they're afraid that the judge will deny them custody (or because they already have been denied custody). Others abduct their children to exact revenge on their ex-spouse, to force a reconciliation with their ex, or to keep their children away from what they regard as a dangerous parent. Abducting spouses may flee with their children to another state or, worse yet, to another country.

All states and the federal government have laws to prevent childnapping, and in most cases, parents who kidnap their child are committing a felony. Parents convicted of childnapping can end up in prison. (Turn to Chapter 18 for more information on the laws that apply to childnapping, the specific steps you should take immediately if your child is missing and you fear he or she has been kidnapped, and some of the organizations that can help you in such a situation.)

If you and your spouse are separated, your spouse takes off with the kids, and you have no idea where they are (and neither of you has a temporary court order for custody), immediately call a family law attorney. The attorney can initiate the appropriate legal actions to get you temporary legal custody of your missing children so that you can get your children returned to you.

Visiting with restrictions

When you have good reason to believe that the noncustodial parent will harm or endanger your children, that parent's visitation rights should be restricted or even prohibited. Examples of when this restriction may occur include when the noncustodial parent has a history of

- Alcohol or drug abuse
- Child neglect
- Criminal activities
- Exhibiting explicit sexual behavior in front of children
- Mental or emotional instability
- Mental, physical, or sexual child abuse

Usually when a court restricts a parent's visitation rights, a designated adult must be present whenever that parent spends time with the children.

If you have custody of your children and you think that the court should restrict your ex-spouse's visitation rights, ask the court to change the terms of your ex's visitation. Don't take the law into your own hands; if you do, you'll be breaking it.

As a way to deny a former spouse access to his or her children, some parents cruelly and maliciously make unwarranted accusations of child abuse or molestation. If you're unfairly accused, get legal help from an attorney.

Usually if allegations of abuse surface in a divorce, the court appoints a guardian *ad litem* or attorney *ad litem*. Ad litem is a Latin term meaning "for the lawsuit or legal action." Therefore, in a divorce, a guardian ad litem or an attorney ad litem is someone who protects your children's interests in your divorce proceedings. When there are allegations of parental abuse, this individual conducts an investigation into the allegations and prepares a report that a judge uses to rule on custody, visitation, and what to do about the alleged abuse.

Grandparents have visitation rights, too

Many states have laws that give grandparents the right to court-ordered visitation when the children's parents get divorced. However, like with other legal matters in divorce, those laws vary from state to state. In most states, if the custodial parent doesn't allow the grandparents to spend time with their grandchildren after a divorce or if the grandparents are fearful that the custodial parent will try to exclude them from their grandchildren's lives, they can ask the court to grant them formal visitation rights. Like with other issues related to children and divorce, the court determines whether or not spending time with their grandparents is in the children's best interest. If a court grants a grandparent that right and one or both divorced parents interfere in his or her exercising it, the grandparent can ask the court for help.

More and more grandparents have gone one step further and sought custody of their grandchildren. Usually this happens when a grandparent thinks that both parents are unfit to raise the children or when the grandparents have been acting as *de facto* parents.

If you think your ex is abusing one of your children

If you think that your ex-spouse is abusing your children, talk to an attorney immediately. The attorney can advise you on the appropriate steps to take, which may include any of the following:

✔ Contacting the police

✔ Filing a criminal lawsuit against your former spouse and stopping all communication with your ex

✔ Asking the court to prohibit your ex-spouse from having any future contact with your child until your allegations are investigated

✔ Having your child examined by a doctor

✔ Having your spouse undergo evaluation and treatment for chemical dependency, alcohol abuse, psychiatric problems, or anger management

✔ Taking photos of any unusual marks, bruises, or cuts on your children that you believe are evidence of the abuse or molestation

You should also report your ex-spouse to your local Child Protection Services office immediately. In fact, you may be held criminally liable if you don't report your spouse.

Chapter 11

Child Support: Taking Care of Your Kids' Financial Needs

As a parent, you have a moral and legal responsibility to support your minor children (younger than age 18 in most states) so that they at least have the basics — a roof over their heads, clothes to wear, enough food to eat, and an education. Divorce doesn't change this obligation, whether your children live with you or with your former spouse after your marriage ends. If you have minor children, deciding how you and your spouse will share the cost of raising your kids is a key issue that you must resolve before your divorce can be final. And, if you separate and have minor children, you and your spouse should negotiate a temporary child-support agreement.

In this chapter, we explain which parent usually pays child support to the other and how to use state child-support guidelines to determine a minimum level of support. We also help prepare you to negotiate your own child-support agreement and explain what a judge may decide if you and your spouse can't work things out yourselves. In addition, we cover other child-related expenses beyond the basics that you and your spouse may want to include in your divorce agreement or that a judge may order you to pay, along with the tax implications your agreement will have.

Defining Child Support and Figuring Out Who Pays It

Child support is a fixed amount of money that one parent pays to another parent after the couple divorces to help cover the cost of raising their minor child or children. The agreement is different for various living arrangements, which we discuss in this section. You can negotiate your own child-support agreement, taking into account the support guidelines in your state, or you can let a judge decide about child support if you and your spouse are unable to come to an agreement about it. (The section "Negotiating Your Own Agreement," later in this chapter, provides advice for how to work out the terms of that agreement on your own, and the "Taking state guidelines into account" section gives you the lowdown on state guidelines in general.) Contact your state's child-support enforcement office or a divorce attorney for specific information about the guidelines in your state.

If you're the parent who receives child support, you're expected not to use the money to enhance your lifestyle — to pay for your vacation, to help finance the sexy little sports car you always wanted, to pay for the cost of a personal trainer at your gym, and so on. You're expected to use those payments *only* for the benefit of your child or children.

When one parent has primary custody

Usually if one parent has primary custody of the children, the other parent (the *noncustodial* parent) is obligated to pay child support. The court usually considers the parent with primary custody to be meeting his or her child-support obligation by raising the couple's children. But the custodial parent typically spends up to three times the amount of money he or she receives from the noncustodial parent in child support paying for their children's necessities.

Although some states deduct *reasonable living expenses* from the income of the parent who will pay child support before determining how much support that parent must pay, in primary custody arrangements especially, most states calculate child support based on the gross income of the noncustodial parent.

When parents share custody 50/50

When parents share custody of their children on a 50/50 basis, depending on their individual incomes and assets, neither parent may pay child support to the other. Instead, they may agree (or the court may order) that whenever their children are living with one of them, that parent pays for the children's day-to-day care, although they should have an agreement regarding how they will share the cost of the big stuff — health insurance, private school or college, private lessons, summer camp, and so on.

Sometimes, however, depending on each parent's individual circumstances and the needs of their children, one parent may pay the other parent child support in a 50/50 custody arrangement. For example, if one of the custodial parents earns much more than the other parent, the higher-earning parent may agree that it would be fair if he or she paid child support to the parent who earns less. If the parents don't see eye to eye on this matter, they may go to court and let a judge decide. If a judge decides that the higher earning parent must pay child support to the other parent, the amount of the court-ordered support will probably be less than it would be if the parents didn't have a shared 50/50 custody arrangement.

If you and your spouse negotiate your own child-support arrangement and decide to share custody on a 50/50 basis, but your incomes aren't equal or close to equal, one way to determine how much each of you should contribute toward the care of your children is to calculate the percentage of each of your individual incomes relative to your combined income, and then apply that percentage to the total cost of your children's day-to-day care.

When a shared custody arrangement isn't 50/50

In some shared custody situations, each parent's financial contribution to child support is a function of their individual income relative to the combined total income of both parents and of the amount of time the children will spend with each parent. For example, a couple's children may spend more time with the parent who earns less — maybe because the other parent travels a lot for business. Therefore, the parents may agree (or the court may order) that the parent who travels should pay the other parent child support. Exactly how much support depends on what the parents decide or what the judge rules is fair to both spouses and necessary to take care of their children's needs. But the amount of the payments will probably be smaller than they would be if the parents weren't sharing custody.

If you and your spouse decide to share custody of your kids but agree that one of you will stay at home to care for them until they all reach a certain age, you should negotiate child support as though you had decided on a sole-custody arrangement. (Chapter 10 discusses various child-custody arrangements.)

Calculating and Paying the Child-support Check

You and your spouse can negotiate your own child-support arrangement based on how you will share custody of your kids, your individual estimated post-divorce budgets, and the financial needs of your children. Or, you can ask the court to decide which one of you should pay child support to the other and how much the support will be. When determining an appropriate amount of support, the court takes into account your state's child-support guidelines, and it may factor other considerations into its decision as well, such as whether any of your children have special needs, whether one of you makes much more money than the other, and so on.

If one of you is also asking to receive spousal support (or alimony), that request takes a backseat to child support because, in the eyes of the law, child support is more important than spousal support. Therefore, the judge won't order one spouse to pay so much spousal support that he or she won't be able to pay an adequate amount of child support. Similarly, if you and your spouse are negotiating your own divorce agreement, you should make child support a higher priority than spousal support if you're addressing both types of payments.

Taking state guidelines into account

In the late 1980s, Congress passed a law requiring all states to establish guidelines (formulas, really) that family court judges must use to calculate the appropriate amount of child support in a divorce. One of the reasons for the guidelines was to try to bring some consistency to the amount of child support paid from state to state. Even so, a considerable amount of variability still exists among states, which means that parents in some states pay more in child support than parents in other states who make the same amount of money.

Most states express their child-support guideline amounts as a percentage of a parent's income. Usually, the more dependent children a couple has, the larger the percentage.

- ✔ When calculating the amount of child support to be paid, some states consider only the income of the noncustodial parent, whereas other states consider the incomes of both parents.

- ✔ Some state guidelines base the amount of child support on a parent's *gross income* (income before taxes and other deductions), but others base the amount on *net income* (actual take-home pay).

✔ Some states cap the total amount of income that their guidelines can apply to; that is, the states only apply the guidelines to income up to a certain dollar amount, which means that the court doesn't consider any income a parent earns that's more than that amount when determining how much child support he or she must pay. Also, some states apply a different percentage to income over a certain amount. The percentage may be higher or lower depending on the state.

✔ State guidelines even differ in their definitions of *income*. For example, some states consider only a parent's wages, whereas others take into account *all* sources of income, including wages, investment income, trust income, royalties, government benefits, and so on.

Accessing your state's guidelines

You can get the info you need to figure out the minimum amount of child support you'll have to pay (or receive) in several ways:

✔ Ask your attorney about your state's child-support guidelines.

✔ Call your state attorney general's child-support division for your state's guidelines.

✔ Go online to `www.acf.dhhs.gov/programs/cse/extinf.htm`, which is located within the U.S. Office of Child Support Enforcement's Web site. You can also access brochures and fact sheets about your child-support rights at this site.

✔ See whether the family law court in your area can provide you with a child-support worksheet for calculating the amount of child support that you're likely to receive or may have to pay based on your state's guidelines.

 If you have custody of your children and you move to another state where the cost of living is higher than where you used to live, you can ask the court that issued the original order for child support to increase the amount of support that your former spouse must pay you.

Needing more than the guidelines allow

If your spouse will be paying you child support and you believe that you need more support than your state's guidelines provide for, prepare a post-divorce budget for your children that clearly demonstrates just how much you need to care for them. Bring the budget to your negotiations if you and your spouse are resolving the issue of child support on your own. If your attorney is helping you resolve that issue or if you're going to court to resolve it, make sure that your attorney has a copy of your budget.

When you're preparing this budget, include expenses such as your mortgage or rent payment, your car payment, phone service, cable, and other similar expenses as well as expenses that are directly associated with your children — clothing, day care, and so on. Be sure to figure in your income, too.

To make preparing your children's budget as painless as possible, try using the budget worksheet found at `www.free-financial-advice.net/budget.html` or flip to Chapter 3 where you'll find an example of a budget that you can adapt to your needs.

Leaving special circumstances to judges' discretion

In most states, under certain circumstances family law judges have the flexibility to order more or less child support than the guideline amounts dictate. Those circumstances may include when

✔ The custodial parent earns considerably more than the other parent or has considerably more assets, or the assets of the noncustodial parent are worth relatively little.

✔ The couple's children have emotional, physical, educational, or other special needs.

✔ During the couple's marriage, their children enjoyed a standard of living that was higher than what the guideline amount provides.

✔ The noncustodial parent has the ability to pay much more than the guideline amount or makes too little to pay the guideline amount.

✔ One of the parents must incur substantial childcare expenses in order to be able to earn a good living.

✔ One parent assumed a lot of the couple's debt in their divorce.

✔ One parent experiences a significant amount of positive or negative cash flow from his or her real or personal property.

✔ The noncustodial parent makes substantially less than his or her full earnings potential.

In this case, the judge may decide to order an amount of support based on how much that parent *could* earn, not on how much money the parent *is* earning. For example, if a former corporate executive trades his or her high-stress job (and six-figure salary) for less-lucrative but more relaxing employment as a woodworker, the judge may order that parent to make child-support payments that are more in line with what he or she earned when the parent was a corporate executive.

✔ The noncustodial spouse becomes unemployed.

The judge may order the noncustodial spouse to pay less support or none at all until that parent finds a job. However, if the court has reason to believe that the parent's unemployment is little more than a ruse to avoid paying child support, the judge may set a date by which the parent must begin paying an amount of support equal to what he or she would pay if that parent were working at his or her full earnings capacity. Even if the judge doesn't think that the unemployment is a ruse, he or she may order the unemployed parent to pay what the parent would have to pay if he or she were employed or to pay up after the parent lands a job.

✔ The children will be living full time with the noncustodial parent during a certain time of the year — for example, during the summer.

In such an instance, the judge may allow the noncustodial parent to pay less child support during that time.

Considering the payment method

If you and your spouse have more than one minor child, the judge may order the noncustodial parent to

✔ Pay a per-child amount of child support.

✔ Make a lump-sum payment of child support. (However, most courts don't like the lump-sum option because judges realize that many people have trouble managing a large chunk of money.)

✔ Purchase an annuity calculated to cover the financial needs of all your children.

✔ Set aside specific property so that it can be administered for the benefit of the children.

✔ Combine all these options.

If you have only one child, many of these same methods also apply, including a lump-sum payment, an annuity, setting aside property to be administered for your child's benefit, or some combination of these options.

Unless you and your spouse agree to a different arrangement or the judge orders otherwise, a noncustodial spouse with child-support obligations must pay support year-round, not just when the custodial parent has the children.

If you pay your child support by check, note exactly what the payment is for on the bottom of each check because a canceled check provides proof of payment in the event that some question arises in the future about whether you failed to make a payment or didn't make a full payment.

Negotiating Your Own Agreement

Like most everything else to do with divorce, negotiating your own child-support agreement without the help of a judge has its advantages:

✔ **You split the responsibility:** The negotiation process encourages you and your spouse to assume equal responsibility for deciding how your children's financial needs will be met.

Mothers often end up being their children's financial advocates in child-support negotiations and, sometimes, it can appear to their husbands that they're really arguing on their own behalf, not for their kids. If you're a mother in this situation, a good way to avoid this problem is to be prepared to justify what you ask for on behalf of your kids with receipts, check-register entries, and with anything else that helps prove that what you're asking for makes financial sense.

✔ **1 + 1 = 2 parents:** Negotiating together reinforces the fact that, even though your marital relationship is changing, you and your spouse still have a relationship as parents and that you're both legally responsible for your children's welfare.

✔ **The child support gets paid:** Working things out together makes it more likely that after you're divorced, the parent who's obligated to pay child support will actually do so.

If you decide to negotiate the agreement yourself, make sure that you spell out all the details of your child-custody and -support arrangement in writing, including the amount of child support, how often each payment will come, and the date by which you or your ex must pay it. After you have a draft, hire a divorce attorney to review it so that you can be sure that the agreement covers all the bases and leaves little in question. Later, if you and your former spouse disagree over exactly what you agreed to in terms of child support, you have the agreement to refer to, and if a judge decides your dispute, he or she can read your agreement to determine exactly what both of you were intending at the time of your divorce.

Agreeing on how much is enough

Although you may both agree that one of you should pay child support to the other, deciding on the exact amount of the support payments can be a challenge. Start by reviewing the following: a budget that reflects the cost of raising your children; your estimated post-divorce budget and your spouse's; and your state's child-support guidelines, which you can obtain from your divorce attorney or from your state's child-support enforcement agency. But most likely, you and your spouse will want to provide your children with more than what the guidelines indicate because they generally define the minimum amount of support to be paid.

Slacking off on child-support payments leads to . . .

If you're the parent who will receive child support, try hard to negotiate a child-support agreement with your spouse rather than have a judge decide how much your spouse must pay. Your spouse is more apt to meet his or her child-support obligation if he or she has a say in the amount of those payments. And, if the support checks keep coming, you're better able financially to provide your children with what they need. The following facts emphasize the value of you and your spouse negotiating your own child-support arrangement:

✔ About 59 percent of custodial parents, or 8 million parents, had child-support agreements in 2002, most of which were court-ordered, according to the Census Bureau. Of those parents, about only 45 percent received the full amount of child support they were due; 29 percent received only some of that money; and 26 percent received nothing.

✔ In fiscal year 2003, the total amount of past-due child support owed to custodial parents for all previous fiscal years was a whopping $95.8 billion.

✔ In 2001, 1.5 million custodial parents were living below the poverty line and were due child support. Among those parents living in poverty who had received some child support, the average amount of that support was $3,000.

✔ In 2001, about 36.5 percent of all custodial parents contacted a government agency for help collecting their child support.

Don't forget to factor inflation into your child-support agreement, because increases in the inflation rate ultimately decrease the value of the child support that one spouse pays the other. A practical way of dealing with this issue is to build nominal increases in the amount of child support into your agreement. If those increases don't keep pace with the inflation rate, your agreement can state that you and your former spouse will negotiate a different amount of child support. (If you do, be sure to get a new court order that reflects the revised amount.) Another option is for the spouse who receives child support to ask a judge to order an increase in the amount of the support payments.

If you initiated your divorce and feel guilty about how it may affect your kids, don't try to ease your guilt by agreeing to pay more child support than you can truly afford. Otherwise, if you have a tough time meeting your child-support obligation after your divorce, you can find yourself in court if your former spouse takes legal steps to enforce your child-support agreement.

Providing for adjustments as your lives change

Another advantage to negotiating your own child-support agreement is that you and your spouse can craft one that readily allows you to anticipate and accommodate changes in your lives and in the lives of your children over the years. For example, you can spell out how to deal with possible future expenses related to your children — such as orthodontia, sports, extracurricular school activities, clubs, the cost of the prom, an opportunity to study abroad — and how any salary increases or decreases either of you may experience will affect your child-support agreement. If the future brings any changes in the amount of support to be paid or when it will be paid, be sure to get a new order from the court that reflects those changes. Otherwise, the changes are not enforceable.

When you go to the family law judge and ask to revise your existing child-support court order, assuming you and your ex-spouse are both in agreement about the changes, the judge will probably approve your request without any delays or problems. However, to help ensure that things go smoothly, involving a family law attorney is best.

State courts aren't bound to honor provisions you may include in a prenuptial or postnuptial agreement concerning the custody or support of your children.

Being prepared for obstacles in negotiation

Despite the benefits of negotiating your own child-support agreement, doing so is easier said than done if you don't ground your negotiations in reality or if you let your emotions get in the way. Before you tackle those discussions, you need to be in the right frame of mind, and being aware of the following thinking patterns that can derail your child-support discussions with your spouse is important:

- The spouse who will pay child support may view it as nothing more than spousal support in disguise. Therefore, he or she may argue for as little child support as possible and against any extras.

- The spouse who will receive the child support may demand an unreasonable amount of support as revenge for having to get divorced, to "protect" the children, or out of fear for the future.

✔ Looking forward to being single again, some spouses begin dreaming about the exciting new lifestyles they'll enjoy. Because living that kind of life takes money and because money is usually in short supply after a divorce, the parent who will be paying the support wants to pay as little as possible, and the other parent wants as much as possible.

Going Beyond Basic Child Support

Child support isn't the only expense that a judge can order you, your spouse, or both of you to pay for the benefit of your minor children. Also, if you negotiate your own support agreement, child support isn't the only expense that you and your spouse may decide should be paid. For example, depending on your state, a judge can order the noncustodial parent to contribute to the cost of the other parent's work-related day care and the children's college or trade-school education (assuming that the parent can afford to do so). A judge can also order the noncustodial parent to provide health insurance for the children, unless the parents have worked out another arrangement that's acceptable to the court.

Making your children your life insurance beneficiaries

If you're obligated to pay child support, you can help ensure that your children's financial needs are taken care of if you die while they're still minors by purchasing a life insurance policy and making them the beneficiaries of the policy. If a judge is involved in your divorce and orders you to purchase such a policy, he or she may also order you to provide your ex-spouse with annual proof that the life insurance policy continues to be in force. If you and your spouse decide to share the cost of raising your children, you should both purchase life insurance policies.

If you purchase life insurance, you must designate an adult to manage the policy proceeds on your children's behalf because, legally, minors cannot manage more than a very small amount of money or other assets. Depending on the kind of estate planning you've done, this adult can be the trustee of the living trust you may have set up for your children, or the trustee can be your children's property guardian if you write a will. Whomever you choose, this person may be your children's other parent, a relative or friend that you trust, an attorney, and so on. You should discuss how best to use life insurance to benefit your minor children with an estate-planning attorney.

Ensuring uninterrupted child support with disability insurance

Disability insurance provides a working parent with a percentage of his or her income if that parent is unable to work due to a debilitating illness or injury. Therefore, the court often requires the parent who's paying child support to purchase disability insurance, particularly if he or she is self-employed.

Disability insurance is especially important if a parent's business is a sole proprietorship, a partnership, or a small, closely held corporation. In such businesses, the active involvement of the business owner is critical to the business's financial success. Therefore, if the owner becomes physically or mentally incapacitated, the business can falter or fail, leaving the owner with little or no income. As a result, the owner probably won't be able to meet his or her child support obligation after a period of time.

Taking care of medical expenses

Having health insurance for your children is important. Usually if one parent has employer-sponsored health coverage, he or she maintains the children on that plan. However, if either parent can provide their children with comparable coverage at a lower price through a different insurance plan, the court will probably accept that alternative.

Health plans may not cover all your children's medical expenses — for example, dental or orthodontia expenses, and eyeglasses — and don't pay 100 percent of the expenses they do cover. For this reason, as part of your negotiations, you and your spouse (or the judge if he or she is involved) must decide how you will share those costs. If you will be the custodial parent, don't overlook these expenses during your divorce negotiations or trial. Otherwise, you may have to cover them yourself.

If you're going to be the custodial spouse and, as part of your child-support agreement, your spouse agrees to provide your children with health coverage, don't consent to the arrangement until you're very familiar with the details of your spouse's health plan.

Some health plans provide a lower level of reimbursement if you use health providers outside the plan's network. This point can be important if doctors who aren't in the plan's network are currently treating your children. Therefore, you and your spouse or a judge need to decide how to deal with these and other possible issues related to the scope and cost of the health plan that will cover your children.

Funding a college education

These days, sending a child to a four-year institution can cost a small fortune, and education is getting more expensive all the time. So, when negotiating your child-support agreement, don't overlook how you and your spouse will pay for your children's college educations. Neither you nor your spouse can probably afford to take on that expense by yourself, especially if more than one of your children will be in college at the same time. You may both agree to begin putting a certain percentage of your monthly income in a special account for your children's college educations or you may agree upfront how much each of you will contribute to your children's education funds and that whatever you can't pay, they will have to come up with by working and getting student loans.

Paying for life's little extras

Gifts, vacations, clothes, lessons, summer camp, and anything else that you give to your children because you *want* to (and not because you *have* to) don't necessarily count as child support when you have a court order for support. Therefore, if you're paying child support, you usually *cannot* deduct such expenses from the total amount of support that you're obligated to pay. But, to be certain, check with your attorney.

Under state guidelines, child support is essentially an average dollar amount that is presumed to provide adequate support for a child. But it really provides a minimum amount of support and probably doesn't cover the "extras" you may want your children to have — private school, special classes, summer camp, vacations, or tutoring, for example. If a judge is deciding child support in your divorce and you want certain extras to be included in the court order, you must ask the judge to consider those special expenditures when calculating how much child support your spouse must pay.

Even if you and your spouse agree that each of you will be responsible for paying the basic day-to-day costs of your children's care, depending on where your children are staying, you must still decide on which extras to fund and how to split the cost of any big-ticket extras you both feel your kids need.

Calculating how you will split the cost of special activities and other extras for your kids is a good idea. One easy way to calculate the split is for each of you to pay a *pro rata share* — that is, a percentage of the cost of the extras based on your individual incomes relative to your total combined income.

For example, assume that the total annual cost of the extras you want to fund is $10,000. Also assume that you earn $40,000 a year and your spouse earns $45,000 a year; this gives you a total combined annual income of $85,000. In this case, your income would represent 47 percent of the total, and your spouse's income represents 53 percent of the total. If you applied these percentages to the $10,000 total cost of the extras, in order to pay for them, you'd contribute $4,700 a year, and your spouse's share would be $5,300.

Realistically speaking, given the cost of maintaining two households, you may not have enough money left over to give your children all the extras they are used to — or paying for them will require some cutbacks in your post-divorce budgets.

If you do *not* have a court order for child support, then gifts, vacations, lessons, and so on are considered in-kind child support. Their costs may be applied to your child-support obligation.

Child-support payments aren't tax deductible. Therefore, if you're paying child support for tax purposes, treating any extra money you contribute to help cover the cost of extras for your kids as spousal support — not as child support — makes sense. Talk to your CPA about how to do this and what sort of records you should keep. For details about the ins and outs of spousal support, turn to Chapter 9.

Making Sure You Receive the Support You're Owed

You have no way of knowing what the future will bring, and, the truth is, being single again sometimes changes the priorities of a previously devoted parent. As a result, that parent may begin to take his or her child-support obligations less seriously and fall behind on them or stop making them entirely. Or, your ex may decide to withhold one or more payments in order to get back at you if you've had a falling out with one another. Other developments that can affect your former spouse's commitment to your child-support agreement include

- ✔ A new marriage
- ✔ A new or failing business
- ✔ Another child
- ✔ Excessive debt
- ✔ Substance abuse problems

If you find yourself in this situation, don't hesitate to take action — your responsibility is to your children, and that means providing for them financially, including doing what you can to ensure that your child-support payments keep coming.

Getting a court order from the get-go

The best way to ensure that you receive the child-support payments you're entitled to on a timely basis is to submit the agreement you and your spouse negotiate to the court and to ask the judge to formalize it through a court order. This precaution is critical even if you believe that your spouse is totally trustworthy and you're certain that your spouse will live up to your agreement. If anything, submitting it to the court may help you sleep better at night.

Without a court order for child support, you don't have the full force of the law behind you if your former spouse stops making regular child-support payments, begins paying less than he or she is supposed to, or fails to make any payments at all. (Chapter 18 has additional information on what you can do if you begin having trouble collecting your child support.)

Securing the payments with automatic wage withholding

To help custodial parents collect their child support, all new and amended child-support court orders written after December 31, 1993, must provide for each payment to be automatically deducted from the paychecks of the parent who must pay child support, unless both parents and the court agree to a different arrangement. (Legal limits dictate how much can be deducted from each paycheck.)

To begin automatic wage deductions, the employer of the parent who's obligated to pay child support is served with a court order for the deduction. If the employer fails to comply with the court order, the *employer* is violating federal law.

If your former spouse has a stable work history, the automatic wage deduction ensures that you get the child support you need. But, this strategy isn't as effective if your ex changes jobs a lot because each new employer must be served with a new automatic wage deduction court order. With each job change, you need to make certain that the new employer is served with an automatic wage deduction court order. Doing so can be a challenge, particularly if you constantly have to try to track down what company your ex is working for.

The automatic wage deduction won't help you collect if your former spouse is self-employed.

You and your spouse can agree to waive the automatic wage deduction; however, your attorney should structure your court order so that if your former spouse gets behind on his or her support payments, after a period of time, the automatic wage withholding activates without you having to go back to court.

To help deal with potential problems with the automatic wage deduction, your divorce decree should order your former spouse to let you know whenever he or she changes jobs, which can be an iffy proposition for some ex-spouses. However, the court order for automatic wage deduction requires your former spouse's employers to inform you and the court of any change in your ex's employment status. Despite these safeguards, sometimes you still don't receive notification of such change or the notifications aren't sent on a timely basis.

Helping to ensure payments if your spouse is self-employed

If your spouse is self-employed, a good way to help ensure that your child-support checks keep coming is to ask the court to order your spouse to post a bond to secure the support. Another option is to ask the court to order your spouse to secure the obligation with a liquid asset, such as a checking or savings account, rental income, a profit-sharing plan, or other asset. Then, if the child-support checks stop coming, you can begin drawing the money you need from the collateralized asset until the payments resume.

If your spouse has a history of writing bad checks, agreeing to accept your child support in the form of a personal check is a bad idea. However, the judge can issue a court order that requires that your ex make the payments in the form of a cashier's check or money order.

Knowing When Child-support Obligations Cease

A parent's child-support obligation ends when a child becomes a legal adult (18 years of age in most states). However, depending on your state, that obligation can continue while your child is a full-time college student or is attending a trade school. But, diploma or no diploma, your responsibility to provide child support typically ends when the child reaches his or her early 20s.

Your obligation to help support a child may end before your minor child becomes a legal adult if he or she

- Becomes an *emancipated minor*. Emancipated minors are children who become legal adults before they turn age 18 or 21. They must initiate a legal process to become emancipated.

- Is on active duty in the military.

> ✔ Takes a full-time permanent job.
>
> ✔ Gets married.
>
> ✔ Dies.

If an unmarried dependent child becomes a parent, that unmarried child's noncustodial parent still has to help support that child. However, the noncustodial parent is *not* legally obligated to support his or her grandchild.

If you're paying child support and the minor child you're supporting moves in with you on a full-time, permanent basis, ask the court for a court order canceling your child-support obligation. If you do not, your legal obligation to pay child support to your former spouse continues.

Heeding Uncle Sam

As far as adjustments to taxable income go, if you're paying child support, you *cannot* claim your payments as a tax deduction on your federal tax return. If you are receiving child support, you do not have to claim it as income.

Although the IRS assumes that the custodial parent will claim his or her dependent children as tax exemptions, as part of your divorce negotiations, you and your spouse can agree to split up that deduction. For example, each of you can claim them in alternate years, one of you can claim one child and the other can claim another child, and so on.

Generally, the parent with the higher income realizes the greatest benefit from claiming his or her children as tax deductions. Discuss how to handle the deductions with a tax CPA when you are working out the terms of your divorce.

By agreement, a custodial parent can transfer his or her dependent-child exemption to the noncustodial parent by completing IRS Form 8332, which can be financially beneficial to both parents. You can use this transfer as a bargaining chip in your negotiations — possibly creating a win-win situation for both of you — if you give your spouse the deduction in exchange for getting more support. (The court cannot order this transfer, because taking the tax deduction for children is a privilege granted by the federal government.)

Part IV
Coming to an Agreement: Negotiating the Terms of Your Divorce

The 5th Wave   By Rich Tennant

"Okay, but when I was in law school we relied on state guidelines and a meeting of the minds when negotiating a divorce agreement."

In this part . . .

Working out the terms of your divorce can seem downright daunting. But after reading the chapters in this part, you should feel more confident about your ability to meet that challenge. For example, if you and your spouse want to negotiate as much of your divorce as possible on your own, Chapter 12 provides a framework for negotiating, tells you when negotiating on your own may not be such a great idea, and advises you on the instances when you should seek legal help. If you'd rather hire a divorce attorney to work out the terms of your divorce, Chapter 13 provides advice on how to find a qualified and affordable attorney and explains what your attorney expects from you and what you should expect from your attorney. Chapter 14 provides an overview of the information that your attorney needs from you in order to negotiate your divorce. It also explains how your attorney and your spouse's attorney will work together to reach an agreement that both parties can live with.

In Chapter 15, we explain the important role that mediation can play in helping you resolve the sticky issues in your divorce so that you can avoid the expense and emotional trauma of a divorce trial (where a judge decides the terms of your divorce for you). In the event that you and your spouse aren't able to reach a negotiated settlement, the last chapter in this part prepares you for a divorce trial.

Chapter 12

Doing the Negotiating Yourself

*N*egotiating your own divorce agreement (or at least some of it) can definitely save you money on attorney fees and court costs. But it does require that you work cooperatively with your soon-to-be ex-spouse, which can sometimes be a challenge. No mediator will be in the room with the two of you to help keep your conversations civilized and productive, nor will you have an attorney to do the negotiating for you. It will all be up to the two of you. Nevertheless, negotiating your own divorce terms doesn't have to degenerate into a shouting match or a stalemate.

Although this chapter doesn't tell you *what* to decide (that's up to you), it does prepare you to make good decisions by suggesting how to plan and organize your negotiation sessions and by offering some basic negotiating advice. In this chapter, we also provide a primer on the basic issues that you may have to resolve before you and your spouse can make your divorce legal.

Note: This chapter touches on negotiating spousal support, child custody, child support, and the division of your property — topics that we cover in more depth in other parts of this book. For more specific information on these topics and how the law addresses them, see the related chapters in Part III.

First, a Word of Caution

When you read this chapter, keep in mind that the plan of action it describes is an ideal scenario to shoot for. Realistically, you may not have the desire or inclination to do *everything* this chapter recommends, which is okay. Just accomplish what you can, and you can still save yourself some time and money.

Be aware that negotiating on your own isn't for every person or every couple, and it can be downright dangerous for some spouses. You may end up with a divorce agreement that gives you less than you're legally entitled to, a custody arrangement that can be emotionally harmful to your children, an agreement that's completely unenforceable, or some other problem.

What you say to your spouse during your negotiations can be used against you if you end up in court, unless you and your spouse have a written agreement that guarantees that whatever you say during your one-on-one negotiations remains confidential. If you don't have such a written agreement, what you say to your spouse may come back to haunt you. For all these reasons, you want to go into your negotiations prepared.

Being on Your Best Behavior

Successful divorce negotiations take hard work, a commitment to the negotiation process, and a willingness to act like mature adults. That can be a tall order for many happily married couples, let alone those who are splitting up. For your negotiations to be productive, you and your spouse must be able to sit down together; talk honestly; figure out in a calm, rational manner how to end your marriage; and be willing to give as well as take.

You must also be willing to treat one another fairly and politely during your negotiations, which may be the last thing you really feel like doing. If you don't, your negotiations are apt to become little more than a painful reminder of why you're getting divorced in the first place.

Negotiating your own divorce means that both of you must

- Let reason, not emotions, rule.

- Be polite.

- Avoid using your negotiations as an excuse to replay old, angry, and hurtful accusations.

- Listen to one another without interrupting. Waiting to have your say can be tough to do, especially if you don't like what your spouse is saying.

- Resist forming a response to what your spouse is saying while he or she is still talking. Instead, try to really listen to his or her words.

- Allow your spouse to express his or her opinions and respect what your spouse has to say. Ridiculing your spouse's choice of words is one way to put your spouse on the defensive and shut down two-way communications entirely.

✔ Be open to compromise. Neither of you will get everything you want from your divorce, so be ready to make some trade-offs.

✔ Stay cool. If something your spouse says or does during a negotiating session upsets you, just bite your tongue. Try not to respond in the heat of the moment. If necessary, take a bathroom break, leave to get some coffee, or do something else to give yourself time to chill out.

✔ Avoid using intimidation and threats to get what you want. Tactics like that will backfire on you.

Preparing for the Process

Taking time prior to your negotiations to plan how you will negotiate is a good idea. Laying the right groundwork can mean the difference between progress and frustration. Therefore, ideally, before you actually begin your formal negotiations, you and your spouse should decide the following:

✔ How you will structure your negotiation sessions.

✔ When and where to negotiate.

✔ What issue(s) you plan to address at each negotiation session.

Unless your divorce is very simple — with little to divide up, no minor children, and no spousal support — you will probably need more than one session to negotiate your divorce.

✔ What information and documentation you need and what kind of record-keeping system you're going to use to record your progress.

If you're concerned that working out the ground rules for your negotiations may lead to a fight, you may want to discuss the preliminaries in a public place, such as a coffee shop or restaurant. Your discussion is less apt to degenerate into name-calling and anger if you have it in a public place. (Wherever you meet, make sure that no one can overhear your conversation.) Of course, if you're worried that working out the ground rules of your negotiations may be filled with strife, you may want to reconsider whether negotiating your own divorce is a good idea because you're likely to face more difficult issues to resolve during the actual negotiations than deciding what rules to follow.

Because a deadlock is always possible, no matter how hard you try to come to a meeting of the minds, you should also decide ahead of time what to do if your decision-making reaches an impasse. Your options include mediation, arbitration, and hiring attorneys to do your negotiating. You should also decide ahead of time where you will go to get information or clarification when a matter of law arises that you don't understand.

If you and your spouse negotiated a prenuptial agreement prior to your marriage or a postnuptial agreement after you were married, you have less to negotiate. (For an explanation of how these agreements work, turn to Chapter 19.)

Educate yourself about your divorce-related legal rights and responsibilities before you begin negotiating. You can do that by scheduling a meeting with an attorney (which we discuss in the "Involving an Attorney" section later in this chapter) and by reading divorce-related literature (such as this book).

Planning a method of negotiation

There's no one right way to negotiate. A method that works for one couple may not be appropriate for another. However, prior to starting your negotiations, you and your spouse should come to at least a general agreement about how you want to structure your negotiation sessions to make them as efficient and effective as possible. The following steps outline one plan of action that may work for you:

1. **Prior to tackling a major new issue in your divorce — child custody, child or spousal support, or the division of your property — share your goals and priorities with one another and discuss any special concerns you have.**

   Try to speak in terms of your realistic needs or your children's realistic needs. Then, identify where you agree or disagree and where your shared interests lie.

2. **Develop a list of possible options for settling the issue you're discussing, keeping in mind your individual goals, priorities, and areas of agreement and disagreement.**

   When identifying your options, try to be creative and avoid automatically rejecting any ideas. A seemingly silly idea may inspire a new, more practical one that works for both of you. You may each want to develop your own list of options and share your lists with one another.

3. **Eliminate all the ideas on your list that you both dislike or both agree are unrealistic.**

   Identifying the options that you don't like or that seem impractical to both of you helps you focus on the ones that you both feel are more feasible.

4. **Using the options that still remain, develop written proposals for resolving whatever issues you're negotiating.**

   You can each develop your own proposal for an issue, present it to one another, and respond with counterproposals, or you can write a proposal together. When you settle on a decision, put it in writing. Each time you concur on a specific issue, you're that much closer to a final divorce agreement.

The negotiating process you use doesn't have to be as formal as the one just described. Find a method that you both feel comfortable with and that facilitates a fair resolution of each issue in your divorce.

Choosing the right setting

When deciding on a place for your negotiation sessions, pick a quiet, comfortable (but not too comfortable) location that's relatively free of distractions. That probably rules out negotiating in front of the television set or any time at home when your children are up and about. Wait until they've gone to sleep or, better yet, do your negotiating away from home in a neutral location — in a corner of your local library, at a coffeehouse, or in a park, for example.

When you negotiate in a public place, you're more apt to be on your best behavior, which means that you're less likely to yell at each other, burst into tears, or stomp away in a huff.

Scheduling the time

Negotiating your divorce agreement will probably take a couple of sessions, depending on what you have to resolve and how quickly you and your spouse can come to a consensus on things. Therefore, schedule your sessions ahead of time and make them a priority in your life. They should be every bit as important as business meetings, doctor's appointments, parent-teacher conferences, and your kids' birthdays.

Chill out before you storm off

When negotiating tough issues related to your divorce, keeping your cool can be tough to do, no matter how hard you try. Old hurts and insecurities may resurface during your negotiations, especially if your spouse exhibits an uncanny knack for pushing your emotional hot buttons and deliberately or unwittingly hurts your feelings or makes you angry. Rather than letting your emotions get the best of you and, maybe even derail the negotiations, try these alternatives instead:

✔ Take a short timeout. Walk around the block, fix a snack, listen to calming music, or read a magazine. Then, resume your negotiating.

✔ If you need more than a quick break, tell your spouse you can't continue negotiating, and reschedule for another time.

✔ Acknowledge that you need third-party help.

Set a time to begin and end each session. Generally speaking, your sessions shouldn't run more than two hours. Longer sessions will probably become unproductive.

Don't back out of a scheduled session without a very good reason. (Incidentally, wanting to play golf, having dinner with friends, or "just not feeling like it" aren't good reasons.) However, the unexpected does come up. So, if one of you has a legitimate reason for rescheduling, try to provide the other with at least a few days' notice.

Don't rush your negotiations. Take all the time that you need — you're making important decisions that will affect your life and the lives of your children for years to come.

Deciding on the order of business

Develop written agendas for your negotiating sessions and determine ahead of time who will prepare them. You can take turns writing the agendas or one of you can agree to prepare them all. Whatever you decide, make sure that both of you have a copy of the agenda well in advance of the next negotiating session.

Plan on taking up the major issues in your divorce in the following order:

- **Child custody and support:** Your number-one responsibility in your divorce is your children's well-being.

- **Spousal support:** Assuming that any money is left after you decide how you'll meet your children's financial needs, consider the issue of spousal support.

- **Division of your marital property:** Negotiating this issue includes any outstanding debts you have.

Using written agendas may sound like needless work but, in fact, preparing them ahead of time means that you

- Know what sort of "homework" you have to do before your next session

- Can get down to business at the start of each session instead of trying to decide what you will discuss

- Are more apt to stay on track during a negotiating session because you have a written reminder of what you're supposed to be talking about

When you can't resolve an issue the first time out, agree to return to it later or to get outside help. An issue that initially seems irresolvable may be easier to address the next time you tackle it, especially after you and your spouse have successfully resolved a few other issues.

Making your negotiations as painless as possible

Obviously, negotiating the end of your marriage isn't going to be a barrel of laughs. But consider your options: staying married or turning your entire divorce over to someone else. So buck up and get busy. We offer some suggestions that may make negotiating the terms of your divorce easier:

✔ Start your negotiations off with some easy stuff — something both of you can probably agree on. Early success is a confidence-builder and helps create momentum for continued progress.

✔ Don't lose sight of your goals: a less-expensive divorce, an agreement that you can both live with, an agreement that's in your children's best interests, and a mutual commitment to making your agreement work after your divorce is official.

✔ Avoid over-reaching, threatening, or posturing to gain control.

✔ When your spouse makes a concession that benefits you, acknowledge it. (Go on, swallow your pride and do it!) By doing so, you help encourage your spouse to make yet more concessions and compromises. But don't forget: In order to keep the concessions and compromises coming, you must make some yourself.

✔ Be sure that your spouse doesn't mistake your willingness to concede a few points as a desire to get back together, unless that's definitely what you want.

✔ Try not to make important decisions in the heat of the moment or when you're feeling especially depressed or guilty about your divorce because you're more likely to make decisions that you'll regret later.

During your negotiations, keep an accurate record of what you agree and don't agree on. Without a written record of your discussions, you don't know where each of you stands in the negotiating process, and writing a final divorce agreement will be difficult, if not impossible. Decide which of you will keep records of your negotiations. If one of you agrees to be responsible, make sure that the records are always readily available to the other spouse. Better yet, whichever spouse is the record-keeper should mail or e-mail his or her notes to the other spouse after each negotiating session.

Getting expert advice (and how to pay for it)

Before your negotiating gets underway, you and your spouse need to determine what sort of information you need in order to make intelligent decisions and which of you will be responsible for getting that information. First, make a list of what you need, and then take turns choosing a research topic. Next, you may need to hire any or all of the following professionals:

✔ **A certified public accountant (CPA):** A CPA can help you understand the possible tax implications of your financial decisions and how to plan for them.

✔ **A certified divorce planner (CDP):** A CDP can help you evaluate your options and make informed decisions. For example, a CDP can conduct cash-flow analyses to help you determine how much spousal support you may need or can afford to pay and how much child support is reasonable. The CDP can help you evaluate various scenarios when dividing your marital assets and debts, too.

✔ **A therapist or religious advisor:** During your negotiations, times may arise when you need the help of a therapist or your religious advisor to cope with your emotions.

✔ **An appraiser:** An appraiser can help you value your home, other real estate, collectibles, fine art, and so on.

✔ **A financial planner:** A financial planner can help you determine what to do with the assets you may get in your property settlement.

If you're going to share the cost of outside experts, you need to decide who to use and how to pay their fees. Any of the following options may be feasible:

✔ Liquidate a marital asset. For example, sell one of your cars, sell some stocks or bonds, or dip into your savings.

✔ Suggest bartering (or trading) your professional services, skills, or labor in exchange for outside professional help.

✔ One of you pays the costs associated with using an outside professional in exchange for getting an equivalently larger share of your marital property or assuming less of your marital debt.

✔ One of you pays all the expenses associated with the experts you hire and gets reimbursed by the other spouse. The other spouse may pay his or her share right away or in installments over time — whatever you both agree on. Of course, if the spouse who's doing the paying back is unreliable and you're the spouse who's going to pay the experts, agreeing to this payment method probably isn't wise.

✔ You split the expenses 50/50, 60/40, 75/25 — whatever you both agree is fair.

✔ One of you pays the full cost of hiring one expert, and the other pays for hiring another expert. However, for this agreement to be fair, the costs associated with each expert should be about the same if you both earn about the same amount of money. If you don't, the amounts you each pay should be equivalent relative to your individual incomes.

So that you have no doubt about the fairness of an outside expert's advice, choose experts who have no personal or business relationship with either one of you. Meet with the expert together (not separately) and make sure the expert understands that he or she is working for *both* of you.

Involving an Attorney

If you're like most people, one of the key reasons you may want to negotiate your own divorce is so that you can keep your legal costs down. However, entirely excluding attorneys from your divorce can be penny-wise and pound-foolish. Lawyers have a valuable role to play in *all* divorces. (For information about how to shop for legal counsel, see Chapter 13.)

You and your spouse should each hire your own attorney. No ethical lawyer will accept both of you as clients. In fact, a code of ethics in most states prohibits attorneys from working for both spouses in a divorce.

Getting some basic information

Meeting with your divorce attorney prior to starting your negotiations is a good idea. Use the meeting to acquire an overview of the divorce laws and guidelines in your state, to gain an understanding of what your divorce agreement must include, and to determine the issues and trade-offs you may want to consider during your negotiations. Unless you read law books just for the fun of it or have been divorced a number of times, these are subjects that you probably know little or nothing about.

Be sure to get advice about any special concerns you may have related to the decisions ahead of you and find out about potential legal pitfalls or problems. After talking with an attorney about the issues in your divorce, you may decide that your divorce is much too complicated to negotiate on your own.

You may also want to use an attorney to help you with specific tasks during the negotiating process — for example, to review financial documents, to provide you with feedback about a proposal your spouse has made, or to review the counteroffer you're considering. Another and, probably less-expensive, option is to hire a CDP to help you with these types of tasks.

Be upfront if money is an issue for you. Tell the attorney that you can afford to purchase only an hour or two of his or her time.

Hiring an attorney to review or draft your final agreement

If you and your spouse are able to resolve all the issues in your divorce and draft your own divorce agreement, ask your attorneys to review the draft before you sign it. That way, they can assure you and your spouse that you haven't overlooked anything important and that your agreement does not create the potential for future problems between the two of you.

If you decide not to draft a final agreement but instead to provide each of your attorneys with a written list of everything you've agreed to, you will have to decide which of the two attorneys will draft your final agreement. You can make that decision with a coin toss or the spouse with greater financial assets can agree to pay his or her attorney to prepare it. However, the attorney representing the other spouse should review the agreement before the other spouse signs it.

The lawyer you hire can tell you whether or not the agreement you and your spouse negotiate by yourselves is equitable to both of you under the law. For example, although the agreement may sound fine to you, your attorney may tell you that you're entitled to more than you're getting. If this is the case, you can decide that you're happy with what's in the draft agreement or you can try to get more. Your attorney also can make sure that the agreement doesn't overlook certain issues that may create problems (with taxes, for instance) down the road and that it's legally enforceable.

Attorneys are conditioned to assume that each case is a worst-case scenario and to provide legal advice to prevent or mitigate all potential problems. So, if an attorney says something that alarms you or makes you question whether you should negotiate your divorce on your own, don't panic. The attorney is legally obligated to inform you of all possible outcomes, and the scenario you find alarming may have little chance of actually occurring.

If you and your spouse decide to go back to the drawing board to work out any problems in your draft agreement that your attorney may have called to your attention or to address issues you may have overlooked, you can try to resolve them using whatever approach worked for you and your spouse when you were negotiating your draft agreement. Or, you and your spouse can ask your attorneys to help resolve the remaining problems and issues, if you feel you and your spouse will have trouble reaching an agreement on those matters by yourselves. However, involving your attorneys increases the cost of your divorce, and a chance always exists that if one of you is working with an aggressive attorney, the attorney could turn your amicable divorce into an angry one. Mediation is another option when you and your spouse don't see eye to eye on the remaining issues in your divorce and want to avoid spending a lot of money on legal help. Chapter 15 explains how mediation works.

Negotiating an Agreement Everyone Can Live With

When you and your spouse are ready to sit down and begin working out the details of your divorce agreement, you and your spouse may have to figure out how to deal with the custody of your children; whether one of you will pay child support to the other and, if so, how much the payments will be; whether one spouse will pay spousal support to the other and the amount of those payments; and how you will divide up the assets and debts from your marriage. The following sections provide guidance for negotiating each of these issues.

Creating an agreeable custody arrangement

If you're like most divorcing parents, you want to be actively involved in your children's lives after your marriage ends, as you should be. Therefore, your custody negotiations will probably focus on determining how you and your soon-to-be ex can each continue spending time with your children, how you can continue sharing parenting responsibilities with one another after you no longer live together, and how you can both assure your children of your continued love. (For more on the subject of custody, see Chapter 10.)

The custody arrangement you finally decide on may not be as good as having two parents under the same roof, but it can be the next best thing. And, if your marriage was tense and full of strife, parenting under two roofs rather than one may end up being better for your kids.

As you and your spouse evaluate various custody options and prepare a written proposal (or proposals) for the custody of your children, you should consider

- ✔ Your children's individual requirements, both practical and emotional.

  Develop a written list of your children's day-to-day needs, activities, and so on. Writing everything down can help both of you become more realistic about what you actually need to do to meet your children's needs.

- ✔ Your individual strengths and weaknesses as parents.
- ✔ Your post-divorce lifestyles.

  Describing what your life will be like after your divorce takes some guesswork, but you probably at least have a general idea of what your life will entail. For example, you may know that you'll be working at your current job for a while and, therefore, that you'll have to travel a great deal; that you won't be able to afford to quit the night shift for several more years; that you have to begin working outside the home after your divorce and will be juggling a job and childcare; or, that you'll be returning to school so that you can upgrade your job skills and eventually make more money.

- ✔ How well you think that you can cooperate with one another as divorced parents.

To help ensure that you don't overlook anything when developing your lists, use the Child Care Tasks worksheet at www.divorcehelp.com/WR/ W51kidtasks.htm.

Most judges approve whatever custody arrangement you and your spouse choose, so long as it's consistent with whatever is in the best interests of your children.

Calculating child support

If you and your spouse share dependent children, the decisions you make about child support are apt to be the most important aspects of your divorce negotiations.

Determining a reasonable standard of living

You and your spouse must come to an agreement about the standard of living you want for your children after your divorce. Although you may both agree that you want the very best for them, if you're like most couples, money may be even tighter after your divorce. Therefore, to provide your children with the extras that you want them to have, you and your spouse may have to agree to cut some items out of your own post-divorce budgets. To make certain that you don't overlook any expenses related to your children, turn to Chapter 11, which discusses child-related expenses in detail.

You and your spouse can decide how you will fund college for your kids when you draft your agreement or, if they're very young, you can include a clause providing that you will return to that issue as each of your children reaches a certain age (10 years old, perhaps).

When negotiating child support, don't overlook your state's child-support guidelines. The guidelines help determine the minimum amount of support that one parent should pay the other. Chapter 11 discusses state guidelines in detail.

Getting a court order, even if you and your spouse see eye to eye

Even if your divorce is amicable, if you will receive child support or if you both agreed to share the cost of supporting your children, get a court order to ensure that your spouse upholds the agreement. If your spouse doesn't uphold the agreement, the full force of the law can help you collect what you're entitled to.

Securing a court order is an important just-in-case step because, without one, your options for getting the agreement enforced are quite limited. Although you can get a court order for child support after the fact, the process takes time and, while you're waiting, you and your children may suffer financially. (Chapter 11 talks more about enforcing child-support agreements.)

In your agreement, don't forget to spell out exactly how you or your spouse will pay the child support — personal checks, direct deposits, automatic withdrawals, and so on. Also, before you sign a child-support agreement, hire an attorney to review it so that you can be sure what you and your spouse agree to is legally enforceable and fair to both of you.

Discussing the subject of spousal support

If you need financial support after your marriage ends and can present solid reasons why your spouse should provide it, your divorce negotiations should address how much spousal support you should receive and how long the payments will last. (For more in-depth information on spousal support, turn to Chapter 9.) Be aware, however, that many couples have a difficult time negotiating spousal support, so don't give up if you can't come to an agreement right away.

If you're the spouse who wants spousal support, in order to make your case, compare your post-divorce financial needs and resources with your spouse's. Note the contributions you made to your marriage or to your spouse's career. Steer clear of phrases such as "I must have," "I require," and "I deserve." (Those words won't get you the results you want.) Don't act resentful about the sacrifices you may have made in the interest of your spouse or marriage. At the time you made those choices, you probably believed they were for the best.

If possible, frame your arguments in terms of how your spouse, not just you, will benefit from any spousal support that he or she may pay to you. For example, you need support so that you can develop marketable job skills and earn a better living. You may be able to argue that after you have a good job, not only can your spouse stop paying you spousal support, but you can also begin contributing more to the support of your children. In other words, your spouse may trade a short-term sacrifice for a long-term gain!

When preparing your projected post-divorce budget and estimating your monthly income without spousal support, do *not* include any child support you will be receiving in your income figure. Child support is for your children, not for you.

Dividing up your property and debts without a court battle

If you don't have any young children to support and you and your spouse both earn good money, the only decisions you may have to make in your divorce may relate to the division of your marital property and debts. Before you can actually get down to deciding who gets what, you must come to an agreement about what is and isn't marital property and what percentage of the value of that property each of you is entitled to. Obviously, developing a comprehensive inventory of your marital assets and debts and assigning accurate values and amounts to each is critical. (See Chapter 3 for information on creating inventories for your personal and marital assets.)

If you're divorcing after just a short marriage, you and your spouse may have few, if any, joint assets and debts to divide up, so you may be able to divide up your property in a single negotiating session. Usually, the longer your marriage, the more you own and owe together, so the more time you will need to reach a property settlement agreement that's fair to you both.

Split it down the middle or not?

For simplicity's sake, many divorcing couples decide to split up their property and their debts 50/50. Depending on the circumstances of your marriage as well as your assets and debts, this method may or may not be fair. (For more information on ways to divide property, turn to Chapter 8.)

Unless you and your spouse negotiate a different arrangement, if you live in a community property state, you're legally entitled to half the value of all your marital assets when you divorce. Also, you're legally responsible for half your marital debts. Therefore, even if your spouse agrees to pay all or a portion of your marital debts, if he or she fails to do so, the creditors can look to you for payment.

The following factors can suggest that a non-equal split is fairer than an equal division of property:

- ✔ One of you was significantly more responsible for the assets you acquired during your marriage or for the debts that you ran up.

- ✔ One of you has a greater need than the other for more than half the assets or less than half the debts. For example, one of you makes much less money than the other or has a limited capacity to earn money because he or she has never worked outside the home, has a chronic illness, and so on.

- ✔ A significant disparity in your ages is going to affect the ability of the older spouse to replace the assets that he or she would give up.

- ✔ One of you has a significant emotional investment in certain assets.

As a point of reference or a reality check, find out what criteria a family law judge in your state would use if it were up to him or her to divide your marital property and debts. You can get this information if you meet with an attorney.

Regardless of what percentage split you use to divide up the value of your marital property and debts — 50/50, 60/40, 80/20, for example — both of you should be 100 percent clear about and comfortable with the rationale for the percentage. Otherwise, a number of things may result:

- One of you may feel cheated or swindled in some way and stay mad at the other or even go to court later to get the arrangement changed. If that was to happen and you share custody of your children, you could find it difficult to cooperate on their behalf.

- The disgruntled spouse may refuse to pay off your marital debts according to your agreement, and the other spouse may get stuck paying them.

- The spouse who feels cheated may seek revenge by being late with his or her child- or spousal-support payments or stop making them all together. (Not paying them is illegal but, unfortunately, people do it all the time.)

Divide up the big assets first

Dividing up your property in two stages — for significant assets and miscellaneous personal property — can make practical sense.

Focus on the division of your most significant marital assets first — your home, other real estate, bank accounts, pensions, investments, vehicles, and so on. To be sure that you don't overlook the tax consequences of your decisions during this stage, consulting with a tax CPA is a good idea. What looks like a good deal may not be so good after you factor in taxes. Be open to selling some of your marital assets if doing so will help create a win-win situation for you and your spouse. (You're most likely to need the help of outside professionals during this phase.)

When you divide up assets that secure loans — your home, vehicles, and so forth — look at both the debt associated with each asset and the asset itself. Value that asset according to the amount of *equity* you have in it, or its market value less the amount you owe on it.

When you divide up your miscellaneous marital property — household items like your CD player, big-screen TV, furniture, computer equipment, kitchenware, linens, lawnmower, power tools, and so on — assigning them specific values may be difficult. Approximate values will probably do. Also divide up your credit card debts and other miscellaneous unsecured joint debts that you may have during this stage.

Don't overlook your family pets. If you have children, you may want to let the pets live with whichever parent will have the children most of the time after your divorce is final. Having family pets around increases your children's sense of stability and security after your marriage has ended.

If you and your spouse are childless but have multiple pets, you may want to share custody of the animals, giving each of you the pets on specific days, although such an arrangement may be impractical.

Dividing up your miscellaneous marital property can be as simple as

- ✔ Taking turns choosing, asset by asset, debt by debt, until each of you has an appropriate amount of assets and debts given the percentage splits you agreed to.

- ✔ Letting one spouse divide a pile of miscellaneous property in half, and giving first pick of either of the two piles to the other spouse (thus, assuring that whoever does the dividing makes an even 50/50 split).

- ✔ Preparing separate lists of what each of you wants and comparing the two. When some of the same things are on both your lists, you will have to decide what's fair. (One option is described in the upcoming sidebar, "When you both gotta have it: A negotiating secret.")

- ✔ Choosing comparable categories of assets and debts without strict regard to dollar amounts and percentages. For example, you take the dining room furniture and your spouse takes the bedroom furniture; you take the car, and your spouse gets the boat; you take the Visa card debts, and your spouse takes the MasterCard debts.

You can trade off debts for assets or vice versa. For example, you can agree to pay off more of your marital debt in exchange for getting a larger share of your marital assets, or you can agree to take less marital property so that you don't have to pay off as much of your debt.

Consider wiping out as much of your joint debt as you can by selling marital assets. Minimizing your post-divorce financial ties is almost always a good idea. You may also want to sell joint assets to provide both of you with the cash you may need to start your lives as single people. Be careful that in your quest for cash you don't sell items for less than their actual values.

When you both gotta have it: A negotiating secret

So what do you do when you and your spouse both want the same asset? If the asset at issue isn't significant enough to merit scheduling a mediation session or getting legal help to break your stalemate, try one of the following simple, no-cost approaches to reach an agreement:

- ✔ Ask a neutral third party to take two small pieces of paper, write the name of the asset on one of the pieces, fold up both pieces of paper and put them in a hat, box, or some other container. Next, you and your spouse each pull one of the pieces of paper out of the container. The spouse who pulls out the piece of paper with the name of the asset written on it gets the asset; the other spouse gets something else in exchange — another asset or less debt of equal value.

- ✔ Collect all the items you both want and wait to deal with them until after you've divided up everything else. Then, take turns selecting items until nothing remains.

Just think — some people pay top dollar for this kind of advice!

Deciding what to do about your home

If you're like most other couples, your home is probably the most valuable asset you own together. What to do with it when you're divorcing can be a tough decision emotionally as well as financially. Nevertheless, deciding what to do with your home is a bottom-line issue that you should make based *only* on financial considerations. Chapter 8 provides an overview of those considerations.

To help you make that decision, ask yourself the following questions and talk over the answers with your spouse. Getting advice from a financial professional, such as your CPA or certified divorce planner, is also helpful.

- How much does comparable housing cost?
- What emotional ties do each of you have to your home and to your neighborhood?
- How much can you sell the house for?
- Is living in the same neighborhood or school district important to your children?
- Can you and your children move into other houses in the same neighborhood or school district?
- Can you afford to keep the home, taking into account the amount of your mortgage payments, insurance costs, taxes, upkeep, and maintenance? (Don't forget that mortgage interest is tax deductible.)
- What will your spouse get in return if you keep the house?

Don't overlook your income taxes

Don't forget to take your income taxes into consideration when negotiating your divorce agreement. If you'll still be married on December 31, you can file a separate return or a joint return for that year.

Filing a joint return is usually the better option for the spouse with the bigger income, but it can work against the spouse who earns less. Ask your CPA to determine the most advantageous filing method.

Other tax-related issues you may need to consider include

- How you will share any tax refund you may have coming
- How you will share responsibility for any taxes you may owe
- How you will share liability for any interest, penalties, and back taxes you may owe if you're audited some time in the future

Getting to Closure

After you and your spouse think you're close to an agreement on all the issues in your divorce, draft a final agreement that reflects your decisions so far. Then, each of you should hire a divorce attorney to review the draft. The "Involving an Attorney" section earlier in this chapter discusses what the attorneys will look for when they review the agreement. After you have a final agreement, the spouse who initiated your divorce can file the agreement with the court so that a judge can issue a court order or the spouse's attorney can file the agreement instead.

Chapter 13

Hiring a Divorce Attorney

*R*egardless of your opinion about attorneys — that they're sage and savvy legal counselors or a necessary evil — you almost always need to hire a lawyer when you're getting a divorce. In complicated and contentious divorces, an attorney's help is absolutely essential. In more straightforward and amicable breakups, a lawyer's input and assistance is advisable, even if you and your spouse handle most of the divorce negotiations yourself.

Unless your divorce is extremely simple — for instance, you and your spouse were married just a short period of time and have few, if any, marital assets or debts; no minor children; neither of you wants spousal support; and you're in total agreement with one another about how to end your marriage — *not* getting an attorney's help is penny-wise but utterly pound foolish.

After you read this chapter, you should feel a little less intimidated by attorneys and much more confident about hiring one. We show you what to look for in an attorney, how much they charge, and how to begin your search for a trustworthy and affordable lawyer. We also explain the issues that you should consider when hiring an attorney and tell you what you have the right to expect from the one you hire and what he or she can expect from you.

What to Look for in an Attorney

You can involve an attorney in your divorce from start to finish or work with one on a very limited basis. (If you and your spouse both feel confident about your abilities to draft your own divorce agreement, you may be able to limit your use of an attorney to initial advice and information and the final evaluation of your agreement; see Chapter 12 for advice on negotiating your own agreement with your spouse.)

When you do hire a divorce attorney, choosing one should be more than a matter of running your fingers through the lawyer ads in the Yellow Pages until you spot the word "divorce" or simply hiring the lawyer who helped you negotiate your office lease or draw up your will. The right attorney can make your divorce easier, but the wrong attorney can add to the stress you're already feeling and make your divorce more difficult for you than it already is.

Among other things, the attorney you hire should

- ✔ Be experienced in family law.

   In some states, attorneys can become *board-certified* in family law, meaning that these lawyers specialize in family law matters including divorce. To become board-certified, lawyers must have significant experience handling family law cases, and they must pass a rigorous test. To maintain their certification, they must receive substantial continuing education in family law each year.

   Although a board-certified family law attorney tends to charge more and demand a higher retainer to handle a family law case than one who isn't board-certified, the attorney is usually more experienced. Therefore, the attorney may be able to get things done in your divorce more quickly and may be more adept at finding solutions to any problems in your divorce than an attorney who isn't board-certified in family law.

- ✔ Talk to you in plain English, not legalese. You have a right to understand what's going on in your divorce.

- ✔ Be someone you can trust and with whom you feel comfortable because you may have to reveal highly personal and even embarrassing information about yourself and your marriage.

- ✔ Make it clear that during your divorce you must put your children's needs first and that he or she will not pursue unreasonable demands for child support or help you pursue vindictive child-custody and visitation arrangements.

- ✔ Be affordable.

Appropriate skills and experience

An old adage states, "There are horses for courses." This saying is as true for an attorney as for any other professional. In other words, when you select a family law attorney, you want one with the legal skills, knowledge, and experience required to get the job done for you:

- ✔ If you need help negotiating your divorce agreement, the ideal attorney is a problem-solver who works well with people and is good at working out compromises. Find out what percentage of an attorney's cases go to trial. Unless the attorney specializes in difficult divorces that go to trial, attorneys with high percentages of litigated divorces probably are not great negotiators. The attorney should also be comfortable in court. Although you and your spouse may have no intention of going to court; an attorney's trial record of success in court can have some bearing on his or her success negotiating a settlement with your spouse's attorney.

✔ If you know from the start that you're headed for a divorce trial, you want an attorney who has considerable courtroom experience. Not all lawyers do. Ask each attorney that you meet with what percentage of the divorce cases he or she takes go to trial. When you're getting referrals for divorce attorneys, specifically ask for ones who are good in the courtroom.

✔ If your financial situation is complex, hire a lawyer who has a solid understanding of the issues and laws that pertain to your financial affairs or one who works closely with other lawyers or financial experts who have that knowledge, such as a CPA or appraiser. Remember, negotiating your divorce agreement is as much about financial matters as it is about ending your marriage. If your finances are especially complicated — maybe because you and your spouse have a lot of investments, share a business, and so on — ask the attorneys you meet with what financial experts he or she would involve in your divorce and exactly what those experts would do to help your case.

Don't base your hiring decision on which attorney has the nicest office. A fancy office in an expensive building says nothing about a lawyer's legal skills. At the same time, don't assume that just because an attorney charges a lot of money that he or she is highly skilled or will meet your needs. Also, don't let a lawyer's physical appearance influence your hiring decision — great fashion sense doesn't necessarily mean he or she has great legal skills.

Personal style

If you're relying on an attorney to do more than simply review your divorce agreement, be prepared to share details about your personal life, marriage, and finances. For example, you may have to let your attorney know that you have way too much credit card debt, that your spouse is a philanderer, or that you've been hospitalized in the past for emotional problems. Sharing that sort of information with a virtual stranger can be embarrassing. Therefore, feeling comfortable with your lawyer is key.

In addition, your attorney should share and support your basic philosophy about your divorce. For example, if you want to keep things as calm, cooperative, and nonadversarial as possible, avoid attorneys who like to "go for the jugular."

Don't confuse your attorney with your therapist or religious advisor. Your attorney's clock is usually running regardless of whether you call with a legal question or to complain about your spouse. If you need emotional advice and support, meet with a therapist.

Affordability

Most family law attorneys bill for their services on an *hourly* basis. Some agree to charge a *flat fee* based on the total amount of their time they think it will take to complete your divorce. Estimating upfront can be financially costly for an attorney because he or she can't possibly know exactly how any divorce will play out. For example, a divorce can start out very cooperatively but end up being contentious and taking far more time than the attorney thought it would. Attorneys who charge flat fees usually limit the services they provide and charge extra for any work outside of the scope of the original agreement.

You're more apt to find an attorney to take your case for a flat fee if your divorce is 100-percent amicable and if the tasks the attorney will perform are very well defined (such as review your divorce agreement or fill out some legal paperwork) and very limited (such as you just need some paperwork filled out and filed).

Among other things, an attorney's hourly rate depends on your region of the country and whether your community is rural or urban. If you live in large cities on the East and West Coasts, you can expect to pay higher fees. Depending on where you live, the services of a divorce attorney can cost you anywhere from $100 to $500 an hour, although some attorneys charge much, much, more. Also, the attorney you hire will charge you for the expenses associated with your case and for the cost of his or her legal staff, which helps with your divorce. Your legal expenses are likely to include court fees, copying, courier services, the cost of a court reporter for depositions, the cost of a mediator, and so on.

If you don't have a lot of money to spend on legal help, you may have to hire a relatively inexperienced lawyer rather than a seasoned professional. New attorneys tend to cost less than lawyers who've been practicing law for years and already have solid reputations. However, working with an up-and-coming or novice attorney has a potential advantage, aside from monetary savings: The attorney may be willing to work a little harder for you than a more-seasoned lawyer would in order to build up a good reputation.

Finding a Reputable Attorney (And Avoiding the Bad Ones)

The best way to start your search is to develop a list of potential attorneys by

✔ **Asking friends and family members who've gone through a divorce and were happy with their attorneys.** Referrals from trusted friends or family members who've gone through a divorce similar to what you anticipate yours will be like are particularly valuable.

✔ **Asking attorneys you've worked with in the past to recommend some divorce attorneys.** When you contact attorneys you've worked with, be sure to explain the nature of your divorce — amicable or contentious, minor children or no kids, and so on — and to indicate the kind of legal help you think you need.

✔ **Checking with your local, county, or state bar association.** Many bar associations can refer you to attorneys in your area who can help you.

✔ **Consulting an online lawyer referral service, like** www.lawyer.com, **(a service of LexisNexis Martindale-Hubbell).** Some attorneys pay to be part of an online referral service as a means of building their visibility and gaining additional business. When you use one of these services, you provide information about yourself — usually your geographic location — and the service sends you the names of attorneys who practice law close to you.

A referral to an attorney by a bar association, online referral service, or other organization is not the same thing as an endorsement by that organization. You must still meet with the attorney and check out him or her to make certain that the attorney is right for you.

✔ **Calling the American Academy of Matrimonial Lawyers (312-263-6477) for a list of attorneys in your area who specialize in divorce and family law.** For an attorney to become a member of this association, 75 percent of his or her practice must be in matrimonial law. Additionally, the attorney must have been a member of the bar for at least ten years; be board-certified in matrimonial law, when possible, or have at least 15 hours of continuing education; pass a national exam; and submit to a stringent screening process. You can head to the academy's Web site at www.aaml.org.

✔ **Asking your mental health counselor, religious advisor, or social worker to recommend an attorney.** Having counseled other individuals going through a divorce, mental health professionals may know who the good divorce attorneys are.

✔ **Asking members of a divorce support group for names.** Some members, based on personal experience, are likely to have strong opinions about who is or isn't a good divorce attorney.

If you feel more comfortable being represented by a female attorney, contact the women's bar association in your area, if one exists, or other female lawyers in your community. If you want a male attorney to represent you, you may want to get in touch with a father's rights organization in your area, which may be able to refer you to a father-friendly attorney.

If you anticipate an especially rancorous divorce, you want an attorney who will act as your legal ally and your advocate, not one who's merely interested in collecting a fee. Steer clear of attorneys who

✔ Brag about themselves

✔ Don't pay attention to you when you're speaking

✔ Trivialize your questions by not answering them or telling you "not to worry about that"

✔ Ignore your questions entirely

✔ Ask you few, if any, questions about your marriage, your finances, or your divorce goals at your initial meeting

✔ Talk down to you

✔ Don't ask you any questions

✔ Are constantly interrupted by phone calls or conversations with people who come into their office while you're meeting

✔ Ask you few, if any, questions about your marriage, your finances, or your divorce goals at your initial meeting

If you don't find an attorney right away who fits the bill, don't get discouraged or give up. Some great divorce attorneys who truly care about their clients are out there.

Interviewing Potential Attorneys

After you compile a list of divorce attorneys, schedule a get-acquainted meeting with each of them. Don't hire an attorney just because someone you know and respect gives the lawyer a glowing review. Make up your own mind after an in-person meeting.

Request a free consultation

Many attorneys provide free 30-minute to one-hour initial consultations but, when you call their offices, you'll probably have to ask for the free meeting. Don't expect them to offer a free first meeting. Attorneys who don't offer free consultations may charge a nominal sum — $25 to $50 — for an initial meeting or may charge their normal hourly rate. However, the amount of money attorneys charge for an initial meeting has no bearing on their skills in divorce law.

In your consultation, don't be afraid to let the attorneys know where you are emotionally. Although you don't want to use up your entire free consultation explaining how awful your spouse is, how angry you are, or give a blow-by-blow account of the demise of your marriage, a good attorney knows that your emotions will affect your divorce case. Therefore, the attorney will factor your emotional state into his or her assessment of your case and its likely cost. Some attorneys will even suggest resources, such as counseling and support groups, to help you deal with your emotions.

Ask the important questions

Prior to your initial meetings with the attorneys on your list, think about the questions you want answers to and write them down in a notebook. Don't be afraid to ask your questions. Listening to how the attorneys answer your questions and watching their body language is a critical factor in deciding which one to hire. You have no other way to assess whether you like an attorney's personal style, feel comfortable with his or her proposed approach to your divorce, and so on.

Bring to your attorney meetings the notebook you used to record your questions so that you can keep notes regarding each attorney's replies to your questions. Also, as soon as possible after each meeting ends, write down your overall impressions of the attorney you just met with. This information will be important to review when deciding which attorney to hire.

The following questions represent some of the most important ones to ask when you meet with each attorney. (These questions are most appropriate if you're hiring an attorney to help with your divorce negotiations or because you need to be represented in court.)

✔ **How long have you been practicing divorce law, how many cases have you handled, and how many trials have you been involved in?**

Look for an attorney who's been a divorce lawyer for at least three years. If you anticipate that your divorce may end up in court, make sure that the attorney has successfully represented other clients in divorce trials.

✔ **What percentage of your law practice is represented by divorce cases?**

At least 50 percent of an attorney's caseload should be divorce cases.

✔ **Have you ever had a case like mine? How did you handle it?**

Avoid hiring an attorney who has never dealt with the particular issues in your divorce case. Lawyers can't give you specific details about another case, but they can tell you enough for you to determine whether or not they have sufficient experience to deal with a divorce such as yours.

✔ **Who will actually handle my case? You, another lawyer with your firm, or both of you?**

If another lawyer will be involved, ask about that lawyer's divorce-related experience. You should also ask to meet him or her.

Don't assume that you're receiving inferior legal care if a skilled paralegal under the supervision of an attorney works on your case. A paralegal can do a good job of handling certain aspects of a divorce for considerably less money than if your lawyer had taken care of those details.

✔ **What do you think about mediation?**

If you and your spouse reach a stalemate on some aspect of your divorce and you want to give mediation a try, select an attorney who believes in mediation and has used it successfully in divorces such as yours.

✔ **How do you charge, and how do I pay you?**

Find out the lawyer's hourly rate and get an estimate of how much your divorce will cost. This estimate is a best guess on the lawyer's part — the final cost depends on how smoothly your negotiations go, whether or not you end up in court, and other factors. If another lawyer or a paralegal will be working on your case, get his or her hourly rates, too. If you're worried about how to pay for the legal help you need, be upfront about your concerns.

✔ **Will I have to pay you a retainer and, if so, how much will it be?**

Most lawyers require a *retainer,* or down payment, on the cost of their services. The cost of the time the attorney actually spends on your case is then credited against the retainer.

✔ **If the cost of your services exceeds the amount of your retainer, how am I expected to pay what I owe? Monthly billings? A lump-sum payment? Under what circumstances is the retainer refundable?**

Most attorneys do not consider a retainer to be refundable unless money is left over after they've completed a client's divorce or if you fire the lawyer and the entire retainer has not been spent.

✔ **How do you calculate your billable hours?**

Many attorneys round up fractions of hours, which increases their total cost. In other words, if the attorney spends five minutes talking with you on the phone, he or she may round it up to 15 minutes of billable time. Over time, rounding up to quarter-hours can really add to your costs.

✔ **Will you provide me with an estimate of my expenses and an explanation of what those expenses include?**

You may have to pay the cost of long-distance calls, faxes, copying, delivery fees, outside expert fees, court costs, and so on. Some lawyers may also bill you for expenses not directly related to your divorce, such as the cost of working dinners and cabs. If you object to paying certain expenses, ask for an explanation of why you should be billed for them. If the expenses aren't essential to your case, tell the lawyer that you refuse to pay for them.

✔ **How often do you bill for your expenses and will I get an itemized bill?**

Expect to receive an itemized monthly expense bill.

✔ **If I have questions about my case, can I call you? How quickly can I expect you to return my calls?**

A reasonable amount of time to expect to have your calls returned is within 24 hours, unless you're calling with an emergency. Then, your attorney should return your call within an hour or two.

✔ **Based on what you know about my divorce, what is your game plan?**

The attorney should provide you with an assessment of the strengths and the weaknesses of your case (and your spouse's case) and a clear explanation of how he or she intends to exploit the strengths and minimize the weaknesses in order to get you the best divorce possible. Steer clear of attorneys who emphasize "playing hardball" rather than negotiating and trying mediation. Hardball tactics cost big bucks.

✔ **If my divorce goes to trial, will you continue to represent me or will you recommend another attorney?**

If you think that your divorce may go to trial, you want an attorney who has trial experience and who can handle your divorce from start to finish. Switching to a trial attorney midstream increases the cost of your divorce because that attorney will require a separate retainer to take your case. Your divorce will also take longer because the trial attorney needs time to get up to speed on your case.

✔ **What can I do to minimize my legal expenses?**

Some lawyers are amenable to letting you handle certain aspects of your case yourself — picking up documents, copying, conducting simple research, and doing other tasks that don't require special training.

Before you agree to take care of some of the simple, nonlegal tasks that are involved in a divorce case, be sure that you have the time to accomplish them in a timely manner. You don't want to be responsible for slowing down your divorce.

✔ **If I become your client, what will you expect of me?**

Any reputable attorney expects a client to fully disclose all facts that are relevant to his or her legal problem, provide information on a timely basis, return phone calls promptly, be honest, pay bills on time, and obey the attorney's directives regarding what to do or not to do in terms of the case.

Provide financial documentation

When you meet with prospective attorneys, bring along information regarding your family's finances. Although the attorneys probably won't study the information carefully, they may want to take a quick look at it. Examples of information to bring with you include

- An inventory of your assets and debts
- Copies of your current will and your spouse's
- Deeds to your property
- Recent tax returns
- A copy of any prenuptial or postnuptial agreements that you may have signed

  Chapter 3 discusses the types of information you should have already prepared and assembled in preparation for your divorce. After you hire an attorney, he or she will probably ask you to provide additional information and documentation. For example, your attorney may request that you provide him or her with any divorce-related correspondence that you've received from your spouse or from your spouse's attorney.

Be prepared to answer the attorneys' questions

You won't be the only one asking questions at your initial meetings with the attorneys. They'll need to get information from you before they can answer your questions to help them decide whether or not they want to take you on as a client and to determine whether your divorce goals are reasonable and legitimate.

The attorneys also ask you questions to determine whether you're using your divorce as revenge against your spouse. Many attorneys want to steer clear of clients who tend to spell trouble unless they really need the work or figure that the money they'll earn from the case is worth the headache of dealing with such a client.

Reputable attorneys also try to assure themselves that they won't have a conflict of interest if they represent you. For example, a conflict of interest would be that their law firm represents your spouse's business.

The following questions give you an idea of what you can expect an attorney to ask you:

- Why are you getting a divorce?
- Do you have any minor children from your marriage?
- Do you work outside the home?

- ✔ How long have you been married?

- ✔ Are you and your spouse still living together? If not, with whom are your children living (assuming you have children)?

- ✔ Do you and your spouse have a prenuptial or postnuptial agreement?

- ✔ What major assets do you and your spouse own, and what would you estimate that each of those assets is worth?

- ✔ What are your marital debts?

- ✔ What kind of employment-related benefits do you and your spouse have?

- ✔ Do either of you have a drug- or alcohol-related substance abuse problem?

- ✔ Are you and your spouse retired or do either of you have plans to retire soon?

- ✔ What are your goals for your divorce in terms of spousal support, a property settlement, child custody and visitation, and child support?

- ✔ What kind of relationship do you have with your young children and what role do you play in their day-to-day lives as a parent?

- ✔ Why do you think you deserve to have custody of your children?

- ✔ Do any of your children have special needs?

- ✔ Has your relationship had any violence in it?

- ✔ What else do you want me to know about you, your spouse, your children, or your marriage?

Be prepared to provide honest answers to questions that may make you squirm, such as, "Are you having (or have you had) an affair?" and "Is your spouse aware of your affair?"

If you aren't 100 percent honest with the attorney you end up hiring and the attorney finds out later that you lied or withheld important information from him or her, your relationship with one another may be damaged and your attorney may not work quite as hard on your behalf. Also, by not being honest with an attorney when you're interviewing him or her, you may end up hiring one who isn't the best attorney to represent you given your circumstances. In other words, by withholding information, you can shoot yourself in the foot.

Getting a Written Agreement

Be sure to get a written agreement or letter of understanding from the attorney you decide to hire before you pay any money, give the attorney a lien on any of your property in lieu of cash, or make any other kind of payment. The document should detail all the specifics you and the attorney agreed to during any of your meetings, including financial arrangements, the services the attorney will provide, payment arrangements, and so forth.

Don't hesitate to take a day or two to thoroughly read the contract or agreement before signing it. Ask the attorney about anything you don't understand and keep asking until he or she has answered all your questions to your satisfaction. If you and the lawyer agree to add or delete anything, make certain that the document reflects those before you sign it. Keep a copy of the final signed contract or agreement for your files.

What If You're Unhappy with Your Attorney?

Your divorce attorney is working for you, so if you're unhappy with something the lawyer does or doesn't do, let him or her know. But be reasonable; don't complain about insignificant matters or constantly call the office to gripe. If you become an irritant, your behavior may impact your lawyer's commitment to your case.

If you feel that your lawyer isn't doing a good job for you, you can fire him or her whenever you want. However, you must pay the attorney for any work that he or she has performed up to that point and for all expenses that the attorney incurred on your behalf.

Also, be aware that firing one attorney and hiring a new one slows the progress of your divorce and will probably increase your legal costs. Therefore, don't take that step without giving it some thought. Try to objectively analyze why you're unhappy with your current attorney. Is it because the attorney consistently seems unprepared, ignores your wishes, or never responds to your phone calls or letters? Is it because your attorney is giving you advice that you don't want to hear or because you're letting your emotions get in the way of rational thinking?

Before you fire your attorney, consider getting a second opinion from another lawyer. Your attorney may be doing the very best job possible under the circumstances and you may not be any happier with a different attorney.

The further you are in the divorce process, the greater the potential harm you may do to your case if you fire your attorney. Your case will grind to a halt until you find a new attorney; your new attorney will need time to get up to speed; your divorce will cost more; and your new attorney may have a different strategy than your first attorney, which could take your divorce in a whole new direction.

What If You Can't Afford Legal Help?

Not everyone can afford to pay the fees of even a relatively inexperienced attorney. If you've checked your wallet and come up short, some legal resources may be available to help you with your divorce case.

When money is tight, you may be tempted to cut corners by getting a divorce online or by purchasing do-it-yourself divorce software. Unfortunately, these options won't work for you if your divorce is contested, and they can be downright dangerous if your divorce is complicated. If you have child-custody and support issues to resolve, if you and your spouse own a substantial amount of marital property and/or you owe a lot of debt, or if you want to share in your spouse's retirement benefits, these divorce options aren't right for you. To protect your legal rights, to get all that you're entitled to for yourself and your kids, and to minimize the potential for post-divorce problems, you need an attorney's assistance, even if that assistance is simply some upfront advice and a review of the divorce agreement that you and your spouse hammered out together.

Try a legal clinic

You may be able to use the services of a nonprofit local, state, or federal legal clinic in your area. Not all these clinics take divorce cases though and, if they do, your household income must be very low (usually some percentage of the U.S. poverty level) to qualify for their services. Furthermore, if your divorce is complicated, you need more help than a legal clinic can provide. You can get the names of nonprofit legal clinics in your area by calling your state or local bar association.

For-profit legal clinics are another source of low-cost help. These clinics tend to rely heavily on standardized legal forms and paralegals and usually charge set fees for certain types of cases — typically in the $200 to $500 range plus court costs. However, if your case is particularly time-consuming, the amount you actually pay can be more than the standard fee. Check out your local Yellow Pages for the names of for-profit legal clinics.

Although the price may be right, a for-profit legal clinic isn't the place for you if your divorce is complicated. Its staff may not have the expertise or the time to give you the legal help that you need.

Your state or local bar association may have a program that provides afford-able legal representation to people of limited financial means.

Explore alternative ways to pay

If you don't have a lot of cash, the attorney you want to hire may be willing to work out an alternative way for you to pay for his or her services:

- **Trade or barter:** If you have a special skill or talent that's worth a signifi-cant amount of money or is of particular value, the attorney may be will-ing to negotiate a trade — your expertise in exchange for legal services. This avenue may be a long shot, but it's worth a try. Such services may include computer trouble-shooting and repair, marketing, graphic design, data entry, and so on.

- **Payment plan:** The attorney may let you pay for his or her services over time, depending on your future earnings potential.

- **Lien on your property:** If you own real property or other significant assets that aren't marital property, the attorney may be willing to take a lien on that property. If you sell the property, the attorney is in line to receive all or some of what you owe him or her from the sale proceeds.

You can reduce your divorce-related expenses by finding an attorney who will let you do your own copying, picking up and delivery of documents, and so on.

Chapter 14

Working with Your Attorney to Get the Best Results Possible

In This Chapter

▶ Giving your attorney the necessary information

▶ Requesting temporary orders

▶ Using discovery to get the facts of the case

▶ Having your attorney negotiate the details of your divorce agreement

▶ Finalizing the agreement

*W*hen you hire a divorce attorney to negotiate the details of your divorce with your spouse's attorney or to represent you in court if a judge is deciding the details, you and your attorney become partners, and the outcome of your divorce depends, in part, on how well you work together. Because the divorce process becomes much more formal when you hire an attorney, being familiar with the legal procedures and processes that your attorney may use to obtain a final agreement is helpful. Also be prepared to provide your attorney with the information and legal documents that he or she will need to work out the best divorce agreement possible for you. Chapter 3 provides a detailed list of the kinds of financial information and documents you should already have pulled together in preparation for your divorce, and Chapter 13 highlights some of the legal documents and information your attorney will want to review as well as the questions your attorney is likely to ask.

In this chapter, we fill you in on what to expect when you work with a divorce attorney by highlighting the kinds of personal, financial, and legal information your attorney will want from you. We also explain how your attorney can use the discovery process to fill in the blanks if you're unable to provide the information that he or she needs and what your attorney may do right away if your divorce is hostile. Finally, we explain how settlement conferences and the draft agreement process works and what happens after you have a final divorce agreement (also called a settlement agreement).

Providing Your Attorney with Essential Information

In order to represent you well in your divorce and to get at all the facts involved, your attorney needs a lot of information, including basic information about your family, marriage, finances, reason(s) for divorce, and so on. Although you probably shared some of this information with your attorney during your initial get-acquainted meeting (which we discuss in Chapter 13), when you're actually working together, he or she will need much more.

You provide your attorney with much of the necessary information through one-on-one interviews, by filling out forms, and by providing your attorney with as much backup documentation as you can — tax returns, credit card statements, titles to property, insurance policies, lease agreements, phone bills, loan applications, business profit-and-loss statements and balance sheets, records of investments, household budgets, and so on.

Don't second-guess whether or not your attorney really needs the information that he or she requests. Try to provide everything your attorney asks for, and don't withhold anything because you think the information is unimportant or irrelevant. You can derail your attorney's negotiating strategy or complicate your divorce in other ways by failing to share that information. For example, if you withhold information from your attorney and your spouse's attorney introduces it into evidence during a hearing related to your divorce, you may damage your case. Also, your attorney probably won't be very happy with you.

If you read Chapter 3 and followed its advice, you're a couple of steps ahead of the game. But if you're not familiar with the details of your family's finances and don't know where your family's legal and financial information is kept — maybe because pulling it together and reviewing it sounded oh-so-tedious and time-consuming (which it is), you have a lot of work ahead of you. That information is essential to negotiating the terms of your divorce and, if you're unable to provide it to your attorney, he or she will have to use the discovery process to get it, which means that your divorce will cost more. We discuss this process later in this chapter and again in Chapter 16.

The following sections of this chapter provide a rundown of some of the things that your attorney needs to know.

Writing it all down: The story of your marriage

Your attorney may ask you to prepare a written narrative describing your marriage: how you and your spouse shared child-care responsibilities, your individual personal habits, what you think led to your divorce, what you would like from your divorce and for your life after divorce, and what you believe your spouse wants.

The narrative can be a good way for your attorney to get the facts related to your divorce that may not be apparent from a review of the financial, legal, and personal documents and other information you provide or from your client-attorney interviews. The information you write down can help fill in the gaps for your attorney and provide him or her with a fuller picture. Plus, you may find that recording the story of your marriage is cathartic and healing. The process may help you gain new insights on what went wrong with your relationship and why you're getting a divorce.

Personal stuff

To help develop a strategy for ending your marriage and to determine what you may be entitled to in your divorce, your attorney needs information on your personal history, your marriage, and your minor children. For those reasons, among others, expect your attorney to question you about

- ✔ Why you're getting a divorce
- ✔ Whether you and your spouse are separated
- ✔ The history of your marriage, including the number of years you've been married, whether any violence occurred in your marriage, and so on
- ✔ Biographical information about you and your spouse
- ✔ Your individual health histories, including whether either of you has a history of serious medical or emotional problems
- ✔ Your minor children, including their ages, where they're living, whether they have special needs (educational, physical, emotional), whether they attend public or private school, and so on

Legal and financial stuff

Your attorney will also spend time studying the details of your finances and reviewing any legal agreements that you and your spouse may have entered into during your marriage. Your attorney will want to know

- ✔ Whether you have a separation agreement. If you have one, your attorney will want to read the agreement. (See Chapter 4 for more details on separation agreements.)

✔ Whether you and your spouse own any real estate, including homes, buildings, or land. Be prepared to provide your attorney with the *deeds of record* to this property and any loan documents related to the property if you owe money on any of it.

✔ Whether you signed a prenuptial or postnuptial agreement. (For the full scoop on prenuptial and postnuptial agreements, turn to Chapter 19.)

✔ Whether you or your spouse have done any estate planning, such as writing wills, buying life insurance, or setting up living trusts.

✔ Whether you and your spouse own a closely held business together, have other shared business interests, or own separate businesses.

✔ What assets and debts you and your spouse have from your marriage as well as where you got the money to pay for any of the real property you may own. *Real property* includes your home and any other homes, buildings, or land that you own.

✔ How much each of you earns annually from all income sources, including salaries, commissions, bonuses, and other employment-related income as well as from trusts, annuities, royalties, rents, and so on.

✔ Whether either of you made any special contributions to one another's career or business. For example, you may have helped finance your spouse's business or worked in the business without pay; your spouse may have supported you through college or graduate school; or you may have used your separate funds to purchase assets for your marriage or to help pay your family's living expenses.

✔ Whether either of you has wasted marital assets by gambling; engaging in phone sex or extramarital affairs; or through an addiction to drugs, alcohol, or even the Internet.

✔ Your current and post-divorce household budgets. (Chapter 5 provides information about developing a budget as well as a budget worksheet.) In addition, if you filed a fault divorce, the attorney will want you to provide proof of the fault. Conversely, if your spouse filed a fault divorce against you, the attorney will want proof of your innocence.

Other important stuff

Your attorney will ask you questions in order to understand what you expect from your divorce and what you're willing to do or not do to get what you want. Your attorney needs this information not just to help you get a divorce agreement that meets your needs, but also to be certain that your expectations for what you may get from your divorce are realistic. So, you can expect your lawyer to ask you about

✔ Your divorce goals and priorities

✔ Your expectations for your divorce

> ✔ Why you feel you should receive spousal support, if that's something you want from your divorce
>
> ✔ Why you feel the custody arrangement you want is reasonable and why your spouse's desired custody arrangement isn't reasonable, assuming that you and your spouse don't see eye to eye on how to handle the custody of your minor children
>
> ✔ Under what, if any, circumstances you are willing to go to trial to get what you want

Taking Special Action for a Contentious Divorce

If your divorce is hostile, one of the very first things your attorney may do when you begin working together is to file motions asking the court to grant *temporary orders* on your behalf. Temporary orders can help you make sure that certain things do or don't happen while you're working out the terms of your divorce. For instance, your attorney may request temporary orders for spousal support; child support; custody and visitation; or an order giving you the right to remain in your home or to use certain property, like a car and the funds in a bank account. See Chapter 16 for more information about temporary orders.

Using Discovery to Get at the Facts of Your Divorce

Attorneys use the *discovery* process to help them determine the facts of a case. This process can be informal or formal. If it's *informal,* you and your spouse, working through your individual attorneys, willingly provide one another the documents and information each of you needs to work out the terms of your divorce. If it's a *formal* process, depending on what you or the opposing side wants to learn through discovery, the attorneys may use a variety of legal tools (most of which we describe in this section) to get the information they need. These tools include subpoenas, depositions, interrogatories, and motions to produce documents.

Your attorney is apt to rely on informal discovery if

> ✔ The two attorneys agree in writing to willingly exchange all the information they need to work out the terms of your divorce
>
> ✔ Your divorce is amicable

Your attorney is likely to use formal discovery if

- ✔ Your divorce is contentious
- ✔ Your attorney has to force your spouse's attorney to provide certain information related to your divorce
- ✔ Either attorney needs to formally acquire additional information related to your divorce from other sources

The discovery process may take just a short amount of time, especially if the facts of your divorce are clear and undisputed and most of the discovery is informal. However, if your attorney (or your spouse's attorney) uses formal discovery to get at the facts of your case, the discovery process can last many months. The process can last many months because obtaining information through the formal discovery process is time-consuming, and reviewing the requested information can take time. Also, court hearings related to your attorney's discovery requests or the requests of your spouse's attorney may occur as well as other potential complications that may slow down the process.

In some states, the amount of formal discovery is limited. For example, your attorney may be able to use discovery to get at only the financial facts of your divorce.

Depending on the issues that have to be resolved before your divorce can be finalized, any number of individuals may be involved in the discovery process: you, your spouse, your financial advisors, your business associates, appraisers, your children's teachers and baby-sitters, mental health professionals, your friends, relatives, and neighbors — basically, anyone who may be able to provide information about your marriage, your children, your finances, and so on.

Uncovering the facts with informal discovery

Informal discovery occurs when your attorney asks your spouse's attorney (or vice versa) for financial, legal, medical, or other information and the opposing attorney provides that information voluntarily. The particular types of information your attorney asks for depend on the issues involved in your divorce.

Ideally, most of the discovery in your divorce will be informal because the more frequently either side uses formal discovery, the longer your divorce will take and the more it will cost. For example, in formal discovery, your attorney or your spouse's attorney may have to complete extra paperwork, formulate questions to ask your spouse or others, conduct interviews, and then review and analyze all the information. More hearings take place as well.

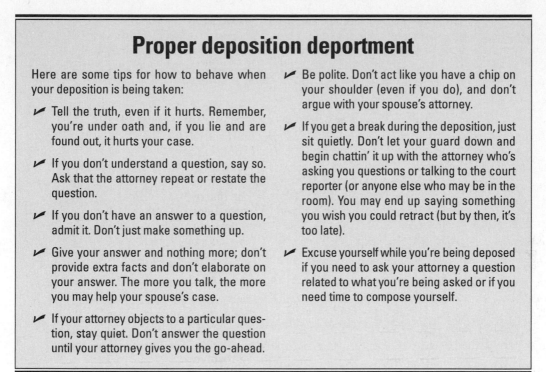

Proper deposition deportment

Here are some tips for how to behave when your deposition is being taken:

✔ Tell the truth, even if it hurts. Remember, you're under oath and, if you lie and are found out, it hurts your case.

✔ If you don't understand a question, say so. Ask that the attorney repeat or restate the question.

✔ If you don't have an answer to a question, admit it. Don't just make something up.

✔ Give your answer and nothing more; don't provide extra facts and don't elaborate on your answer. The more you talk, the more you may help your spouse's case.

✔ If your attorney objects to a particular question, stay quiet. Don't answer the question until your attorney gives you the go-ahead.

✔ Be polite. Don't act like you have a chip on your shoulder (even if you do), and don't argue with your spouse's attorney.

✔ If you get a break during the deposition, just sit quietly. Don't let your guard down and begin chattin' it up with the attorney who's asking you questions or talking to the court reporter (or anyone else who may be in the room). You may end up saying something you wish you could retract (but by then, it's too late).

✔ Excuse yourself while you're being deposed if you need to ask your attorney a question related to what you're being asked or if you need time to compose yourself.

Using formal discovery to dig for the details

Formal discovery is most common in divorces involving spouses who are unwilling to cooperate with one another. Depositions, interrogatories, formal requests for the production of documents, and subpoenas are all formal discovery tools. The following list tells you what each of these terms means:

✔ **Subpoena:** A legal document requiring someone to provide testimony about something or someone at a court hearing or a trial. Anyone who ignores a subpoena faces legal penalties.

✔ **Deposition:** A statement by a witness, taken out of court and recorded by a court reporter. The witness is under oath. Your spouse's attorney may ask you to be a witness as part of the formal discovery process in your divorce. Others with knowledge related to an issue in your divorce may also be deposed. Although you may wish you didn't have to give a deposition, unless you want to risk being held in contempt of court, you must comply with the request. Your attorney will be by your side during the deposition. The "Proper deposition deportment" sidebar in this chapter provides tips on how to behave if you're deposed.

✔ **Interrogatories:** Written questions prepared by the plaintiff's attorney for the defendant or vice versa in order to obtain information related to an issue that's in dispute in your divorce. Other individuals, such as your family's financial advisor, friends or family members, a business associate of your spouse's, and so on, may also have to respond to an interrogatory.

✔ **Notices to produce documents and other information:** Your attorney may use these notices to obtain such things as the deed to your home, financial information related to your spouse's business, your spouse's cellphone records, and so on.

A notice to produce documents is also known as a "request for production of documents and other tangible things."

Even if your divorce is amicable, your attorney may do a limited amount of formal discovery in order to

✔ Narrow the scope of your negotiations by identifying exactly where you and your spouse agree or disagree and the particulars of your agreements and disagreements. The more that you agree on, the less the attorneys have to negotiate or litigate later and the less your divorce costs.

✔ Assess the strengths and weaknesses of your position versus your spouse's.

✔ Assess how well your spouse is likely to perform on the stand if your case goes to trial and your spouse must testify.

✔ Get your spouse to admit to certain facts. If your divorce goes to trial and your spouse provides testimony while on the stand that differs from what he or she said during discovery, your attorney can use the discrepancy to undermine your spouse's credibility.

Using Your Attorney to Work Out the Details of Your Divorce Agreement

After your attorney briefs you on key points and legal issues in your divorce, he or she may suggest that you and your spouse work out the terms of your divorce on your own instead of having him or her and your spouse's attorney do that for you (assuming that you and your spouse are communicating with each other). Chapter 12 provides how-to advice for negotiating an agreement with your spouse; nailing down the terms of your divorce on your own will save you a considerable amount of money. After you and your spouse complete your negotiations, you draw up your own written divorce agreement and have your attorneys review it. After you have a final divorce agreement, the attorney working for the spouse who initiated the divorce files the agreement with the court so that the court can issue a final divorce judgment, which gives your agreement the force of law. After that task is done, you're officially divorced.

If you and your spouse put your attorneys in charge of drawing up your divorce agreement, your attorneys work together to negotiate the terms of your divorce in consultation with you and your spouse. After they've worked out all the terms of your agreement, the attorney for the spouse who initiated the divorce drafts a final divorce agreement and files it with the court.

Working out an agreement with the help of your attorney

If you're the spouse who filed for divorce, your attorney contacts your spouse's attorney to begin discussing the terms of your divorce. When the attorneys come to an agreement on an issue in your divorce, your attorney sends the other attorney a letter stating what they agreed to; assuming that your spouse's attorney feels that the letter accurately reflects their agreement, the attorneys put that issue aside and move on to another issue.

If your spouse's attorney wants to change anything, he or she calls your attorney to convey the change. Your attorney consults with you by phone before offering anything to your spouse's attorney or accepting anything he or she may offer to you. This back-and-forth process continues until all the issues in your divorce are worked out or until you and your spouse reach a stalemate on one or more issues. If that happens, you and your spouse may agree to use mediation to try to resolve your differences or, worst-case scenario, you have to go to court to resolve the sticking points

Expect your attorney to consult you throughout his or her negotiations with your spouse's attorney. Do not agree to anything that makes you feel uncomfortable, that you don't understand, or that you don't think you can live up to. You're not obligated to agree to anything that you don't like. You can accept or reject something that your spouse's attorney may offer to you through his or her attorney, or you can use the offer as the basis for additional negotiations.

You may be tempted to threaten your spouse with taking your divorce to trial in order to pressure him or her to give in on certain points that are important to you. But, before you try this tactic, consider which scenario is more likely: You holding your ground and your spouse agreeing to a compromise, or your spouse holding his or her ground and calling your bluff.

After you and your spouse feel that you're close to a final agreement, the attorney representing the spouse who filed for divorce drafts a formal divorce agreement that reflects everything you and your spouse have agreed on for your approval and your spouse's approval.

Evaluating an offer or counteroffer from your spouse

Whenever you receive an offer or counteroffer from your spouse proposing how to resolve one of the issues in your divorce, you must decide whether or not you like it. When you do your evaluating, ask yourself the following questions:

- ✔ How close is the agreement to what I'm asking for?

- ✔ Does the offer reflect most, if not all, of my divorce priorities? Is anything missing from the agreement that's worth the cost and the time involved in continued negotiations?

- ✔ Is the agreement fair?

- ✔ Is the agreement in my children's best interest?

- ✔ Can I afford the agreement?

- ✔ Given what I know now about my legal rights and responsibilities, the value of the marital property that my spouse and I own, and how my divorce is affecting my children, am I likely to get more if I reject the proposal?

- ✔ Is my spouse likely to make any additional concessions if we continue negotiating?

- ✔ How much have I already spent on my case, and can I afford to spend any more?

- ✔ Am I willing to take the offer just to end this protracted and expensive legal process?

- ✔ Given what I know about the judge and his or her past rulings, am I likely to do better if I go all the way to trial than if I were to accept what my spouse is offering? What is the worst that could happen? (Your attorney should be able to give you a strong sense of how a judge would be likely to rule on your case given your state's laws and guidelines and the past decisions of the judge who's likely to preside over your divorce trial.)

- ✔ If I really push for whatever is missing, what may I have to give up in order to get it? Is it worth it to me? What are the risks of not settling now?

- ✔ If I don't settle now, how long will it take for this case to come to trial and how long is the trial likely to last?

- ✔ Do I not want to settle yet because I'm unhappy with the agreement, because I'm not sure that I can live up to the agreement, or because my emotions are getting in the way?

✔ What kind of financial and emotional toll is not settling likely to take on my children and me? Discuss the pros and cons of whatever agreement you're evaluating with your attorney. Share your thoughts and concerns with him or her and find out what your attorney thinks. Your attorney may tell you that what your spouse has offered is about as good as you're going to get, that you can probably get a few more concessions if you keep negotiating, or that you should not accept what your spouse is offering because it's not in your best interest. In the end, however, it's your call whether to accept the offer or not.

Settling disputes at a settlement conference

If your divorce is very complicated and contentious and you and your spouse both feel as if you have at least the beginnings of an agreement, your attorneys may schedule a *settlement conference* to try to work out the issues that are unresolved. The settlement conference usually takes place at one of the attorneys' offices and usually occurs after the discovery process is complete. However, the conference can take place whenever you and your spouse are ready to make a deal.

The settlement conference offers your attorneys an opportunity to sit down face to face to hammer out the final specific details of your divorce agreement. You and your spouse may or may not participate. Before the settlement conference, you should talk with your attorney about whether you should attend. It may or may not be in your best interest if your divorce is contentious or if you have a hard time keeping your emotions under control. But you may want to be there so that you can hear everything that's said at the settlement conference and so that you can provide your attorney with immediate feedback.

A successful settlement conference involves some old-fashioned horse-trading. So, if you haven't been clear with your attorney about your divorce priorities and what you're willing to give up to get them, your attorney will not be able to bargain effectively for you.

Don't get impatient with all the back-and-forth negotiations. Getting all the terms of your divorce agreement just right is essential because, after you and your spouse sign it and file it with the court, the agreement becomes a legally binding contract, which means that you must live up to what it says, like it or not.

If you and your spouse simply cannot agree on something, no matter how hard your attorneys try to craft a mutually acceptable compromise, they may recommend mediation or even arbitration, both of which we describe in Chapter 15. If you don't want to give these options a try and you don't want to keep negotiating, either, your only other option — assuming that you and your spouse still want to get divorced — is to have your case tried in court. For more on what happens if your case goes to trial, see Chapter 16.

Making a deal: The final settlement

After you and your spouse have a final divorce agreement (or final settlement agreement) detailing the terms of your divorce, your lawyer or your spouse's lawyer drafts a formal document stating everything you agreed to. The final agreement includes a lot of standard provisions and boilerplate language — stuff that's in every settlement agreement. Whichever attorney does the drafting submits the agreement to the other attorney for review. The other attorney may make some minor tweaks to the agreement but, at this point, no substantive changes should occur.

After you sign the settlement agreement, depending on your state, you and your spouse (or just one of you) may have to appear at a court hearing in order to have a judge officially dissolve your marriage. In other states, a hearing takes place only if your divorce is a fault divorce. (Chapter 1 explains the difference between a fault and a no-fault divorce.) If a hearing is scheduled, it's more of a formality than anything else, and it won't last long. Your attorney will attend the hearing with you.

Concluding Your Divorce: Filing the Divorce Decree

After your attorney (or your spouse's attorney) submits your final divorce settlement agreement to the judge, the court reviews its terms. Then, the judge signs your divorce decree (a final judgment of divorce).

Some states allow judges to modify negotiated settlement agreements. Others allow judges to only accept or reject an agreement. If the judge rejects your agreement, you can go back to the drawing board to work out a new, more acceptable one. A judge may reject your agreement because he or she doesn't think it's fair to one or both of you, because it's unenforceable or violates your state's laws, or because it isn't in the best interests of your minor children, among other reasons.

After the judge approves or modifies your settlement, he or she returns your *divorce decree* to your attorney who, in turn, forwards the decree to your spouse's attorney. At that point, you and your spouse have a certain amount of time to review and, if necessary, appeal the court's judgment (usually ten days).

Realistically, unless you have a last-minute change of heart or unless the judge makes changes to your divorce agreement that you don't like, an immediate appeal is unlikely. However, you or your spouse may try to get something changed later after you've had a chance to live with the agreement and have identified problems with it or if changes occur that merit a modification. (Chapter 18 covers the topic of modifying divorce agreements.)

You and your spouse become officially divorced when the judge signs your divorce decree or *judgment of divorce* and enters it together with your final settlement agreement into the court records.

Keep a copy of your final settlement agreement and your divorce decree in a safe place. You may need it if you have to prove that you're divorced, if any questions arise about what you and your spouse agreed to, or if you want to change something in your divorce agreement later.

Chapter 15

Using Mediation to Resolve the Sticky Issues in Your Divorce

*W*hen you and your spouse are working out the terms of your divorce, no matter how hard you both try, you may encounter issues that you just can't resolve on your own. If that happens, you and your spouse don't have to tear your hair out in frustration or toss in the towel and brace yourselves for a trial. Instead, you may be able to use mediation to work out the sticky issues standing between you and a final divorce agreement.

In this chapter, we explain how mediation works and describe the role of a divorce mediator. We also highlight the benefits of mediation, describe the role of your attorney when you use mediation, and discuss what will happen next if your mediation is successful.

Deciding Whether Mediation Is Right for You and Your Spouse

Mediation is a dispute-resolution method that uses the open exchange of information, ideas, and alternatives to help individuals problem-solve with the goal of resolving their differences outside of court. It encourages mutual understanding, cooperation, and problem-solving, *not* winning.

At the time of this writing, more than half the U.S. states' laws require divorcing couples under certain circumstances to participate in mediation before heading for a divorce trial. Those circumstances usually relate to unresolved custody issues. For the sake of the children, courts prefer that parents make their own decisions regarding custody and visitation rather than letting a judge decide.

Mediation is most apt to work for couples who can discuss their divorce calmly and clearly. If you or your spouse feels a lot of anger or other strong emotions about your divorce, you or your spouse may need to work with a mental health professional before you can use mediation successfully.

If you and your spouse decide that mediation is right for you, don't begin the process until each of you has spoken with a divorce attorney about your legal rights. Otherwise, you may end up agreeing to something during a mediation session that isn't in your best interest.

The following sections outline the basic benefits of mediation and warn you about situations when mediation may not be the best option for you.

Considering the benefits of mediation

It takes two to tango, to sing a duet, and to make mediation work. So, if your spouse isn't serious about mediation, you're probably wasting your time as well as the mediator's (we discuss the mediator's role in the "Working with a Mediator" section later in this chapter). However, if your spouse is uncertain about whether or not to mediate, ask him or her to consider these important mediation benefits:

✔ **Using mediation to work out the sticky points in your divorce can be a lot cheaper than going to trial to resolve them.** In fact, mediation may cost hundreds to thousands of dollars less, depending on how many sessions you and your spouse have with the mediator, the complexity of the issues you're trying to resolve, and the cost of the mediator versus the cost of an attorney's help.

Depending on where you live and the experience and reputation of the mediator you work with, expect most mediators to charge between $60 and $300 an hour.

✔ **Working out your issues with a mediator is a lot less stressful and intimidating than working them out in a courtroom.** Sitting in a mediator's office and attempting to work out the issues in your divorce with your spouse is much better than sitting in a courtroom, taking the stand during your divorce trial, and having a judge decide those issues for you.

✔ **You will get divorced faster.** Depending on the caseload in your area's family court, months — or even a year or more — may pass before your trial date arrives. On the other hand, when you decide to mediate, you can probably schedule your first session within a month — although just how long you and your spouse take to work things out is in your hands.

✔ **Mediation encourages you and your spouse to brainstorm creative options for resolving the issues in your divorce.** The benefit? You and your spouse may come up with resolutions that you may have never thought of otherwise.

✔ **You and your spouse control your divorce.** In mediation, you and your spouse make the tough decisions, not a judge.

✔ **You preserve all your options.** If mediation doesn't work, you and your spouse can always go back to the drawing board with your attorneys and try to negotiate the terms of your divorce with their help or take your divorce to trial.

✔ **Mediation maintains your privacy.** If you end up in court, anyone in the courtroom can hear your dirty laundry. But, with mediation, only you, your spouse, the mediator, and maybe your attorneys are in the mediator's office.

✔ **You and your spouse are more likely to be satisfied with and honor your agreement because you came up with it together.** The agreement that comes out of mediation isn't something that a judge imposes on you both — it's something that you and your spouse agree upon.

Sometimes mediation isn't such a hot idea

Mediation isn't for everyone. It's not right for you if

✔ Your spouse intimidates you.

✔ You have a hard time standing up for yourself.

✔ You haven't clarified your divorce priorities and goals, so you don't know what to negotiate for.

✔ You don't have the information you need to negotiate on an equal footing with your spouse; for example, you suspect that your spouse is hiding assets. (A good attorney won't let you go into mediation unprepared; see the section "How Your Attorney Can Help with Your Mediation" later in this chapter.)

✔ You and your spouse can no longer communicate effectively.

If you or your spouse decides that you don't want to try mediation, but you don't want to let a judge decide the terms of your divorce through a divorce trial, you may want to consider using arbitration, which is another noncourt dispute-resolution method. See the sidebar "Arbitration: Another out-of-court option" to find out how the process works.

Arbitration: Another out-of-court option

When you hear the word "arbitration," you may think of labor union disputes. But did you know that you can use arbitration to resolve marital disputes as well?

Arbitration is an out-of-court dispute-resolution method that's more formal than mediation but less formal and less costly than a trial. During arbitration, your attorney represents you, witnesses can testify, your attorney can present written evidence, and so forth, just like in a trial. But during arbitration, you're not constrained by the formal rules of evidence or the usual courtroom procedures. You and your spouse, working with your attorneys and the arbitrator, set your own rules.

If you want to resolve the issues in your divorce through arbitration, your attorney will choose the arbitrator who's best for you. Choosing an arbitrator is an important decision, so let your attorney's experience work for you.

A fundamental difference between arbitration and mediation is that you and your spouse won't make the final decisions. The arbitrator does. Although the arbitrator is not a judge, his or her decisions are legally binding and *can* be legally enforced, and you *cannot* appeal them.

Some states allow couples to have any of their divorce-related disputes arbitrated, although special arbitration rules may apply when a dispute relates to custody or child support. Other states prohibit any and all child-related issues from arbitration.

Arbitration can be a good alternative if

✔ You don't want to try mediation or have already tried it and failed to reach an agreement.

✔ You don't want to run up big legal bills or want to be divorced sooner than if you had to wait for your day in court.

✔ You're willing to let an arbitrator — often a retired judge or lawyer — decide the outstanding issues in your divorce.

✔ You're willing to live with the arbitrator's decisions, even if you're not happy with them. Remember, unlike a judge's decision, you cannot appeal an arbitrator's decisions.

Working with a Mediator

When you and your spouse want to use mediation to work out the terms of your divorce, you must decide which mediator to hire. Don't take this decision lightly! If either of you is uncomfortable with or doesn't trust or have confidence in the mediator you use, mediating your divorce may not work for you. Hiring a mediator who has experience mediating divorces is important because the issues involved can be extremely emotional, and you must be certain that whatever you and your spouse decide complies with the divorce-related laws of your state. Not every mediator has the skills and knowledge to help couples negotiate the terms of their divorce. Therefore, in this section, we provide information and advice to help you choose a mediator who's not only qualified to help you, but who also has the trust and confidence of you and your spouse.

If you and your spouse are already working with attorneys when you decide to try mediation, each of your attorneys will recommend a mediator based on their past experience resolving marital disputes through mediation. Each attorney will want a mediator who has achieved positive results for their divorce clients in the past. If you're lucky, your attorney and your spouse's attorney will agree on which mediator to use but, if they don't, you may have to go to court to let a judge decide.

Selecting a great go-between

Mediators are neutral third parties who may be mental health professionals, social workers, attorneys, clergy members, financial professionals, and even volunteers. However, if you use a mediator to help with your divorce, that person should be a family law attorney or a nonlawyer mediator who has specific experience in divorce mediation.

Your choice of mediators is important because you want to be sure that whatever decisions you and your spouse agree to comply with the laws of your state and are legally enforceable. Also, a mediator who understands your state's divorce laws and processes is better able to diffuse potentially explosive situations during your mediation. For example, if your spouse threatens to storm out because you asked him exactly how much he makes, a mediator can remind your spouse that your attorney can get that information through formal discovery anyway if it isn't provided voluntarily (see Chapter 16 to find out how formal discovery works).

If you're not working with divorce attorneys yet and are choosing a mediator on your own, both of you should meet with the prospective mediators to find out about their backgrounds and training and to ensure that their personalities mesh with yours. You can meet with them together or separately. Either way, you should both agree on which mediator you want to work with.

In most states, mediators don't have to be certified or licensed. Also, no national certification standards exist for mediators. Therefore, even if a mediator who your attorney recommends isn't certified or licensed by your state or a professional organization, that person may still be highly qualified to help you and your spouse resolve your differences. Nevertheless, do some investigating before you hire a mediator. When you meet with each mediator, ask the following questions in order to get the information you need to select a mediator who has experience mediating divorces, who you and your spouse both feel comfortable working with, and who is affordable:

- How much do you charge for your services? Do you charge by the hour or do you charge a flat fee?
- What is your professional background?

✔ Do you have any special mediation training and are you certified by any organizations?

✔ Do you belong to the Academy of Family Mediators (800-292-4236) or another professional mediator organization? (The Academy of Family Mediators is a membership organization that sets standards of practice for its members and investigates complaints against them.)

✔ Can you mediate all the issues that my spouse and I need to resolve or just some of them?

Some mediators handle the full gamut of divorce-related issues; not all mediate financial matters or custody battles.

✔ How many times have you mediated issues like mine? What is your success rate, and how have you helped other divorcing couples who were dealing with the same issues that we have come to closure?

During the screening process, be sure to ask each potential mediator for client references — and check them, too! References can give you insights into a mediator's personality and style, which may suggest that another mediator would be a better choice for you. You wouldn't find out that information if you relied only on what you gleaned from your meeting with the mediator.

Knowing what to expect during a session

After you and your spouse have decided on a mediator, that person will work with you to schedule a convenient time for your initial mediation session as well as a place for you to meet. Most likely, you will meet at the mediator's office, but the meeting can also take place at some other neutral location. The mediator will handle making all the arrangements.

During a mediation session, the mediator acts as coach, consensus builder, facilitator and, if necessary, referee, with the goal of helping create an environment in which you and your spouse will feel comfortable calmly expressing your opinions, talking over your differences, and working out your problems together.

The mediator won't take sides with you or your spouse, interject opinions, or provide legal advice. Also, a mediator won't make decisions for you or order you or your spouse to do anything that you don't want to do.

A mediator

✔ Clarifies the issues that you and your spouse need to resolve

✔ Establishes the ground rules for your mediation

✔ Sets an agenda for your discussions

✔ Keeps the discussions moving forward

✔ Provides legal information, as necessary (but not legal advice). For example, the mediator may provide you with a written explanation of your property rights so that you and your spouse have a clear understanding of what each of you is legally entitled to when the time comes to divide up your marital assets.

Your attorney can accompany you to the mediation sessions or may just be available to consult with you by phone as needed. (See the section "How Your Attorney Can Help with Your Mediation" later in this chapter.)

Depending on the complexity of the issues that you and your spouse need to resolve and how well you both work together, you may be able to resolve the issues in a single mediation session or you may need a few sessions before you reach an agreement.

How Your Attorney Can Help with Your Mediation

If you decide to use mediation, your lawyer won't simply hand you off to a mediator and wait for you and your spouse to resolve all your outstanding divorce issues. At a minimum, your lawyer will prepare you for mediation by helping you

✔ Develop a list of the specific issues you want to resolve.

✔ Assess your options.

✔ Review any information that your spouse may share with you prior to mediation so that you understand all of it and know the right questions to ask about it.

✔ Develop a mediation game plan or strategy.

Depending on your ability to negotiate with your spouse during a mediation session, the complexity of the issues you want to resolve, and your attorney's preferences, your attorney may help you in other important ways:

✔ By serving as a sounding board before and after your mediation sessions

✔ By being at your side during mediation

✔ By serving as your onsite mediation consultant, brainstorming with you, and providing you with feedback

✔ By confirming or denying any information that the mediator or your spouse may give you

✔ By reviewing any written agreement that the mediator may have drafted before you sign it

✔ By negotiating for you

You Agree! Now What?

If mediation works for you and your spouse, the mediator prepares a written document that details everything you and your spouse agreed upon. The mediator gives a copy of the agreement to your attorney so he or she can review it before you sign it. After you sign it, the mediator provides your attorney with the signed agreement and does the same for your spouse and your spouse's attorney.

You and your spouse's attorneys incorporate the mediation agreement into your final divorce agreement and, after the attorneys file the final divorce agreement with the court, you and your spouse are legally bound to comply with everything that you both agreed to during mediation.

Chapter 16

Divorce Court: Letting a Judge Decide the Terms of Your Divorce

- -

In This Chapter

▶ Determining whether you really want a divorce trial

▶ Settling your divorce out of court

▶ Resolving your issues at a pretrial conference

▶ Preparing for your trial

▶ Knowing how a trial works and the role of the judge or jury

▶ Weighing the pros and cons of an appeal

- -

*W*e're going to give it to you straight: Resolving the terms of your divorce by going through a divorce trial isn't a pleasant experience. Compared to working things out with your soon-to-be-ex by yourselves or with the help of attorneys, turning your divorce over to a judge is much more stressful — not to mention substantially more expensive. In fact, the cost of having your divorce litigated will probably come out of your marital property, which means you and your ex each end up with less of it. Plus, when you go through a divorce trial, you and your spouse have no guarantee that you'll like what the judge decides.

Unlike negotiating the terms of your divorce through cooperation and compromise, a divorce trial is about winning and losing, and both attorneys will do whatever they can to be on the winning side. Therefore, be prepared for your spouse's lawyer to negatively portray you and to use highly personal information against you. People you consider friends may testify on your spouse's behalf, and your spouse's attorney may mischaracterize your past mistakes or blow them out of proportion. Your attorney will use the same tactics against your spouse, which may make you gloat or feel terrible about how badly your marriage is ending.

If a divorce trial sounds like a kind of hell on earth, you're getting the picture. Divorce trials are serious business. If you're headed for a trial, fasten your seat belts, because you're in for a bumpy ride.

To help prepare you for some major turbulence in your life, this chapter discusses out-of-court settlement opportunities and how to evaluate any offers that your spouse may send your way. This chapter also explains what happens prior to a trial and offers you general advice about proper, in-court behavior and how to dress for a court appearance. Last, you find an overview of the trial process and information on appeals — in case the outcome isn't what you'd hoped for.

Making Certain You Really Want a Trial

Before you move full speed ahead with a divorce trial, think long and hard about its financial and emotional costs. (Remember, you still have time to change your mind and get serious about a negotiated settlement!) Maybe the time has come to swallow your pride, compromise, and do whatever is necessary to avoid the pain and expense of a trial.

Weighing your options

Bear in mind that putting your divorce in the hands of a judge is a gamble because he or she may not see things quite the way you do. Therefore, the terms of your divorce may not be what you'd hoped for. Don't assume that your side of the story is so strong that the judge will automatically decide in your favor. Prepare yourself to be disappointed.

Before you commit yourself to a divorce trial, ask yourself the following questions:

- ✔ Because the judge may not see everything my way, does the risk of not getting what I want from my divorce outweigh any benefits I may receive from going to court?

- ✔ Would I be better off compromising with my spouse to get at least some of the things that are really important to me in my divorce rather than rolling the dice and hoping that I come up with the lucky number?

- ✔ Do you have the time to devote to a lengthy trial? Getting divorced takes longer when you go to court. Not only does preparing for the trial take a great deal of time, but you may also have to wait months for a trial date — as long as a *year*, depending on how many other cases are ahead of yours in the pipeline and whether you have to postpone your original trial date. If you're looking for a speedy divorce, going to trial isn't the way to get it.

- ✔ Are you willing to put your children through the emotional stress of a divorce trial? Although they may not fully understand what's going on, they will at least sense that you're under an unusual amount of pressure, which may scare them.

Despite all the negatives associated with a divorce trial, sometimes it's your best or only option. For example:

- ✔ Your spouse refuses to negotiate with you.

- ✔ You and your spouse have tried to negotiate an agreement and have gotten nowhere.

- ✔ Your spouse is hiding information essential to a fair settlement.

- ✔ Your spouse is insisting on a custody arrangement that you don't think is in your children's best interests.

- ✔ You need more spousal support than your spouse will agree to.

- ✔ You think that your spouse may be wasting or hiding your marital property or other assets.

- ✔ Your spouse has an alcohol or drug problem or has abused you or your children.

If, after reading all this information, you're beginning to have second thoughts about whether going to trial is such a hot idea, you can still resolve the outstanding issues in your divorce outside of court. "Deciding to Settle After Beginning Your Trial Preparations" discusses what happens if you and your spouse agree to let your attorneys work out a negotiated divorce agreement for you rather than pursuing a trial.

Don't let your selfish wishes to have your children live with you all the time, your desire for revenge against your spouse for ending your marriage, or your discomfort with having your children live with your ex and the new person in his or her life cloud your thinking about the best custody arrangement for *your kids*. If you do, you may end up in a painful custody battle that's totally unnecessary.

Temporary orders: A pretrial taste of the courtroom experience

You may have already gotten a taste of what being in a courtroom and having a judge make decisions that affect your life and/or the lives of your kids is like because your attorney or your spouse's attorney may have filed motions for temporary court orders early on in your divorce. If so, then you had to attend court hearings related to those motions. Your attorney may have asked the court to issue a temporary court order to

- ✔ Give you the right to receive temporary spousal support.

- ✔ Settle issues related to child support, custody, and visitation until the final details of your divorce are worked out.

- ✔ Give you the right to remain in your home.

> ✔ Give you the right to use certain property, such as a car or the funds in a bank account.
>
> ✔ Prohibit your spouse from certain types of improper behavior. For example, your attorney may ask the court to prohibit your spouse from selling your marital property or from making certain decisions related to a business you own together.

Your attorney may also request that the court issue a temporary restraining order if your spouse is threatening your safety or your children's safety or has already been physically violent. The order bars your spouse from coming near you and/or your children.

If you're concerned that your spouse may disappear with your children, your attorney can ask the court to mandate supervised visitation if your attorney can provide evidence to the court that your spouse may attempt to flee with the kids.

Although the judge's decisions address these motions on a temporary basis, the motions can become a permanent part of your divorce judgment or decree. In other words, some aspects of your divorce may actually be decided at the temporary-order level. For this reason, a hearing on a temporary court order can be just as stressful and nerve-wracking as a divorce trial. (For more information on temporary court orders, see Chapter 14.)

After your attorney files a motion with the court requesting a temporary order, a court hearing is held to discuss the motion. At this hearing, your spouse (actually your spouse's attorney, assuming that he or she hired one) probably will argue why your motion should *not* be granted because, in a contentious divorce, most spouses object to whatever the other spouse is asking for.

If you have need for an immediate court order — for instance, you have reason to think that your spouse is about to sell some of your marital assets or flee with your children — your attorney may be able to get a court order issued on an *ex parte* basis. *Ex parte* refers to a legal action ordered on behalf of one party without the other party being notified about it or having an opportunity to participate in the action.

With an *ex parte* order, your spouse doesn't find out about the court's decision and a hearing doesn't take place until after the court approves your attorney's motion and issues its order. Therefore, an *ex parte* order usually has a very short duration. After the court grants the order, usually both parties must attend a hearing to determine whether or not the court should extend the terms of the order.

If you request an *ex parte* order, you may have to post bond to protect your spouse against any harm, such as a financial loss, that he or she may suffer because the court issues the order without a hearing. However, in many family law situations, the court waives the bond requirement.

Taking a financial hit

Divorce trials aren't cheap. The exact cost depends on a number of factors: what part of the country you live in (divorcing in a major metropolitan area on either coast costs more than divorcing in the Midwest, the South, or a rural area); the specific issues the judge will decide; your attorney's legal strategy; and the legal strategy of your spouse's attorney.

You can expect your legal bills alone to run into the five- or six-figure range — as much as four times the cost of a negotiated divorce.

At a minimum, be prepared to incur the following expenses related to your divorce trial:

- ✔ Lawyer fees
- ✔ Filing fees
- ✔ Court reporter fees
- ✔ Expert fees
- ✔ Discovery fees
- ✔ Subpoena fees
- ✔ The cost of preparing exhibits for the trial if an outside firm is hired to create them
- ✔ Miscellaneous legal expenses — copying, long-distance charges, postage, delivery fees, and so on

Keep in mind that this list covers only the monetary costs of a trial. We can't begin to calculate the cost to your family's health and happiness if you're embroiled in an ugly divorce trial.

Deciding to Settle after Beginning Your Trial Preparations

For various reasons, most contested divorces never get to trial, although they may get as far as the courthouse steps. So, while your attorney and your spouse's attorney prepare for your trial, they may also try to negotiate an out-of-court settlement agreement. Also, you and your spouse may have a change of heart about going to trial after the trial preparations have begun.

Big business in Splitsville, Nevada

During the first half of the 20th century, divorce was legal in all states, but people generally frowned upon it as something "nice people" didn't do. Plus, getting divorced was considered somewhat scandalous. In fact, to discourage couples from divorcing, state laws made certain that the divorce process would drag out as long as possible. But the law in one state was an exception to this rule. Nevada, a freewheeling, cash-poor frontier state at the start of the last century saw divorce as a potential source of considerable revenue. At the turn of the century, Nevada allowed a man or a woman who lived within its boundaries for a minimum of six months to walk into a courthouse, tell a judge why he or she wanted a divorce, and walk out a divorced person. As a result, countless unhappy couples, including the rich and famous, flocked to Nevada to obtain their divorces. But the city's reputation as America's divorce capital didn't really take off until 1920, when America's sweetheart Mary Pickford obtained her Reno divorce and immediately returned to California to marry Douglas Fairbanks, Sr.

In 1931, to capitalize on the income potential from the state's new divorce mecca, the Nevada legislature shortened the residency period from six months to a mere six weeks, putting a Reno divorce within the financial reach of the average person. After that point, Reno's divorce business grew steadily, reaching a peak of more than 19,000 divorces a year by 1946.

Visitors to Reno in search of a quickie divorce included debutantes, movie ingénues, preachers, truck drivers, waitresses, businesspeople, and Hollywood executives. Some spent their six-week waiting period living in hotels and boarding houses, whereas others spent their time at one of Reno's "divorce ranches." Male and female guests at a divorce ranch rode horses, swam, or skied (depending on the time of year) during the day and wagered money at Reno's gambling casinos or whiled away the hours at the divorce ranch bar in the evening. Local cowboys who worked at these ranches were on hand to help the female guests forget their troubles and maybe even indulge in a little romance while they waited to end their marriages.

With America's eventual acceptance of divorce and the liberalization of state divorce laws throughout the country, the divorce ranch rode off into the sunset.

If your attorneys are trying to hammer out a negotiated settlement agreement while they prepare for a divorce trial, the process they use is much like the negotiation process we describe in Chapter 14. In other words, communicating via phone and letters, the attorneys try to hammer out resolutions to the outstanding issues in your divorce using a back-and-forth negotiation process. Your attorney consults with you and keeps you up-to-date throughout the negotiations. Eventually, you and your spouse may arrive at an agreement on the final terms of your divorce and avoid a trial.

When your attorney tells you about an offer your spouse may have made to you in order to settle one of the outstanding issues in your divorce or a counteroffer your spouse may have made in response to your offer, consider it carefully so that you can decide how to respond. Your spouse's offer may not be close to what you're legally entitled to, what your spouse can really provide, or what you think you need, but it may be close to what you want. Although your attorney should provide you with his or her opinions about what you should do, the final decision is yours. Chapter 14 provides a series of questions to ask yourself to help you decide how to respond to what your spouse may offer you.

Working Out Your Differences through a Pretrial Conference

If you and your spouse are unable (or unwilling) to resolve your differences by negotiating and your trial preparations move forward, the next step in those preparations is for your attorney and your spouse's attorney to participate in something called a *pretrial conference,* sometimes called a *pretrial hearing.* You and your spouse may or may not attend the pretrial conference.

During the pretrial conference, a judge (who may or may not be the same judge who will hear your case at a trial) listens to the attorneys present information about the unresolved issues in your divorce. The judge may ask the attorneys questions to clarify exactly what your divorce trial will focus on. Also, during the pretrial conference, your attorney and your spouse's attorney review what witnesses they intend to call during the trial and, in cooperation with the judge, they create a schedule for *discovery.* (See the "Gathering in-depth Information" section of this chapter for more information on the discovery process.)

In some jurisdictions, pretrial conferences are mandatory; in other jurisdictions, they're used rarely. And, in some jurisdictions, before a divorcing couple can get a court date for their trial, they must use mediation to try to resolve the outstanding issues in their divorce. This requirement is particularly common in custody battles.

After listening to both attorneys, the judge may signal that he or she is unhappy that you and your spouse haven't been able to agree on the outstanding issues in your divorce. Your attorney may also get the impression that the judge is apt to rule against you on some of those issues. After the pretrial conference, your attorney will convey to you whatever information he or she gained during that meeting and, if your attorney has the impression that the judge wants you to settle your divorce out of court or may not rule in your favor on certain issues, your attorney is likely to strongly encourage you to try to reach an agreement with your spouse instead of moving forward with a divorce trial.

If you and your spouse are unable to reach a negotiated settlement in your divorce prior to the start of your trial, you can come to an agreement even after your trial begins. If you find yourself in this situation and want to know what to anticipate, see the section "Deciding to Settle after Beginning Your Trial Preparations" earlier in this chapter.

Getting Ready for the Trial

Preparing for a divorce trial is time-consuming, which is why trials are so expensive. Your attorney must gather and review all the information related to your case, develop and refine his or her legal strategy, coordinate the production of exhibits, prepare your witnesses to take the stand, and make other preparations.

Deciding on a strategy for the courtroom drama

Preparing for a trial is somewhat like staging a dramatic play, but with you and your spouse as the reluctant "stars." The witnesses who take the stand are your supporting, or not-so-supporting actors, depending on whether they testify for or against you.

To help stage your trial, your attorney outlines a trial strategy. The strategy provides an overview of everything your attorney will do to get you a favorable out-of-court settlement as quickly as possible, assuming that's a realistic goal, or to win your case, assuming it goes all the way to trial.

Your lawyer's strategy is either aggressive or nonaggressive:

- An *aggressive strategy* involves bombarding your spouse with claims of abuse, indifference, child neglect, infidelity, marital instability, hiding or wasting assets, and so on. To a lesser extent, an aggressive strategy can involve pressuring your spouse by filing a lot of pretrial motions, interrogatories, requests for depositions, and requests to produce documents, among other things.

  The tactics used in an aggressive strategy are intended to encourage your spouse to agree to an early out-of-court settlement. Under such pressure, your spouse may agree to settle, especially if his or her financial resources are very limited. On the other hand, such tactics may make your spouse all the more determined to go to trial. Although an aggressive divorce strategy almost always means that you and your spouse will have a lot of bad feeling between you for a long time, if not forever, sometimes it's your only option.

✔ A *nonaggressive strategy* is less hostile than an aggressive one. A nonaggressive strategy relies more on informal discovery to get at the facts of the case and cooperation between attorneys to work out the terms of your divorce.

The strategy that your attorney chooses depends on several factors, including

✔ Your own desires and financial resources

✔ What your attorney thinks is best for your case

✔ The strategy that your spouse's attorney is likely to use

✔ Your attorney's style and the style of your spouse's attorney (some are scrappy street fighters and others are wily tacticians)

If you have concerns about the strategy your attorney proposes, speak up. Find out why the attorney feels that the strategy is appropriate and express any reservations you have about it. If you speak your mind and your attorney's response doesn't quell your concerns, you may want to consider hiring a different attorney. However, changing attorneys, particularly at this stage of your divorce, is expensive and will delay the completion of your divorce. The best way to ensure that you and your attorney see eye to eye on a trial strategy is to carefully select your divorce attorney. Chapter 13 discusses how to screen attorneys to find the right one for you.

Gathering in-depth information

One of the ways that your attorney (and your spouse's attorney) can gather information related to your divorce is through informal or formal *discovery*. *Informal discovery* occurs when you and your spouse, working through your attorneys, willingly share information related to your case with one another. That information may include legal documents, financial records, medical files, and so on. Formal discovery involves the use of legal tools, such as depositions, requests to produce documents, and interrogatories to obtain that same kind of information. Discovery done to prepare for your trial is in addition to any that both attorneys may have already done — formally or informally — to try to work out a negotiated divorce agreement for you and your spouse. Chapter 14 discusses the role that discovery can play when you and your spouse are working with attorneys to negotiate the terms of your divorce. It also provides additional information about the legal tools used during the formal discovery process.

Discovery costs can skyrocket in a litigated divorce. Ask your attorney what he or she can do to keep those costs down.

In order to make the discovery process less overwhelming and less costly, many state legislatures have passed discovery reform laws. These laws' provisions include requiring the parties to any lawsuit to exchange basic information and documentation upfront in the process. Usually, such exchange includes basic financial information, such as bank statements and business records.

One of the reasons your attorney may use the formal discovery process is to find out about the witnesses that your spouse's attorney will be calling. Your attorney may also be able to get a short summary of what each witness knows about your divorce. If you know anything about the backgrounds of your spouse's witnesses that could undermine their credibility on the stand — alcohol or drug problems, spousal abuse, or criminal records — be sure you share that information with your attorney.

If you contest the validity of a prenuptial or postnuptial agreement, a judge has to rule on that issue before he or she can decide how to divide up your marital property and debts or decide whether one of you has to pay the other spousal support. (See Chapter 19 for more on prenuptial and postnuptial agreements.) To save time and money, your attorney should try to resolve this issue as quickly as possible because the judge's decision on the matter determines exactly what issues your trial will address and influences how much discovery your attorney may need to do.

Producing physical evidence

Your attorney may use physical evidence to bolster his or her arguments or to undermine your spouse's position. Your attorney also must figure out how to address physical evidence that's damaging to your case that your spouse's attorney may introduce. Among other things, physical evidence can include

- Financial records
- Police reports
- Property appraisals
- Doctors' records
- Depending on your case, photos, letters, diaries, video tapes, and audio tapes
- Psychological evaluations

Calling all witnesses

Your attorney and your spouse's attorney are likely to call witnesses to testify during your trial. In fact, your spouse's attorney may even put *you* on the stand, and your attorney may put your spouse on the stand.

Attorneys use witnesses to help establish certain facts in a case. For example, if you and your spouse are fighting over the custody of your kids, the attorneys may call witnesses to help establish which of you is the primary caregiver and *go-to-parent* — that is, the parent who takes them to the doctor, attends parent-teacher conferences, takes them to and from day care, feeds them, clothes them, chauffeurs them to and from their extracurricular activities, helps them with their homework, and so on. Doctors, psychologists, teachers, childcare workers, teachers, and neighbors commonly serve as witnesses in this situation.

Before the start of your trial, your attorney interviews your witnesses to get a sense of what they will say on the stand and how they're likely to hold up under cross-examination. Although your attorney won't tell your witnesses what to say, he or she may advise them about the points that they should try to make and the best way to get those points across.

The attorneys may call your friends, family members, co-workers, business associates, and even your children as witnesses. The attorneys may also call *expert witnesses* who have special training, education, or knowledge related to some aspect of your divorce, such as psychologists, business valuation specialists, doctors, real estate agents, social workers, and others with professional expertise.

Expert witnesses expect you to pay them for their time. Depending on the kind of witness and his or her reputation, an expert witness may charge several hundred dollars an hour! If you and your attorney ask these witnesses to do certain things to prepare for testifying — review documents or write a report, for example — they will bill you for the time they take to do that work as well as for their time on the stand.

Courts formally order witnesses to appear and testify in court via *subpoenas.* Subpoenaed witnesses who don't show up are escorted to court by a law enforcement officer or are charged with contempt of court.

Rehearsing for your big day (or days)

Prior to the start of your trial, your attorney should prepare you for what's to come. For example, your attorney may

- ✔ Walk you through the trial process.

- ✔ Review his or her strategy with you.

- ✔ Explain the points that you should make when you testify, even suggesting words or phrases you ought to use to help clarify your thoughts or to add weight to your statements.

- ✔ Review the questions that your spouse's attorney is likely to ask you and help you come up with answers for the more sensitive or difficult ones.

✔ Do some role-playing by grilling you as your spouse's attorney might do if he or she were trying to unnerve you or make you angry. Such role-playing can help build your confidence that you can handle whatever the attorney dishes out.

✔ Advise you on how to dress for your trial and how to behave in the courtroom.

Tell your attorney about any concerns you may have about the trial. Your attorney can probably help alleviate your worries.

Dressing for your role

Appearances count in a courtroom. Your appearance can detract from the real issues in your divorce, undermine your credibility, and even weaken your attorney's legal strategy! Therefore, be sure that you and your attorney talk about how you should dress for your trial.

Most likely, your attorney will suggest that you wear something simple and understated (no loud colors, plaids, or prints and no Ally McBeal-style skirts or form-fitting outfits). If you're a man, your attorney will tell you to wear a suit and, if you're a woman, your attorney will probably advise you to wear a tailored suit or dress with a modest hemline. You should also leave flashy jewelry at home, and avoid wild hairstyles and excessive makeup (after all, this is court, not the '80s). Even if understatement isn't your style, make it yours during the trial.

Remaining calm and collected

Feeling nervous about what to expect as your trial date approaches is normal. One way to alleviate some of those pretrial jitters is to visit the court ahead of time so that you can see the courtroom setup and watch and listen to some other divorce trials. If you know which judge is going to hear your case, try to attend a divorce trial that he or she is presiding over.

You may seethe with anger, quake with fear, or feel totally defeated when you're in the courtroom, especially when you're on the witness stand, but try to keep your cool. Also, be polite to everyone — including your spouse's attorney and, yes, even your spouse!

While you're preparing for your day in court, keep a few things in mind for when you take the witness stand:

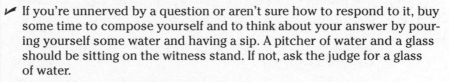

✔ Answer the questions you're asked in as few words as possible. If you give long, involved answers, you may say something that can hurt your case. If the attorney wants to know more, let him or her ask you another question.

✔ Pause before you answer a question so you give yourself time to think about what to say and so your attorney has time to object to the question, if necessary. If your attorney does object and the judge sustains the objection, the judge will tell you not to answer the question. Otherwise, you're expected to answer any question that an attorney asks you.

✔ If you're unnerved by a question or aren't sure how to respond to it, buy some time to compose yourself and to think about your answer by pouring yourself some water and having a sip. A pitcher of water and a glass should be sitting on the witness stand. If not, ask the judge for a glass of water.

✔ Your attorney may tell you not to hold back your tears when you're on the witness stand. Sincere tears can work to your advantage. Fake emotion can work against you, however.

✔ Sit up straight; don't slouch. Keep your hands folded in front of you on your lap and avoid angry hand gestures.

✔ Don't be rude, sarcastic, or argumentative with your spouse's attorney, even if his or her questions are offensive or upsetting. Part of the attorney's strategy may be to make you mad or to get you to break down in tears.

✔ When you get off the stand, don't send dirty looks or expressions of exasperation in the direction of your spouse or your spouse's attorney. Maintain your dignity no matter what.

Understanding the Role of the Benchwarmers: Judges and Juries

Although some states require a judge to decide a divorce trial (this sort of trial is called a *bench trial*), other states let you opt to have a jury trial or a bench trial. When you have the choice, deciding what kind of trial to have is an important strategic decision that you should make with your attorney. If one spouse wants a bench trial and the other wants a jury trial, the spouse wanting a jury trial prevails. However, the basic trial process is the same whether you opt for a judge or a jury trial.

In this section, we tell you what to expect from the decision-makers in both scenarios.

Putting the decisions on one pair of shoulders: The judge

Regardless of whether you have a bench or jury trial, the judge who hears your case is responsible for ensuring that your trial is fair and that the attorneys follow the appropriate trial procedures. He or she also

- Listens to all the testimony and the attorneys' statements
- Reviews any exhibits that the attorneys may enter into evidence
- Rules on any objections that the attorneys may make to the introduction of the evidence
- Resolves any disagreements that may develop between the attorneys and steps in if someone gets unruly
- May ask questions of some of the witnesses
- May take notes during the trial, although a court reporter will be on hand to record every word said

Many family court judges used to be divorce attorneys. Judges tend to have reputations for running a certain type of court and for the way they tend to rule on certain issues. For example, some run their courtrooms with an iron fist; others give attorneys a great deal of leeway; and some tend to favor mothers over fathers in custody battles.

If your attorney knows which judge will hear your case and is familiar with the judge's style and reputation, your attorney should take those things into account when preparing for your trial. If your attorney isn't familiar with the judge, he or she should talk to an attorney who is.

In some jurisdictions, you may not know which judge will hear your case until the day of your trial. Therefore, your attorney won't be able to prepare with a particular judge in mind.

Taking a hiatus from the day job: Jury

Before your attorney and your spouse's attorney can begin presenting their cases in a jury trial, they must select the members of the jury from a list developed by the district clerk in your jurisdiction. The attorneys select the jurors they want through the *voire dire* process. This process involves asking the potential jurors questions in order to assess their biases and prejudices so that the attorneys can decide who they want and who they don't want on the jury. (Each attorney gets to eliminate a certain number of potential jurors.)

After a jury has been selected, the judge swears in the jury members. Jury members are expected to show up on time each day for your trial, to listen carefully to the testimony, and to follow any instructions that the judge gives them. They may or may not be allowed to take notes during your trial, depending on the judge's rules for his or her courtroom.

After the attorneys have presented all the evidence in your trial and each attorney has made his or her final arguments, the jury begins deliberating on the issues in your divorce according to the judge's instructions. The jury members conduct their deliberations in the jury room after selecting a jury *foreperson* — the person who's in charge of the jury's deliberations and decision-making. If the jury has any questions about certain aspects of the testimony during your divorce trial, the jury foreperson writes them down and sends them to the judge. The judge answers the questions in the courtroom in the presence of the jury as well as you, your spouse, and your attorneys.

After the jury completes its deliberations, the jury foreperson lets the judge know, and the jury members are called into the courtroom to announce their decision(s) to you, your spouse, and your attorneys. The jury may reach its decision(s) after just an hour or two deliberating the issues, or they may take a longer amount of time — a day, several days, or even longer. How long the jury spends deliberating depends on the complexity of the issues in your divorce as well as on how well the jury members work together.

Life in the Courtroom

Weeks, maybe even months, after you or your spouse files for divorce, you finally get your day in court (assuming that you haven't reached an out-of-court settlement yet).

In the courtroom, you and your spouse sit with your respective attorneys at tables directly in front of the judge. If you haven't seen or spoken with your spouse in a while, you may feel unnerved and upset having to be in the same room with him or her; on the other hand, you may feel just plain glad that your day in court has finally arrived and that you will be divorced soon.

In case you're wondering, the courtroom dramas that you've read about in books or seen on TV rarely occur. Instead, as anyone who's watched Court TV knows, trials often move slowly with a lot of starts and stops. And, at times, they can be boring and confusing.

No matter how long you think you'll be sitting in front of the judge, never bring food, beverages, or reading materials into a courtroom. Doing such things isn't allowed in court, and the court bailiff will tell you to stop doing them. Furthermore, eating, reading, and so on while you're in court signals that you don't respect the legal process, which can ultimately hurt your case.

Although some trials take some unexpected detours, they all follow a basic sequence of events. To help you make sense of what's happening in your trial, here's a brief rundown of what to expect:

1. **Opening statements.**

   Each attorney makes an initial statement to the judge about what he or she will prove during the trial. The plaintiff's (whoever initiated your divorce) attorney goes first. These statements set the stage for the evidence and arguments to come. However, one or both attorneys may elect to waive making opening statements if your divorce trial is resolving just a few issues.

2. **The plaintiff's or petitioner's case.**

   The plaintiff's attorney presents his or her case first. The attorney presents evidence why the spouse he or she is representing should get what the spouse wants. To do that, the attorney may call witnesses to the stand and question them. Next, the defendant's attorney questions the witnesses during a process called *cross-examination*.

3. **Redirect and re-cross examinations.**

   During your trial, after the attorneys examine and cross-examine a witness, the witness may have to answer follow-up questions during redirect and re-cross examinations. Redirect and re-cross examinations are most likely to occur when a witness damages the plaintiff's case during cross-examination and needs to be *rehabilitated,* that is, something he or she said needs clarified or explained in a way that's more favorable to the plaintiff.

4. **The defendant's case.**

   The attorney for the spouse who's the defendant presents his or her case following the same procedures used by the plaintiff's attorney.

5. **Rebuttal by plaintiff.**

   After the defendant's case has been presented to the court, a *rebuttal* may or may not take place. Rebuttal allows the plaintiff's attorney to respond to comments the defense made. However, the attorney cannot introduce any new evidence during rebuttal.

6. **Surrebuttal by defendant.**

   Surrebuttals are rare in a divorce trial but, when they do occur, they provide the defendant's attorney an opportunity to deny or counter what the plaintiff's attorney said in rebuttal. The defense attorney cannot address anything else during surrebuttal.

7. **Closing arguments.**

   During closing arguments, both attorneys get one last chance to make their cases. The plaintiff's attorney goes first. If only a few issues need to be resolved, the attorneys may decide to waive final arguments, although that is rare.

8. **The ruling.**

    Depending on the complexity of the case, the judge in a bench trial may issue his or her decision right away or may take time to deliberate and return with a decision later. If your case has more than one issue that needs to be decided, the judge makes multiple rulings. If a jury is deciding the outcome of the trial, the jury begins its deliberations after closing arguments. When the jury finishes its deliberations, the jury's decisions are announced in the courtroom. The jury, the judge, or a court staff person may announce them.

Listen attentively to the courtroom proceedings. Take notes and, when you hear someone say something that you know isn't the truth, let your attorney know. The best way to do so is by passing your attorney a note rather than whispering in your attorney's ear. Whispering may make your attorney miss important testimony, and someone on your spouse's side may overhear your comments.

In most states, after you've heard how the judge rules on the issues in your divorce, you have a short period of time, typically from 10 to 20 days (although the specific amount of time varies by state) to file a *motion to reconsider* with the court if you're unhappy with something that the judge decided. (You do not have this right if you had a jury trial.) If you file this motion, you're asking the judge to revisit the decision with the hope that he or she will rule differently. However, unless you can prove that the judge made a mathematical error, overlooked important evidence, or misapplied the law, the judge is extremely unlikely to change his or her mind. If the judge denies the motion to reconsider or hears the motion and decides that his or her ruling was correct, you can always appeal. The section "Making an Appeal" later in this chapter explains the appeals process.

Following the Judgment

Although you may breathe a sigh of relief (or shed some tears) when you hear the judge's (or the jury's) decision(s), your divorce isn't completely over when you walk out of the courtroom. You still have some work to do before your divorce is final. For instance, your attorney and your spouse's attorney must prepare a final divorce agreement and file it with the court, and you and your spouse must do whatever the agreement requires of you. For example, you may have to transfer assets to your spouse, pay off certain debts, and so on.

Putting the terms of the divorce in writing

After the judge issues his or her decision or the jury's decision(s) is announced, usually the attorney for whichever spouse filed for divorce drafts the *divorce decree* (a legal term for the written summary of what the judge ruled and of anything that you and your spouse may have agreed to on your own). The other attorney reviews the draft judgment and notifies the attorney who prepared the draft whether any changes are necessary. At this point, the changes, if any, should be very minor. When a final draft of the divorce judgment is ready, the judge must sign it. This usually happens between 10 and 20 days after the decision by the judge or jury.

After the judge approves your divorce decree, expect the following to happen:

- ✔ The provisions of the decree usually replace any temporary pretrial court orders.

- ✔ Your attorney gives you a copy of your signed divorce agreement. Now you're officially divorced. You will receive a copy of the judgment at a later date after the court processes all the paperwork. Make sure that your copy is certified (which means the copy will usually be pressed with a seal or a stamp).

- ✔ The attorney for the spouse who initiated your divorce files a record of your divorce in the vital records section of your state's Public Health Department.

Tending to final details

Yes, your divorce is finally over and, for better or worse, you're single again. You and your now ex-spouse must comply with all the decree's provisions, including transferring and returning property, paying money, adhering to a specific visitation schedule, and any other terms that may be in your divorce decree.

You and your attorney should review the details of the judge's decision and any aspects of your divorce that you may have negotiated with your now ex-spouse so that you understand your legal obligations to your ex as well as what you're entitled to. Another reason to review the decree carefully is so you're clear about any actions you may need to take as a result of your divorce. For example, you may need to

- ✔ Transfer titles, deeds of trust, and other ownership documents.

- ✔ Exchange cash and other valuables. If your divorce was hostile and you anticipate further problems with your former spouse, you may want to make this exchange in front of a neutral third party so that neither of you can accuse the other of dishonesty.

- ✔ Amend your insurance policies, as necessary, or purchase new ones.

- Revise your will (or write a new one) and review the rest of your estate planning for possible changes now that you're divorced.

- Notify your creditors and the three national credit-reporting agencies about your name change, if you take back your maiden name. (You can find information about how to contact the credit-reporting agencies in Chapter 3.)

You also need to notify the Social Security Administration (SSA) and your employer about your name change so that your earnings are properly reported to the SSA and so that it records that information properly. To get a form to report your name change to the SSA, go to www.ssa. gov or your local SSA office. You need to provide the SSA with identification that shows your old name and your new name; for example, you need a copy of your marriage certificate and your divorce decree. When the SSA receives all the necessary information, it sends you a new SSA card that reflects your name change.

Making an Appeal

If you're unhappy with some aspect of the judge's decision, you can appeal it. But, appealing takes even more time and money and means more involvement with the court. Furthermore, you must file your appeal within a certain period of time; how long you have to file it depends on your state. Your attorney can tell you how long you have to file an appeal, and he or she can also advise you of your chances of prevailing in an appeal case.

You can't appeal a judge's decision just because you want to. You must have a legal basis for your appeal. For example, your attorney may try to use any of the following to justify the need for an appeal, among others: Your spouse withheld information; a witness for your spouse lied on the stand; a legal procedure wasn't followed appropriately during your trial or the judge misinterpreted a law related to your divorce.

Time, money, and more court involvement aren't the only factors you should consider when deciding whether or not to file an appeal. You should also consider these facts:

- A court may not hear your appeal for months.

- While you're waiting to learn the outcome of your appeal, you, your spouse, and your kids are living in a sort of limbo. And, if the appeals court does overturn the judge's decision, its action makes you married again. The result: You're still not divorced, so you face yet another divorce trial.

✔ Everyone in your family may already be emotionally worn out by your first divorce trial. A second one may be more than some members of your family can bear.

✔ You may have to find a new attorney to help you with your appeal, especially if your current attorney thinks that filing an appeal is pointless given the facts of your case.

✔ The appeals court may not throw out the judge's decision. Even if it does, you have no guarantee that you'll be happy with the outcome of your second trial. In fact, you can end up with a judgment you like even less than the first one!

Rather than trying to get the judge's decision overturned, if you don't like one or more provisions in it, you can leave the judgment in place and ask the court to modify those specific provisions by filing a *petition for modification*. Such a process is faster and less expensive than trying to get a judgment overturned and, if you're successful, going to trial again. Chapter 18 talks about modifications to a divorce decree.

Part V
Looking Toward the Future Now That Your Divorce Is Final

The 5th Wave   By Rich Tennant

@RICHTENNANT

"Usually people recite passages from Robert Frost poems during a marriage ceremony. This being a second marriage I guess we shouldn't be surprised to hear quotes from The Geneva Convention and the Miranda Decision."

In this part . . .

In this part of the book, we help prepare you for life after divorce. We advise you on taking care of any final details related to your divorce, on examining your estate-planning needs, and on evaluating your finances. We also provide suggestions for getting the education you need so you can find a good-paying job, and we offer suggestions that can help you become comfortable as a newly single person and a single parent, too.

We alert you to some of the more common (and serious) problems that newly divorced people face and offer advice and resources for dealing with those problems. Finally, for more peace of mind the next time you marry, we give you information on prenuptial and postnuptial agreements (they're not just for rich people!).

Chapter 17

Handling Practical Matters after Divorce

. . . .

. . . .

*Y*our divorce is final, so now what? Depending on the details of your divorce decree, also called a *final judgment of divorce,* you may have plenty to take care of in the way of paperwork and payments. As Chapter 16 explains, the decree stipulates everything you and your spouse agreed to in your divorce or that the judge decided. Also, you face the challenge of managing your own finances, maybe finding a job outside the home, and building a new social life for yourself or resuming your old one. And, if you have sole or joint custody of your children, you also have to figure out how to care for them as a single parent.

All these responsibilities may sound like a formidable challenge but, with the right information and a positive attitude, you can put the pieces of your life back together again. In fact, you can even create a life for yourself that's more satisfying than you ever imagined it could be!

In this chapter, we help you move toward that life by providing you with the information and advice you need to tie up the loose ends of your divorce and to face the challenges ahead. This chapter highlights estate-planning issues to consider, offers information that can help you achieve your educational and career goals, and suggests things you should do to manage your money wisely, no matter how much (or how little) income you have. This chapter also offers some valuable advice about post-divorce parenting and about developing new friendships.

Doing What Your Divorce Decree Requires

Read the details of your divorce decree carefully and do exactly what it requires of you. For example, the decree may require you to accomplish specific tasks by certain dates, such as closing a joint-checking account, paying off certain debts for your ex-spouse, or returning your former spouse's CD collection. You may also have to begin making spousal support and/or child-support payments by a certain date every month. Depending on the terms of your divorce, you may also have to take care of other details (some of which can be a little complicated), such as transferring legal ownership of property to your spouse, selling assets, and so on.

If you thumb your nose at whatever legal obligations (and that's exactly what they are) the divorce decree sets out for you, the battles that may have plagued the end of your marriage are likely to continue. Even worse, your ex-spouse may take you to court if you don't hold up your end of the divorce bargain, which means more involvement with lawyers, more legal expenses, and more hassles and emotional upset. If you're unhappy with something in your divorce decree, comply with it anyway. If you want the terms of your divorce modified due to changes in your life or in your former spouse's life, the court may agree to the change depending on your state and on the nature of the modification you are requesting. For example, most states allow modifications related to child custody, visitation, or child support, but only some states permit changes related to spousal support. Requesting a modification requires that you file a petition with the court. Then, a court hearing follows to consider your request. (See Chapter 18 to find out more details on modifying your divorce decree.)

If your attorney doesn't send you a letter stating exactly what final responsibilities he or she will take care of as spelled out in your divorce decree and which ones are your obligation to handle, ask your attorney to prepare such a letter for you. Use it as a checklist to make sure that you don't overlook any of your legal responsibilities.

Transferring assets

If your former spouse becomes the sole owner of certain real property that you owned together — your home, land, or rental property, for example — you must transfer your interest in it by giving your ex a signed copy of the deed to the asset. The deed will later be recorded in the public records of the county courthouse where the property is located.

If the transferred property has an outstanding debt associated with it, such as a mortgage or a home equity loan, you're still liable for that debt, even if your divorce decree says that your former spouse has to pay it off. (See Chapter 8 for a discussion of the legal actions that you can take to protect yourself if your ex-spouse defaults on a debt associated with the property you transferred.)

If your divorce decree obligates your former spouse to pay you a substantial amount of money, securing that debt with an asset — just as a bank would do if you borrowed a substantial amount of money from it — is a good idea. That way, you increase the likelihood of actually receiving what you're owed. For example, if your former spouse gets the house and, in return, has to pay you $80,000 over the next ten years, you can secure that debt by placing an $80,000 lien on the house. That way, if your ex doesn't pay the money you're legally entitled to according to the terms of your divorce, he or she won't be able to sell, borrow against, or transfer the house without paying you first, assuming that you recorded the lien at the county courthouse.

Another option you have if you have a lien on the house and your former spouse falls behind on his or her payments to you or doesn't make them at all is to foreclose on the home and sell it to get the money that you're owed. This option can be good if you have enough equity in the house that the sale will provide you with sufficient funds to

- ✔ Pay off the mortgage
- ✔ Pay the costs of foreclosing on the house and selling it
- ✔ Provide you with some or all of the money that you're entitled to according to your divorce decree

If you transfer stocks, bonds, or mutual funds to your former spouse, you do *not* have to pay a capital gains tax if their value has appreciated since you first purchased them.

States differ in their requirements for transferring the legal ownership of vehicles, boats, and motorcycles. Your attorney should be able to advise you on your state's requirements.

Paying off debts

If your former spouse takes over some of your marital debts, notifying your creditors in writing of that fact and asking them to transfer the debts to your ex's name is a good idea. Although the creditors aren't legally obligated to comply with your request and, although they can still collect from you if your former spouse doesn't pay, your letters help underscore who's supposed to satisfy those debts. And, as a friendly reminder of what you expect, send your ex a copy of those letters.

If you want to be sure that your ex-spouse is paying off the debts that used to be yours, see whether you can get your ex to provide you with proof of each payment — a canceled check will do. If the debts are still in your name, you can also call the creditors your ex is supposed to be paying to confirm that payment was made, or you can go to the creditors' Internet sites and check for yourself. Most banks and credit card companies provide this information online.

Arranging for your own health insurance

Under the provisions of COBRA (Consolidated Omnibus Budget Reconciliation Act), your divorce decree may allow you to remain on your former spouse's health insurance plan for up to three years, giving you time to get your own health coverage. (You may or may not have to pay the cost of your coverage, depending on the terms of your divorce.) However, continuing your coverage doesn't happen automatically; you must notify your ex's employer of your intentions within 60 days of your divorce becoming final.

If your former spouse agrees to pay the cost of your COBRA health insurance benefits, ask him or her to provide you with a monthly proof of payment so that you're assured that your coverage doesn't lapse due to nonpayment. The same advice applies if your former spouse maintains life insurance on your behalf.

Protecting your pension rights

If your divorce judgment gives you the right to collect a portion of your former spouse's pension benefits, profit-sharing money, 401(k) funds, or other deferred retirement income when your ex becomes eligible to retire, your attorney must prepare a special legal document called a QDRO (Qualified Domestic Relations Order) — a special type of court order — during your divorce. Without it, you cannot be certain that you'll get your share of those moneys when the time comes. Your attorney sends the completed QDRO to the bank or brokerage firm where the funds are located or to the employer who's administering your ex's retirement benefits. (Chapter 8 provides a more complete explanation of QDROs.)

Rethinking Your Estate Planning

If you had a will when you were married, you need to revisit that legal document now that you're divorced.

In some states when you get divorced, your entire will or possibly only the part(s) that relate to your former spouse are revoked automatically. If your state doesn't apply either option, you probably want to excise all mention of your spouse from your will. Furthermore, if you set up a trust in your will with your ex as the beneficiary or if you created a living trust and made him or her the beneficiary, you no doubt want to change that estate-planning document, too. An estate-planning attorney can advise you about your state's legal requirements for changing or voiding any or all of your estate-planning documents.

Other estate-planning documents you may need to revisit include

- Durable powers of attorney for finances and healthcare, if you gave those powers to your spouse while you were married.

- Life-insurance policies, if your former spouse is the beneficiary of those policies.

- Other assets for which you may have designated your former spouse as beneficiary. Those assets may include your IRA, retirement plan, and some types of bank accounts.

For an easy-to-understand primer about estate planning, check out _The Will Kit,_ 2nd Edition, by John Ventura (Dearborn Financial Publishing, Inc.). To help make a potentially intimidating subject interesting and even fun, the book features anecdotes about the estate-planning successes and failures of such notables as John F. Kennedy, Jr.; John Lennon; Marilyn Monroe; Humphrey Bogart; and Elvis Presley.

If you don't have a will, now's the time to write one

Getting divorced is a good excuse for writing a will if you don't have one already. A will is an essential legal document if you own certain types of assets and care about who will inherit them after your death. Without a will, the laws of your state determine which of your legal heirs — your children, parents, siblings, and so on — inherits those assets, which means that they may go to people you would prefer not inherit them. Because an ex-spouse is not a legal heir, he or she will not inherit from you.

If your divorce agreement gave you assets that you and your former spouse owned _jointly with the right of survivorship_ — real estate, for example — and the ownership documents were never changed to make you their sole owner, when you die, your ex will automatically own them 100 percent.

You cannot transfer certain types of assets through a will, including assets for which you have already designated a beneficiary. For example, when you purchase a life insurance policy, you must indicate who you want to receive the policy proceeds when you die — your beneficiary(ies). After you're deceased, the insurance company that insured you pays the proceeds to your beneficiary(ies), regardless of what your will may say about the money. An asset that you own with someone else, like *joint tenants with the right of survivorship,* is another example of an asset that you cannot transfer to someone using your will. When you die, that asset automatically goes to your co-owner(s).

If you have minor children, you have other extremely important reasons for drafting a will:

- ✔ **To designate the adult you want to raise your kids if you die or become mentally or physically incapacitated while they're still minors.** This person is called a *personal guardian.* Most likely, if you're the custodial parent and your former spouse is still alive, he or she would raise them after your death. However, if he or she were already deceased or weren't able to raise them for some reason (like the court decides that he or she is an unfit parent; your ex is in prison; your ex is very ill, and so on), the court will decide who that person will be. And the court may choose someone you don't like or trust to raise your kids. This person could be one of your family members or a close friend or, if no one with a relationship to you were willing to raise them, your children would be placed in foster care until they could be adopted.

  Another reason to designate a personal guardian for your children is if you don't want your former spouse raising them. For example, you may believe that he or she wouldn't do a good job. Be sure to provide the executor of your will with a written statement of your rationale for wanting someone other than your former spouse to raise your kids in the event of your death. (An *executor* is the adult responsible for getting your estate through the probate process after you die.)

- ✔ **To manage the property you've left to your minor children in your will, assuming that the property is worth more than what your state says a minor child can own without having an adult in charge of the assets.** This person is called a *property guardian.* Many parents name the same person to serve as their children's property and personal guardian. However, doing so doesn't always make sense because each job requires quite different characteristics and abilities. For a personal guardian, you want someone who's nurturing, affectionate, a fair disciplinarian, and who shares your values. However, the person you choose for that role may not have the financial management skills and know-how that you want in a property guardian.

All states limit the total value of the assets that minor children can own and handle by themselves. In most states, the maximum amount ranges from about $2,500 to $5,000. If you use a will to leave your minor children more than your state's maximum, their property guardian will manage their assets on their behalf until your children become legal adults. If you don't name a property guardian in your will, the court will name someone to play that role. Most likely, the court would designate your ex-spouse, but the court could name another relative, a friend, a bank, an attorney, and so on instead.

Other estate planning you should consider

You have other options in addition to writing a will for making sure that your minor children are financially provided for if you die while they're still minors. In this section, we highlight some of those alternatives. To find out which ones are most appropriate for you, talk with an estate-planning attorney. Remember that using any of the options discussed in this section does not eliminate the need to write a will to designate a personal guardian for your minor children.

Custodial accounts

One easy and inexpensive option is to set up a *custodial account* for each child according to the terms of the federal Uniform Gifts to Minors Act or Uniform Transfers to Minors Act. You can set up the account at a bank or at a brokerage house, and the process for setting it up is quick and inexpensive. You can make *intervivos gifts* (gifts that you make while you're alive) of assets that you own to each child and transfer them into their custodial accounts. For each account, you must designate an adult *custodian* who manages the account assets and possibly disperses money generated by those assets to your children while they're minors. (While you're alive, you can be the custodian for each account you set up.) When your children become legal adults, they get full control of the assets in their custodial accounts although, in some states, you can set age 25 as the age at which that happens.

Under the Uniform Gifts to Minors Act, you can transfer only cash, securities, and insurance policies to a custodial account. Under the Uniform Transfers to Minors Act, you can transfer any kind of asset to a custodial account, including real estate.

Testamentary trust

You can include a *testamentary trust* in your will. This type of trust exists only on paper while you're alive and is activated by your death. In your trust document, you indicate what assets you want transferred to the trust upon your death. The assets can include jewelry, fine furniture, money, real estate, and so on. You must designate a trustee to manage the trust assets after the trust is activated. The trustee can be someone you know, a trust company, or a bank-trust department. One of the advantages of a testamentary trust is that you can control when your children take possession of the assets you've left to them in the trust after they become legal adults — something you can't do with only a will. For example, you can indicate in the trust document that your children cannot take control of the assets until they reach age 25.

Living trust

Another kind of trust you may want to set up for your minor children is a living trust. This type of trust exists outside of your will, unlike a testamentary trust. A *living trust* is a legal entity that you establish to hold and manage assets for one or more of your beneficiaries. You can transfer assets into the trust while you're alive, and you can also arrange to transfer certain assets into it after your death. You must designate a *trustee* to oversee and manage the assets held in the trust for the benefit of your children. While you're alive, you can be the trustee, but whomever you designate as your successor trustee takes over after your death if your children are still minors. A key benefit of a living trust is that it maximizes the amount of control you have over when your children receive the trust assets as well as what they can do with the assets.

A living trust can be either revocable or irrevocable. When you set up an *irrevocable living trust* and transfer assets to it, you cannot remove any of the assets from the trust, cancel the trust, or make any other changes to the trust. The primary benefit of an irrevocable living trust is that it helps you reduce the amount of estate taxes you may have to pay. A *revocable living trust* is much more versatile and flexible because you can change anything about the trust that you want. Therefore, revocable living trusts tend to be more popular than irrevocable living trusts, even though they provide you with no estate-tax benefits.

If you want to use a living trust to help care for your children after your death (or in the event of your incapacitation), you must decide exactly what kind of living trust to set up. You have many options, including a *common trust* that benefits all your children, a *separate trust* for each child, and a *special needs trust* for a child who's mentally or physically incapacitated. Your estate-planning needs can help you decide which type of living trust is best for you and your children.

Life insurance

You can name your children as the beneficiaries of a life insurance policy that you purchase. If you die while they're still minors, their property guardian will manage the policy proceeds on their behalf. Alternatively, you can provide that, upon your death, the proceeds get transferred to a living trust that you've set up for your children. If that happens, whomever you designated as trustee of the trust manages the other assets.

Other estate-planning options

Naming your children the beneficiaries of your employee benefits plan or IRA are two other ways to take care of your minor children if you die. Again, depending on the value of the benefits, you may have to name an adult to manage them for your children. Depending on whether you arrange to have the benefits paid directly to your children, placed in a trust, or deposited in a custodial account, the adult you name will be the formally titled property guardian, trustee, or account custodian. Your estate-planning attorney, financial advisor, or plan administrator can provide you with helpful advice on this topic.

Assessing Your Financial Situation

If you're like most divorced people, you probably ended up with something less than what you'd hoped for from your divorce. For example, you may have received fewer marital assets, been saddled with more debt, or received less child support and spousal support than you had hoped for. On the other hand, if you're the one making those payments, you may be paying more than you wanted to.

Divorce tends to have a significantly bigger negative financial effect on women than men. Many reasons account for this discrepancy, including the fact that most women end up with custody of the children, the amount of support that they receive is often inadequate (or they don't receive any at all), and working women tend to earn less than men.

Whatever your situation, now that you're divorced, money will probably be tight. Therefore, developing a budget is a good idea so that you can figure out just how much you can afford to spend each month and where you should be cutting back. Your budget will also tell you whether you need to find a better-paying job. You can use the budget form in Chapter 5 to prepare a budget that reflects your current situation.

After you've filled in all your income and expenses on the budget form and compared your current total income to your current total outgo, you may realize that to stay financially afloat, you need to reduce your expenses and begin working outside the home or find a job that pays more than the one you have now (or get a second one). If your children are old enough, ask them for their ideas regarding how they can cut back a little or earn some money to pay for the extras they may want. Maybe they can work a part-time job after school or on weekends to pay for a new pair of athletic shoes, a prom dress, a trip to Florida for spring break, or their portion of gasoline and insurance expenses (if they drive, of course).

If you have enough income to cover your monthly expenditures and debts, focus on paying off your highest-interest debts first. The more interest you pay to a creditor, the longer it will take you to get out of debt because a large percentage of each of your payments on a high-interest debt goes to paying the interest, not the amount of money that you financed. High-interest debts usually include retail store charges, finance company loans, and some credit card debts, too, depending on the terms of the credit cards.

Finding a financial planner

Some of you may be lucky enough to exit your marriage with enough money and other assets to meet your day-to-day financial needs and to help finance your future. However, even though you may not have to worry much about how to pay your bills, you do have to decide how best to maximize the value of your assets so that you can achieve the short-term and long-term goals you have set for yourself and your children.

To best achieve those goals, you may need a financial planner to help you plan and implement an appropriate investment strategy. When you're looking for a financial planner, steer clear of those who sell specific financial products (like insurance) and who make their money from the commissions they get by selling those products. Because these types of financial professionals have a monetary incentive to push you toward what they're selling, their advice and recommendations are apt to be biased and may not be in your best interest.

Working with a financial advisor who makes money by charging you a percentage of the total value of the assets he or she manages or invests for you or hiring a financial planner who charges you by the hour for advice and assistance are far better alternatives. This type of financial planner is more apt to consider *all* your investment alternatives — mutual funds, stocks, bonds, real estate, and so on — than an advisor who makes his or her money by earning a commission from selling you specific financial products. Therefore, the planner who makes commission on selling products has a financial motivation to encourage you to purchase those products even if they're not what you really need.

Shop for a financial advisor just as you would for any other professional you'd hire to help you make important decisions. Get recommendations from trusted friends and family members, your CPA, divorce attorney, and so forth. Then interview several possible candidates. Come to the interviews with a set of questions and learn about the credentials of each financial advisor you interview. And don't forget to get the advisors' references *and* to check them!

Consider wiping out high-interest credit card debt by selling an asset you don't need, transferring your high-interest credit card debts to a lower interest card (as long as the interest rate will not escalate before you anticipate being able to pay off the new debt), or by applying for a bank loan to consolidate or pay off your debt. Getting a bank loan is not a good idea unless the loan's interest rate is lower than the interest rates on the debts you intend to pay off with the loan proceeds. If you get a home equity loan to wipe out high-interest debt, be aware that if you cannot repay the loan, you can lose your home because your home serves as the loan collateral.

As a general rule, your mortgage payment (principal and interest) shouldn't consume any more than 25 percent of your pretax income, and your debt shouldn't exceed 40 percent of that income.

If you're obligated to pay spousal or child support, managing your money is particularly important because, if your former spouse takes you to court to collect support you haven't paid to him/her in the past, arguing that you "just ran out of money" won't cut it with any judge!

For help putting your budget on a diet or increasing your financial IQ, get in touch with a financial planner or a nonprofit debt-counseling organization affiliated with the National Foundation for Credit Counseling, most of which are the Consumer Credit Counseling Service (CCCS) offices. (To locate a financial planner, see the sidebar "Finding a financial planner" in this chapter.) These offices offer low-cost or no-cost debt counseling, money management, and budgeting assistance. Also, if you owe more than you think you can pay given your monthly income, a CCCS counselor may be able to help you negotiate lower monthly payments to your creditors. If you can't find a CCCS office in your local phone book, call the organization's national office at 800-388-2227 or go to www.nfcc.org.

Finding a Job or Landing a Better One

After you take a hard look at your budget and assess all your options, you may realize that becoming financially solvent or living more than a subsistence lifestyle is impossible unless you increase your income by working outside the home or finding a better paying job.

If you're entering the work world for the first time or if you haven't worked outside the home for many years, you may be unsure about what kind of career you're suited for or you may not have a good sense of what kinds of careers are available to you. If this is your situation, meeting with a career counselor or career coach can be a good idea. He or she can assess your job skills and interests, suggest things that you can do to make yourself more marketable, and advise you about the types of jobs for which you may be suited. A career counselor or coach may also help you prepare a resume and hone your interview skills.

If you can't afford to pay for a career counselor or coach, your state's public employment office or job service office may offer job counseling, skills assessment, and résumé assistance. Also, your local community college may offer a course for people who are interested in entering the work world but have few, if any, job skills and little work experience.

If you're not sure what career path to take, check out *Cool Careers For Dummies,* 2nd Edition, by Marty Nemko, Paul Edwards, and Sarah Edwards (Wiley). *What Color Is Your Parachute?* by Richard Bolles (Ten Speed Press) is a classic must-read for job-seekers who want to analyze their strengths and weaknesses prior to joining the work world or are making a career change. Bolles also has a Web site, www.jobhuntersbible.com, which is a companion site to the book. At the site, you can take a wide variety of tests to assess your skills and interests, get assistance with your resume, find out about how to learn about job openings you may be qualified for, which job sites are the best ones, among other things.

To find information on the "hottest jobs" — meaning the jobs with the best growth outlook — get a copy of the *Occupational Outlook Handbook,* published annually by the federal Labor Department's Bureau of Labor Statistics (BLS). Go to www.bls.gov/emp to download the handbook and other BLS publications.

Getting the education you need to qualify for a good job

If you already have a job but need to increase your income, finding more lucrative work may simply be a matter of updating your resume and conducting a job search, especially if you have good job skills and strong credentials. But, if you're entering the work world for the first time, are reentering it after a long absence and your skills are outdated or very limited, or you want to change careers, achieving your employment goals probably means that you need job training or additional education.

Financing your education

Depending on your job skills and education level, achieving your career goals may require getting a degree from a four-year college or university, completing a community college program, or attending a trade or vocational school (see the next section of this chapter for more on choosing a good trade or vocational school). But financing the cost of your education can be a challenge when money is tight, especially if you're trying to put money away for your children's educations. The federal Department of Education's loan, grant, or work-study programs may be just what you need to help fund the cost of your tuition, books, and other education-related expenses.

We recommend reading *College Financial Aid For Dummies* by Dr. Herm Davis and Joyce Lain Kennedy (Wiley), which helps you make sense of your financial aid options and fill out financial aid forms without making costly mistakes. *The Student Guide to Federal Financial Aid,* published by the U.S. Department of Education (DOE), offers a good overview of the full range of federal educational assistance programs that the DOE offers and also describes the application process for each program. You can order a copy of this publication by calling 800-433-3243 or you can download it at www.ed.gov.

Some states offer their own educational assistance programs. Call your state's department of education to find out whether your state is one of them. In addition to government educational assistance programs, you may be eligible for a special scholarship or grant. (You can find a directory of scholarships and grants at your local library or by doing an Internet search.) A financial aid officer at the college or university you're interested in can tell you about the school's tuition-assistance programs.

If you're going to college with the goal of getting a good-paying job after you graduate, select your program of study carefully. Some college majors provide a bigger and more immediate financial payoff than others. Talk to a career counselor or to an advisor at the school you would like to attend to find out which careers are apt to earn you a good living in the future. They tend to change over time.

Choosing a trade or vocational school

You can find good and bad trade and vocational schools. Attending one of the good ones can be a great way to gain very specific job skills that can translate into a well-paying job fairly quickly. But going to one of the bad ones can take your money and give you little in return.

Before you enroll in a trade or vocational school, explore what your community college has to offer. You may be able to obtain the same education there for a fraction of the cost that a trade or vocational school offers. A trade or vocational school is set up to make a profit, whereas a community college is a nonprofit entity funded by students' tuition and local taxes and is specifically established to provide students with an affordable education.

The following tips can help you choose a trade or vocational school program that will give you a quality education for a fair price:

- ✔ Ask for printed information from the school about the program that you're considering enrolling in, the cost of the program, the instructors, and so forth. If the school doesn't have such information, don't enroll there.

- ✔ Visit the school you're interested in and ask to sit in on some of the classes you would take if you were a student there. Check out the condition of the classrooms, the computers, and other classroom resources. Is there enough equipment for all the students? Do things look well cared for? Is the equipment state-of-the-art?

- ✔ Find out whether the school is accredited and/or licensed. Get the name of the accrediting organization(s) and/or licensing agency. For example, the school may be accredited by your state's board of higher education or by another licensing or regulatory agency that accredits trade and vocational schools. Contact the accrediting organization(s) and/or licensing agency to determine that the school is in good standing with them.

- ✔ Contact your state attorney general's office of consumer protection and the Better Business Bureau in the town where the school is located to find out whether the organization has received a lot of complaints about the school.

- ✔ Ask for a copy of the contract you would have to sign if you enrolled in the school. Read it carefully. Among other things, check to see whether you can cancel the contract and, if you can, what you have to do to get your money back and how long it will take. Steer clear of any school that doesn't provide you with a copy of its contract or that doesn't have a contract.

✔ Talk to students who are enrolled in the program you're interested in as well as students who have completed the program. Get their opinions about the quality of school. Ask the graduates how well the program prepared them for a career; if they're working in the field in which they were trained; and, if they are, what kind of salary they're earning.

✔ Talk with the human resources or personnel departments of the companies you'd like to work for after you complete your education to get their opinions of the trade or vocational school program you're considering. Ask them whether they'd be more or less likely to hire you knowing that you had completed that program (or do they recommend any others instead)?

✔ Find out about the kind of job-finding assistance the school offers its students and ask about the school's placement rate. According to the Accrediting Commission of Career School and Colleges of Technology, most trade and technical schools have a placement rate of at least 70 percent.

✔ Ask about the school's default rate. This rate is the percentage of students who attend the school, borrow money to finance their education, and then can't afford to pay back the loan. A school with a high default rate may not be doing a good job of preparing its students to get a job or it may be preparing students to work in jobs where there is little demand.

Students who attend disreputable or unaccredited trade or vocational schools are often unable to find the employment they need to repay their student loans. If you default on your student loan, the lender may have a legal right to place a lien on property you own after getting a court judgment against you. To be on the safe side, call the Federal Information Center at 800-688-9889 to find out about the loan default rate of a particular school.

Looking for the right job

You can use many approaches to find a job. The right method for finding employment depends on your particular job skills, work experience, and the kind of job you want. Here are some job-search methods to consider:

✔ **Visit Internet job sites.** Some of these sites are www.careerbuilder.com, www.hotjobs.com, and www.monster.com, among many other sites. Many of these sites offer more than job listings. You may also be able to post your résumé at these sites, receive e-mails about job listings that match your job-search criteria, and get advice from career counselors.

✔ **Read the classified ads in your local paper.** Your paper may list them online, too.

✔ **Attend job fairs.** Job fairs can be a great way to find out which companies in your market are hiring and what kinds of skills those companies are looking for. You may even be able to get an initial job interview while you're at a fair. To find out about job fairs in your area, read your local newspaper. If you're willing to relocate, you can also find out about job fairs around the country at www.careerfairs.com.

✔ **Talk with some of the larger job-placement or personnel agencies in your area.** They may be trying to find individuals with your exact skills and experiences for some employers in your area.

✔ **Work with an executive recruitment firm.** If you're in the market for a relatively high-level position, contact one of these firms, better known as *head hunters*. Companies and larger nonprofits hire head hunters to locate individuals who might be right for positions they want to fill.

✔ **Check your local, county, or state human resources department to learn about job vacancies.** These government departments can tell you about job openings with your local, county, or state governments. You may be able to access their information online or you may have to visit these departments to get the information you want.

✔ **Visit your state or local job service or public employment service agency to find out about job vacancies in the public sector.** Visit these offices to find out about public sector jobs in your area. These include jobs such as transportation planner, Department of Human Services clerk, social worker for your local health department, and so on. The offices may also have information about job opportunities with non-profits and for-profits in your community and around your state.

✔ **To find a job with the federal government, go to www.usajobs.opm.gov or call 202-606-1800.** For information about jobs with the U.S. Postal Service, go to www.usps.gov.

✔ **Let your friends and professional associates know that you're looking for a new job.** Many companies fill their better-paying jobs via word of mouth.

✔ **Attend professional networking meetings.** These luncheons, breakfasts, and happy hours may be listed in the business section of your local newspaper or in your area's weekly business journal.

✔ **Contact any trade or professional organizations to which you belong.** These organizations may maintain job banks or job hot lines and/or provide information about available jobs on their Web sites.

✔ **Visit the Web sites of companies and other organizations that you would like to work for.** Many of these sites provide information about job openings, and you may even be able to apply for jobs at the sites. Not all businesses and organizations list their job openings in their local newspaper or on job-search Web sites.

Handling Post-divorce Personal and Family Issues

When your divorce is over, you enter a new phase of your life. In this new phase, you may feel happier than you have in a long time now that you're free of the tension and strife that plagued your marriage. Life after divorce can represent a time of personal growth, rediscovery, and new opportunities.

On the other hand, being single again can be an intimidating and lonely experience for many people — particularly if getting divorced wasn't your idea and you're unprepared for life on your own or if you have sole custody of your children. Even if you fought for such a custody arrangement, having full-time responsibility for your children 24-7 can be overwhelming, not to mention exhausting.

Giving yourself a break

As you begin adjusting to life as a single person, avoid placing unreasonable expectations and demands on yourself. Do what's necessary to tie up the loose ends of your divorce and take a breather to regroup mentally and physically. Although you may have big plans for what you want to do with the rest of your life, give yourself the opportunity to recover from what you've just gone through and to gain some perspective on things. Don't make any big decisions like moving to a new town or state, either. Pressuring yourself to make important decisions right away may cause you to make mistakes that you'll regret later.

In other words, chill out and try to take life one day at a time for now. Be a little lazy — it's okay! Let your house get messier than it usually is; eat fast-food dinners once in while; skip a few workouts at the gym. But, continue doing the things that make you feel good about yourself and about life in general and maintain some structure in your life so that you don't feel like every aspect of your life has changed. If you get too lazy or maintain no constants in your life, you may slip into a funk that you can't get out of, which will definitely interfere with your ability to get on with your life.

Taking time to reflect on what happened

Try to put your recent experiences into perspective. Take time to understand why your marriage didn't work out and how you may have contributed to your marital problems. If you don't and you remarry, you may make the same mistakes again. Writing in a journal and getting therapy are two good ways to gain some perspective on what went wrong in your marriage and how you can avoid repeating the same mistakes if you remarry.

You may also want to pick up a book that can help you reflect on your relationship. *Learning From Divorce: How to Take Responsibility, Stop the Blame, and Move On* by Christie Coates and Robert LaCrosse (Wiley) can help you grow from your divorce and help you instill positive changes in your life. *Rebuilding: When Your Relationship Ends,* 3rd Edition, by Dr. Bruce Fisher and Dr. Robert Alberti (Impact Publishers) can help validate the feelings you may be experiencing about the end of your marriage and provide you with useful advice about how to have a more successful marriage the next time around. *On Your Own Again* by Keith Anderson and Roy Macskimming (McClelland & Stewart) is another useful resource for picking up the pieces and moving forward after divorce.

Accept the fact that your life is no longer the way it used to be and that it never will be again. This doesn't mean that your new life has to be less satisfying and less happy than it used to be; it's just different now, and different can be better. Try to identify some benefits of being single again. They may be hard to find at first, but they *do* exist. For example, now you may have more privacy and time to yourself, your relationship with your children may be stronger, you may have less strife in your life, and you may sleep better now because you're not feeling as stressed out as you used to be.

Being with people in your same situation

You may find joining a support group of divorcees just like you helpful. The group's members can help bolster your confidence through the inevitable down times as you rebuild your life and can provide you with advice and feedback when you encounter problems that you're not sure how to handle. Plus, they may also be a source of new friends and a reinvigorated social life. Your church or synagogue may also have a support group for people in your same situation. Or *Divorce Magazine* offers an online state-by-state directory of divorce support groups. Check it out by going to `www.divorcemag.com/XX/support/index.shtml`.

When choosing a divorce support group, steer clear of groups that are full of angry, bitter divorcees. Participants in these kinds of groups tend to reinforce one another's negative emotions, which does little to help them heal and move on. A better choice is a support group that's run by a professional with experience helping divorcees recover from their divorce.

Developing new skills around the house

Being divorced usually means having to take on household chores that you may not have had to handle when you were married — cooking, grocery shopping, balancing the checkbook, taking care of home repairs, mowing the lawn, and so on. Friends and relatives may be able to help you get up-to-speed quickly on some tasks, and don't be ashamed to ask them for the help you need. Also, learning by doing, reading how-to books, watching how-to DVDs or videos, and taking classes are other good ways to acquire new skills. Soon you'll feel proud of what you can accomplish on your own and will gain confidence in your ability to learn even more. However, you should also develop a list of reliable professionals that you can call on for certain kinds of tasks, such as fixing plumbing problems, taking care of electrical problems, repairing appliances, landscaping, and so on.

Giving more to your kids

Following your divorce, all your kids, regardless of their ages, need more of your love, affection, and attention, but don't smother them or act overprotective, because you can create new problems for yourself and your children.

If you and your spouse were separated while you were getting divorced, your kids probably began making the adjustment back then but, now that your divorce is final, they may have to cope with a new set of changes. For example, you and your children may have to move out of your home and, depending on where you move, they may have to attend a new school. If you have young children, focus your energy on making certain that they're alright and on helping them adjust to life after divorce, as necessary. If your children are teens or preteens, keep the lines of communication open with them and make a point of spending time alone with each child. Helping your older kids adjust to life after divorce may even bring you closer together and improve your relationship with each of them.

Research shows that even in amicable splits, the effect of divorce on both boys and girls tends to be greatest during the year immediately following a divorce, and boys tend to have a harder time adjusting overall than girls do.

Parent Soup at www.parentsoup.com offers information and advice for parents of kids from toddlers to teens. The site also features chat rooms and message boards for parents. Chapter 6 provides additional resources that you may find helpful.

Having fun with your kids when you don't have custody

If you're a noncustodial parent, spending time with your children in your new home or apartment and not living with each other day-to-day may feel weird to them and to you. To help everyone feel more comfortable and to make adjusting to your new situation easier, avoid making each time you're together a special event. Instead, do the things you used to do with one another — go to the grocery store, take a bike ride, help your kids with their homework, watch a movie, or read a book with them. Keeping everything as normal and routine as possible should take some of the pressure off everyone and help reassure your kids that some aspects of their lives remain the same.

You can also reassure your kids that you're still going to be involved in their lives by attending their schools' open houses, coming to their recitals and sporting events, and joining in their scouting activities. Even if you live out of town, try to attend some of these activities at least a couple of times a year. When you do, you give your kids moral support and reassure them that they're still very important to you.

 If you're a noncustodial parent, don't be upset if your kids act nonchalant when you pick them up to spend time with you and then act sad to leave you. Their initial demeanor may be their way of protecting themselves emotionally or it may reflect their confidence that you will always be in their lives and that divorce hasn't changed your love and concern for them. Don't make assumptions about the ways that your children should respond to the changes occurring in their lives or set yourself up for disappointment by having unrealistic expectations about how they will act. Instead, simply observe your children and try to understand the true reasons for their behavior.

If your children live with you but spend some nights with your former spouse, give them time to get used to their other parent's home and the different rules your ex may expect your children to follow. They may have a hard time falling asleep when they spend the night at your ex's or may act reluctant to visit him or her at first. However, if you and your ex work together to make the transition from house to house as smooth and as easy as possible for your kids, they'll likely adjust fairly quickly to their new living arrangement.

Developing a new sense of family

As you recover from your divorce, giving your children a sense of family is important. It's particularly critical if your marital problems affected how your entire family functions or if your children no longer see some of their relatives as often as they used to because of your divorce.

Whether you're a custodial parent, a noncustodial parent, or you share custody with your spouse, feeling part of a family is important to your children and contributes to their sense of security and self-worth. To help give your kids a sense of family despite how your divorce has changed their lives, maintain as many of the rituals that you used to observe when you were married, including attending religious ceremonies with your children, celebrating their birthdays in a special way, spending important holidays with your extended family, and so on.

You should also think about establishing new family rituals (going on an annual family vacation, eating pizza and watching a movie every Friday night, or taking up a new hobby together, for example) to make them feel as if their new lives have some benefits and to help your children feel like they're still part of a family when they're with you.

Special family time doesn't have to cost a lot of money. What you do can be as simple as a walk after dinner, weekend bike rides, playing a board game, or decorating the holiday tree. Whether you have a one-parent, two-parent, or blended family, your children will benefit from spending time together and growing up in a household with open communication, humor, clear values and rules, nurturing, and respect.

If your children are preteens or teenagers, be sensitive to their need for peer support but insist that they do something with your family at least once a week. Also, when they're with you, make eating meals together a priority. Getting your older children to participate in family activities is easier if you choose activities that the whole family enjoys or if you let each of them take turns picking something to do as a family. However, if your older children balk at family togetherness, don't make it such an issue that they don't want to be with you at all. Most likely, they will come around eventually.

Getting a Life after Your Divorce

Okay, you've spent hours wallowing in self-pity, watching countless TV shows, and eating way more than your share of junk food. Now the time has come to peel yourself off the couch, brush the potato chip crumbs off your lap, and begin building a new life for yourself as a single person. Yes, there *is* life after divorce! And, in this section, we offer some suggestions on how to get your social life going again and how to find people to date (once you feel ready to do that).

Building a social life for yourself

Getting divorced almost always means losing some of the friends you had when you were married. Most likely, they will be people you knew through your spouse or people you may have socialized with only as couples. Some of those friends may feel the need to choose sides in your divorce, and some will side with your ex-spouse. Others may side with you, and some may drop out of both your lives.

Your relationships with your friends who you continue to be in contact with may also change after your divorce. For example, you may feel awkward going to their dinner parties and other social gatherings by yourself. And, at some point, you may want to begin meeting other singles for possible dates, and this new part of your social life may create some distance between you and your married friends. As a result, you may drift apart from some of them.

Hopefully your most important and significant friendships remain intact. Even so, try to make new friends, too. Meeting new people can be fun and can bring some much-needed energy, excitement, and hope to your life. To make new friends, join a health club, take up a hobby, participate in a book discussion group, or pursue some other new activity that you may be interested in. Rediscover your community and all that it offers you and your kids. The point is to get out of the house and get on with your life!

Avoid alienating your friends and family members by constantly griping about what a raw deal you got in your divorce or about the people your spouse is dating. Although your friends may have been ready to offer you a shoulder to lean on while you were *getting* divorced, they may be less willing to listen now that you've finally split from your ex. If you need to vent, talk to someone who's a patient and impartial listener or seek professional counseling.

Getting back out there: The dating scene

The first rule of post-divorce dating: Don't begin dating until you've given yourself time to put your former marriage in perspective, to pull yourself together emotionally, to rebuild your self-esteem, and to create a good life for you and your children. In other words, learn to be happy as a single person. When you do, you're more likely to make better choices when you begin dating again.

If you begin dating prematurely, you may end up in a destructive relationship or dating someone with the very same characteristics or behaviors that created problems in your marriage. For example, some people tend to be attracted time and again to needy, dependent individuals or to individuals who are prone to violence.

Your children's well-being is another very important reason for not dating right away. They may feel threatened by the fact that you're dating so soon after your divorce. Among other things, they may be fearful that one of your dates is going to interfere with your relationship with them, replace their other parent, or cause some other unhappiness in their lives.

You may find yourself attracted to people simply because they're polar opposites of your former spouse. For example, if your ex was a total couch potato, you may find yourself attracted to people who are perpetually in motion. Or if your ex was very disorganized, you may begin dating someone who's highly regimented. However, being the complete opposite of your former spouse is no guarantee that the two of you will get along.

Welcome to the 21st century: Tips on using an online dating service

The Internet has become a high-tech matchmaker. Millions of singles are using online dating services to find people to date. Although online dating is easy and convenient, it isn't without risks. Most dating services don't run background checks on the people who use their services. Therefore, you have no way of knowing whether that handsome hunk or sexy gal has a rap sheet. Also, because online dating is easy for people to be whoever they want to be online — handsome, rich, accomplished, single, an adult — you don't want to be taken by surprise if and when you meet one another. If you have a bad feeling about someone, trust your instinct and don't spend time alone with him or her. To protect your safety when you use an online dating service, pay attention to the following advice as well.

- ✔ **Don't include any personally identifiable information in your online profile, such as your address or phone number.** And don't share that information with anyone you meet through the online dating service until you've had an opportunity to meet and feel that he or she is someone you can trust and want to get to know better.

- ✔ **If you decide to communicate directly with someone online rather than through the** online dating service, set up an anonymous e-mail account with a service like Yahoo! or Hotmail and don't give out your full name. You should take this precaution because finding out personal information about you, based on the e-mail address you use all the time, isn't difficult to do especially if you've had the account for a long time.

- ✔ **If you decide to have a first date with someone you meet on the Internet, drive yourself to your date location, meet in a public place, and let at least one friend know who you are meeting and where you are meeting.** Arrange to call your friend or have your friend call you at a certain time during the date. You may even want to bring a friend along on your first date.

- ✔ **Consider running a background check on anyone you meet online who you would like to date.** Even if someone is totally charming and good-looking, that person could have some skeletons in his or her closet — maybe even a criminal past — that may cause you to think twice about whether you really want to date him or her.

When your fabulous single self is ready to start dating again, don't be surprised if you feel a little nervous and insecure. The longer you were married, the more likely you'll feel this way. This feeling is normal and, most likely, as you begin to feel comfortable dating, those feelings will subside. In the meantime, don't expect to find a new Mr. or Ms. Right immediately. Just date to have a good time. If remarrying is your eventual goal, you will find that special someone — when the time is right.

Here are some ways to meet new people to date:

- **Let your friends know that you want to start dating.** They may be eager to introduce you to someone, perhaps by inviting both of you to a dinner party or to join them in some other low-stress group activity. Also, because they know you well, your friends are in a better position than others to know the kind of person you would enjoy meeting.

- **Take a class.** An auto repair class is usually a good place to meet both men and women, but other options can include a music appreciation class, an art class, or a class on any subject you would like to know more about.

- **Take up a sport.** Joining a softball team, a bowling league, or a running club that attracts both sexes can be a healthy, relaxed way to meet people you may want to date.

- **Volunteer.** Giving your time and energy to a cause you care about can put you in touch with like-minded men and women.

- **Join a singles group.** You may be able to find some groups listed in your local Yellow Pages or your local newspaper. Your place of worship may also have an organized singles group.

- **Use a dating service.** Some dating services let you create a video to advertise yourself and preview the videos of other people who've done the same. Other services use computers to match you up with potential dates based on your personal profiles. Still other services sponsor social activities designed to help you meet potential dates and make the initial "getting to know you" process more comfortable.

  Before you agree to work with a dating service or pay any money, make sure you're comfortable with its approach to matchmaking. Learn as much as you can about the company by reviewing its literature, scheduling an in-person meeting with a representative of the dating service, and asking for a sample contract to review. Also, be clear about how much it charges for its services (fees can be as high as several thousand dollars for some!), exactly what you get for your money, and under what circumstances you can get your money refunded. Finally, before you sign anything, call your local Better Business Bureau and the consumer protection office of your state attorney general's office to find out whether or not they've had any complaints filed about the service.

- **Place a personal ad or answer one.** Try running an ad in your local daily paper, singles newspaper, or magazine or answer a few personal ads run by people who sound interesting. For the price of running an ad, you may also get to create a recorded message that callers hear when they punch in a special code. When you create your message, don't include your last name, address, or phone number (you probably won't be allowed to do that anyway). Keep your message brief and friendly and mention some of your interests. Don't forget to be realistic about your expectations.

✔ **Find a date online.** Online dating has become relatively commonplace since the advent of the Internet. (See the nearby sidebar, "Welcome to the 21st century: Tips on using an online dating service.") In fact, *Online Dating Magazine* (www.onlinedatingmagazine.com) is totally devoted to the subject.

If you use personal ads or go online to meet potential dates, for safety reasons, always choose a public place for your initial meetings and steer clear of bars. A meeting at a lunch spot, coffee shop, or bookstore is usually a good choice. Do not give anyone you meet through a personal ad your home phone or address until you feel comfortable and safe with that person.

✔ **Try speed dating.** In this fast-paced world where no one has enough time — even to meet fun people to go out with — speed dating has become a reality. Speed dating gives you the opportunity to attend a party organized by a speed-dating service where you meet multiple potential dates in one evening, but just for a short period of time — ten minutes or less. After each encounter, you fill out a card to indicate whether you would like the person you just spent time with to contact you later. If anyone you met is interested in getting to know you more, they indicate that fact on his or her card. The speed-dating service provides you and those interested in contacting you with a special e-mail account provided to communicate with one another.

Chapter 18

Solving the Toughest Post-divorce Problems

Divorce doesn't always end the problems that destroyed a marriage. Some divorced couples continue to replay old arguments and go out of their way to make each other miserable rather than getting on with their lives. Consumed by anger and a desire for revenge, they fight over the outcome of the divorce, withhold court-ordered child and/or spousal support or purposely delay making those payments, interfere in each other's custodial or visitation rights, and renege on other divorce-related obligations.

Some former spouses develop serious financial troubles after they get divorced — so serious that they end up in bankruptcy, a move that can jeopardize the finances of the other former spouse. Some former spouses even use bankruptcy in an effort to avoid having to meet their divorce-related financial obligations. None of this paints a pretty picture but, unfortunately, these situations are reality in many cases.

This chapter can't solve everyone's post-divorce problems, but it does provide specific information about some of the most common (and serious) problems you may face after your divorce is final. It also explains what you can do about those problems.

Your Ex-spouse Makes Seeing Your Kids Difficult (If Not Impossible)

If you're a noncustodial parent and your ex interferes with your visitation rights, he or she is violating the terms of your divorce, plain and simple.

If you're the custodial parent, you cannot force your former spouse to exercise his or her visitation rights. No law requires a noncustodial parent to spend time with his or her minor children, although most parents want to see their children and be an influence in their lives. On the other hand, you can use your former spouse's repeated failure to spend time with your children as justification for why the court should modify your current custody agreement, possibly restricting your former spouse's visitation rights.

Don't retaliate by withholding payments

If your spouse interferes with your visitation rights, you may be tempted to withhold payment for child support or spousal support. Don't do it! Not only are you breaking the law — just like your former spouse is — but you may also jeopardize your children's financial well-being. Two wrongs in this case definitely *do not* make a right.

A far better course of action is to continue paying your child support (and spousal support, too) and to try working things out with your former spouse. Mediation is probably your best bet if you want to resolve the problem outside of court. (See Chapter 15 for more on the subject of mediation.) But mediation won't work unless you and your ex are willing to give it a try. If that's not the case, your only option is to go to court.

Do file a contempt of court complaint

If you and your ex-spouse are so estranged that resolving your problems outside of court is impossible, consider filing a complaint for contempt of court against your ex. You can do so if, for example, your former spouse is interfering in your right to spend time with your children. If you file a contempt of court against your ex, unless your ex can prove that there is good reason why you should not be able to exercise your visitation rights — you've abused them, sexually molested them, you have a drug problem, and so on — the judge will order you to spend time with your children according to the terms of your divorce. From start to finish, the complaint process should take relatively little time — certainly less time than your divorce.

Although you must pay a filing fee and other expenses when you file a contempt of court complaint with the court, if the judge finds that your ex is in contempt, you can probably recover those costs from him or her.

The Child-support Payments Don't Arrive

Millions of divorced parents (mostly mothers) with court orders for child support never receive those payments or receive only sporadic payments. As a result, many of these parents struggle to provide for their children, some go bankrupt, and still others fall into poverty.

The formal term for past-due child support is an *arrearage.* According to a survey by the U.S. Census Bureau, of the 7.9 million parents with some sort of child-support agreement (in most instances, a court order for child support), only 45 percent received every child-support payment they were due in 2001. In that same year, 29 percent received some of their payments. Twenty-six percent received none of the child support they were entitled to in 2001.

If your ex is a *deadbeat,* a person who can pay but won't, you can scream, cry, and tear your hair out or you can use legal means to force him or her to pay up. If you choose the latter option, you can

- ✔ **Get help from your state's Child Support Enforcement (CSE) Program.** Although the CSE office charges you little or nothing for its assistance, don't expect overnight results. In fact, these offices tend to be understaffed, so months can pass before you get the results you're looking for.

- ✔ **Hire an attorney to do much of what the CSE would do for you.** An attorney's help can be expensive, but he or she may be able to get you quick results. Also, you can try to recover your attorney's fees and legal costs from your former spouse. Otherwise, your attorney will probably deduct his or her fee from whatever moneys he or she may collect for you.

- ✔ **Work with a private child-support collection agency.** If you go with this option, select the agency carefully because some agencies take a large percentage of any child support they collect as payment for their services. For solid advice on how to choose a private child-support collection agency, see the section "Using a private child-support collection agency" later in this chapter.

Getting help from the Child Support Enforcement Program in your state

The goal of the Child Support Enforcement (CSE) Program, a joint effort of the federal and state governments, is to increase the number of custodial parents receiving court-ordered child support. (The CSE Program also helps parents obtain court orders for child support.)

The federal Office of Child Support Enforcement (OCSE), which is part of the Health and Human Services Department, oversees child-support enforcement in the United States. Among other things, OCSE helps fund and develop state CSE programs in accordance with federal law. OCSE also operates the federal Parent Locator Service, which uses computer matching to help find noncustodial parents so that child-support court orders can be established and enforced. For more information about the federal child-support enforcement effort, go to www.acf.dhhs.gov/programs/cse.

State social service departments, revenue departments, and the offices of state attorneys general usually coordinate state efforts. To implement their programs, most states work with local prosecuting attorneys, other local law enforcement agencies, and family law courts.

CSE services are available for free or at very little cost to any parent who needs them. However, if you seek help from your state's CSE office, be prepared for delays and frustrations. Working with any government bureaucracy can be frustrating and, given the extent of the child-support collection problem in this country and the amount of funding most CSE offices receive, they tend to be chronically understaffed. Therefore, getting results can take a long time.

You're apt to get better results from your state CSE office if you follow up regularly with the CSE employee you are working with.

CSE programs vary from state to state. To find out about the particulars of your state CSE Program and to get contact information for that program, click on www.acf.dhhs.gov/programs/cse/extinf.htm. When you do, you will see a map of the United States. Click on your state to get to the information you need.

To more fully understand how the CSE office in your state can help you resolve your child-support problems, request a free copy of the U.S. Department of Health and Human Services *Handbook on Child Support Enforcement.* You can obtain a copy of this handbook from your state CSE office or you can read it online at www.acf.dhhs.gov/programs/cse/fctdsc.htm.

How the CSE office collects your past-due child support

Your state CSE office can help you collect your court-ordered child support in a number of ways. It can

- ✔ Order your former spouse to meet with staff from the attorney general office to discuss how your ex can get current on his or her child-support payments.

- ✔ Seize your ex's federal tax refund. If your state has its own income tax agency, federal law requires that the state's tax collection agency intercept any state tax refunds that your spouse may receive.

✔ Ask the IRS to start collection proceedings against your former spouse. (This collection process is the same one that the IRS uses to collect back taxes.) If the IRS responds to the request, it will offer your former spouse an opportunity to negotiate a payment plan to wipe out the child-support debt. If that doesn't work, the IRS may seize assets that your ex-spouse owns, including bank accounts, real estate, equipment, and other property.

✔ Place a lien on your former spouse's real and personal assets, including real estate, vehicles, computer equipment, and so on. (However, most states don't put liens on a parent's primary residence or on any property he or she needs to make a living.) Although a lien is no guarantee of payment, it prevents your former spouse from selling, transferring, or borrowing against the property with the lien on it until he or she pays your past-due child support.

If your former spouse doesn't pay your court-ordered child support and you didn't get the right to place a lien on one or more of your ex's assets as part of your divorce agreement, you can sue your ex in order to get the court's permission to put a lien in place after the fact.

✔ Require that your ex-spouse pledge real or other property to you or give you a lien on any real estate (home, land, or buildings) that he or she may own as a guarantee of payment. In the case of nonpayment, your ex loses the property to you as payment for the back support.

✔ Seize the assets of your former spouse, sell them, and use the proceeds to pay off his or her child-support debt. Because this option also has issues related to the value of the seized property and transfer of ownership, this matter is one to discuss with an attorney; the CSE office; or a private collection agency, if you hire one to help collect on past-due child support.

✔ Use state nonsupport statutes to prosecute your ex-spouse. This option is usually a last resort but, if you do use it and your former spouse doesn't pay up, the judge can order your ex to be jailed.

Other ways the CSE office can pressure your ex to pay up

Your state Child Support Enforcement (CSE) office may use other tools to pressure or embarrass your former spouse into paying up. Depending on where you live, some of those other tools the CSE may use include

✔ Automatic billing, telephone reminders, and delinquency notices.

✔ Electronic fund transfers from your former spouse's bank account to your account. This tool is good to use when the support-paying parent is self-employed because automatic wage deductions aren't possible.

Federal law requires that states report all child-support arrearages of more than $1,000 to the major credit bureaus; states can report smaller arrearages, if they want. When a consumer has this kind of negative information on his or her credit record, the consumer may have a more difficult time getting new or additional credit at reasonable terms.

✔ Suspending or revoking your ex's license to practice law, medicine, or another profession and suspending or revoking his or her driver's license, hunting or fishing license, or other government-issued license. Also, the Department of State will deny a passport to your former spouse if he or she owes you at least $5,000 in past-due child support.

✔ Using local or state "most wanted" campaigns to embarrass parents to pay up and to flush out deadbeat parents. Typically, these campaigns provide the names and photographs of the parents who owe child support.

✔ Using the media to promote "amnesty" campaigns. Parents who come forward to pay their child-support debt during the amnesty period will not be prosecuted or will be punished less severely than they would be otherwise.

✔ Posting information about delinquent parents on the Internet. The information includes a parent's name and community of residence, if known, as well as the amount the parent owes in past-due child support.

The federal government also has a variety of initiatives aimed at increasing the number of custodial parents who receive their court-ordered child support. Those initiatives include

✔ Mandating that court-ordered payments be withheld from the paychecks of noncustodial parents.

✔ Requiring that state CSE offices report child-support delinquencies to the three national credit reporting agencies.

✔ Establishing a federal/state National Directory of New Hires to help federal and state governments keep track of divorced parents who frequently change jobs in order to avoid paying their child support.

Collect Child Support by Susan Herskowitz (E-Z Products) is a practical guide to child-support enforcement. Although trying to collect past-due support on your own is usually a thankless task, the more you know about what to do, the better able you are to make CSE's services work for you or to work productively with the attorney or child-support collection agency you may hire to help you.

Hiring an attorney to collect your child support

Some family law attorneys specialize in helping parents collect past-due child support (and spousal support as well), but paying for more legal help may be unrealistic, given the state of your post-divorce finances. Furthermore, these attorneys cannot do anything that the CSE office in your state can't do. However, they can probably do it a lot faster, which may make the cost of an attorney a good investment for you.

If you want to hire an attorney to collect your past-due support, you can minimize your out-of-pocket legal expenses by finding one who will work with you on a contingency basis. In other words, the attorney agrees to get paid by taking a percentage of whatever money he or she is able to collect for you. If the attorney is unable to collect any money for you, you don't owe the attorney a fee, although you may be obligated to pay his or her expenses, depending on the terms of your agreement.

If you hire an attorney to help you collect your child support, he or she can work with your area's CSE office, coordinating his or her collection efforts with CSE staff to prevent duplication of services and conflicting enforcement decisions.

Using a private child-support collection agency

Many parents with child-support collection problems hire private *child-support collection agencies* to help them get their money. These agencies tend to get quicker results than CSE offices and may cost less than an attorney.

A cross between a detective agency and a traditional debt-collection agency, private child-support collection agencies can help you collect your back support and track down your ex-spouse if he or she has disappeared in order to avoid paying child support. For the services of a child-support collection agency, you pay a percentage of the child support it collects for you. You may also have to pay an upfront fee.

Although most private child-support collection agencies truly want to help, some victimize desperate parents who are already being victimized by their former spouses. These agencies may take a bigger percentage of the child support they collect than they said they would, demand exorbitant upfront fees (and do little or nothing to earn that money), or fail to turn over the money they collect to the parent who hires them.

To protect yourself from getting ripped off, be sure that you get

- ✔ **Written information about the agency's services.** The information should include background on the company's management and its legal expertise.

- ✔ **References.** Check them out, too. Also call your local Better Business Bureau and the consumer protection office of your state attorney general's office to find out whether they have any complaints against the private child-support collection agency on file.

✔ **A written contract from the agency.** The contract should spell out exactly what the agency will do for you, the terms of payment, and how quickly the agency will turn over any money it collects on your behalf to you. Read the contract carefully before you sign and get all your questions answered.

Do not sign a contract that requires you to pay a percentage of your child support until your child reaches the age of 18 or 21 or that prohibits you from seeking help from other resources.

Your Ex-spouse Skips Town

Unfortunately, some parents are so intent on not paying their child support that they move out of state often without leaving a forwarding address. When that happens, enforcing a child-support court order and collecting that support can be particularly difficult.

The federal government requires state CSE offices to pursue interstate cases as vigorously as in-state cases but, in reality, they often get short shrift given the amount of staff time interstate cases take and the many obstacles to success. Nevertheless, Congress has passed laws intended to improve the effectiveness of interstate child support and collections. Those laws include:

✔ **The Uniform Interstate Family Support Act (UIFSA).** This law gives you the right to ask a court in your state to forward your order for child support to the court with jurisdiction in the state where your former spouse now lives. The court in that jurisdiction can enforce the order and provide your ex's new employer with a copy of your child-support court order so that the employer can begin withholding the amount you are due each month from your former spouse's paychecks.

✔ **The Child Support Recovery Act (CSRA).** Under this federal law, a parent who refuses to make support payments to a parent who lives in another state is committing a federal crime and can be prosecuted. However, to be prosecuted under this law, the parent must

• Owe more than $5,000 in back child support or must have owed back support for more than one year.

• Have been aware that he or she had an obligation to pay child support and been able to meet that obligation when it was due.

✔ **The Deadbeat Parents Punishment Act.** This act amends the CSRA by making it a federal crime when a parent owes more than $10,000 in past-due child support or hasn't paid child support in more than two years and/or has willfully moved from one state to another (or out of the country) to avoid paying the support. If your ex is convicted of violating this law, he or she can be fined and imprisoned.

In the past, a parent who was obligated to pay child support could avoid paying or could pay less by moving to a new state and getting that state to modify his or her child-support court order. Now with the Deadbeat Parents Punishment Act, as long as either parent remains in the state where the court order was originally filed, that state has continuing and exclusive jurisdiction over the court order. Also, according to the Uniform Interstate Family Support Act, if you have a court order for child support and both you and your ex-spouse move out of state, your original court order will be valid in your new state. Contact your new state's child-support enforcement office to find out about any paperwork you may need to file to ensure that your support payments continue. You can obtain the phone number for that office by going to www.acf.dhhs.gov/programs/cse/extinf.htm.

Your Ex-spouse Disappears with the Kids

If you have custody of your kids and your ex-spouse kidnaps them or refuses to return them to you, your former spouse is breaking the law. All 50 states, the District of Columbia, as well as the federal government have laws related to parental kidnapping. Under most circumstances, the laws treat such a kidnapping as a felony.

If your ex takes off with your kids, leave no stone unturned. The longer you wait to act, the harder finding them will be. You should

- ✔ **Call your local police department immediately and file a missing persons report.** Under the federal National Child Search Assistance Act of 1990, no waiting period is required before the police can issue such a report. Get a case number and ask them to enter your child into the National Crime Information Computer (NCIC) right away. Ask the police to give you the nine-digit NCIC number related to your missing child.

- ✔ **Talk with your local police department about whether your missing child qualifies for a nationwide AMBER Alert.** If your child does, the police will fax information about your child, a photo of your child, and any information you may have about the type of vehicle your ex may be driving to radio stations around the country and to TV stations as well. Some states also use electronic billboards to alert people about missing children. For more information on the AMBER Alert, go to the National Center for Missing & Exploited Children Web site (www.missingkids.com).

- ✔ **Contact the district attorney for your jurisdiction and ask him or her to issue a warrant for the arrest of your former spouse as soon as possible.** Ask that office to use the Federal Parent Locator Service to try to locate your ex, too. Your local CSE office can also contact this service for you although, if you want to be sure that the contact happens immediately, do it yourself.

✔ **Contact the FBI.** Don't wait for your local police department to contact the agency, but let them know that you have. If kidnapping is a felony in your state, the FBI will help you.

✔ **Contact your elected representatives in Washington.** Sometimes a call from your senator or congressperson can make government offices move more quickly than they would otherwise.

✔ **Get in contact with organizations that can help you.** Those organizations include

- National Center for Missing and Exploited Children (800-843-5678)

- Child Find of America (800-I-Am-Lost)

- Missing Children Help Center (800-USA-KIDS)

- Polly Klaas Foundation (800-587-4357)

✔ **Contact your state's Missing Children's Clearinghouse.** Ask the staff to list information about your missing child. These government organizations collect, compile, and disseminate information about children who have disappeared and provide parents with another way of getting the word out about their missing child. Many of these clearinghouses maintain Web sites with the photos of missing children and other information about them. If you have any ideas about which state your ex and child may be in, provide that information to the organization.

✔ **Provide the local media with photos of your missing child and relevant information.** The media may publicize your missing child on TV, radio, and/or in your local newspaper, and someone who hears or reads about your child may come forward with information about your child's location. You may want to contact the media as soon as you know for certain that your child is missing. Before you do, however, speak with the law enforcement personnel you're working with to make certain that publicizing the fact that your child is missing will not jeopardize any effort they have underway to find your child.

✔ **Ask law enforcement for the phone numbers of the border patrol for Canada and Mexico.** If you have any concern that your former spouse may take your child to either of these countries, notifying the border patrol of that fact is important so they can be on the lookout for your ex and your child and can stop them from leaving the country.

✔ **Get in touch with the U.S. State Department's Office of Passport and Advisory Services (202-955-0377) and ask that it not issue a passport to your child.** To find out whether your ex has already requested a passport for your child, ask the State Department to enter your child's name into its passport-name check system. Of course, doing so helps only if your child applies for a passport under his or her real name.

✔ **Hire your own private investigator.** *Skip tracers,* individuals who track down missing persons using national computerized databases, are very effective at turning up missing people through social security numbers, driver's license numbers, and plenty of asking around. Plus, they're relatively inexpensive.

If you suspect that your spouse may take off with your children, contact your family law attorney, the CSE office in your area, or both to find out what you can do. One option is for your attorney to ask the family law judge in your area to issue a court order barring your ex from leaving the jurisdiction with your children. The judge may be willing to issue the order on an emergency basis. Realistically, however, if your former spouse is determined to take off with the kids, a court order may not be much of a deterrent. Even so, pursuing this option is a good idea because if your ex does violate the court order, your former spouse will have even more problems with the law than he or she already has after taking off with your kids. Those problems are likely to work to your advantage if you want to change your custody arrangement to protect your children from being harmed again by your ex. Also, you should alert your child's school or day-care center about your concerns and instruct them to release your child only to you or someone you specifically designate.

Keeping your kids safe

You have no 100 percent foolproof way to ensure that your ex will not kidnap your children. However, to help minimize the likelihood that a kidnapping will happen, you can

✔ Respect your ex's right to spend time with his or her kids according to the terms of your custody agreement.

✔ Avoid badmouthing your former spouse or treating him or her with disrespect.

✔ Try to work out any problems between you and your spouse in a friendly manner. Use mediation, if necessary.

✔ Immediately report to the police any kidnapping threats your ex may make. Record the date and nature of each threat. You may also want to contact your local district attorney's office about the threats, especially if they persist.

✔ Make your children's teachers, day-care center, babysitters, friends' parents, and so on aware of your kidnapping concerns. Let them know not to release your child to any adult but you without your permission.

✔ Get a passport for your child and let the U.S. Passport Office know that your child is not to leave the country without your written permission.

✔ Contact your local police department about getting your children fingerprinted. The department will keep the prints on file.

✔ Make certain that your younger children know their full names, address, as well as all your phone numbers.

✔ Teach your children how to use a telephone, including a cellphone. Make sure that they know when to call 911 and how to dial the operator. Be sure that they understand that they can call 911 without having to pay anything, even if they place the call from a pay phone.

Your Ex-spouse Owes You Spousal Support

Many former spouses who are legally obligated to pay spousal support fail to make the payments or don't make them consistently, often because they resent having to pay the money because they remarry and their new spouse pressures them not to pay. Other former spouses don't pay because they develop serious money troubles after their divorce and, instead of asking the court to let them pay less spousal support, they simply stop paying anything or pay only when they can afford it.

If your former spouse falls behind on his or her spousal support payments, the Uniform Interstate Family Support Act (UIFSA) may be able to help you. In addition, some courts are becoming more aggressive about enforcing court-ordered spousal support agreements.

In some states, a portion of the wages of an ex-spouse who's fallen behind on spousal support payments can be taken each pay period until the past-due amount is paid in full. In addition, the former spouse can be held in contempt for violating a court order to pay spousal support and jailed as a result.

If contempt of court isn't an option in your state if your spouse doesn't pay spousal support, you may be in the same boat as everyone else your ex owes money to. Making matters worse, your state's debtor protection laws may make all or most of the property owned by your ex-spouse exempt (that is, protected) from your efforts to collect what he or she owes you, effectively making the past-due spousal support uncollectible.

When your spouse isn't living up to your spousal support agreement, your best option is to contact your divorce attorney. Your attorney can lay out your options for collecting the money that you're entitled to and can help you carry out a plan of action.

The ideal time to ask your attorney about the potential problems of collecting spousal support is when you're writing the terms of your divorce agreement. One option your attorney may recommend is requiring that your spouse let you place a lien on some of his or her property as a guarantee of payment.

Your Ex-spouse Files for Bankruptcy

Your former spouse may experience very serious financial problems and end up filing for bankruptcy. If your spouse takes this step, it can jeopardize your ability to collect money that your ex may owe you related to the division of your marital property (see the sidebar "Canceling divorce obligations using bankruptcy isn't all that easy" in this chapter) and to the child and spousal support you are entitled to receive. Even if your former spouse declares bankruptcy, he or she is still legally obligated to make child-support and spousal support payments. Therefore, if your former spouse declares bankruptcy or you believe that he or she may be thinking about it, you should take some legal steps to ensure that he or she continues paying you your court-ordered support payments.

One step you can take is to hire a consumer bankruptcy attorney to help you protect your rights. For example, even though your former spouse is supposed to pay you child support after filing for bankruptcy, he or she may stop making those payments. If that happens, your bankruptcy attorney can file a motion to initiate a *contested matter* — the equivalent of a mini-lawsuit — in order to get the bankruptcy judge to order your ex to resume paying child support.

If the judge orders your former spouse to continue paying you child support and your ex still doesn't pay you what you're entitled to, your attorney can get permission from the bankruptcy court to ask your state attorney general's state's office of child-support enforcement to intervene on your behalf. The earlier section of this chapter entitled, "How the CSE office collects your past-due child support," outlines what this office may do to help you get the money to which you're entitled.

Your attorney may also initiate an adversary proceeding with the bankruptcy court in order to force your former spouse to live up to his or her other obligations according to your divorce agreement. An adversary proceeding is a more complex and difficult process than filing a motion for a contested matter. Also, the proceeding must be initiated within 60 days of the date of your ex's first creditor's meeting and, if you don't know that your former spouse has filed for bankruptcy or you find out too late, you will miss this deadline and be out of luck.

If your ex does file for bankruptcy, he or she can file one of two types of consumer bankruptcy: a *chapter 13 reorganization of debt bankruptcy* or a *chapter 7 liquidation bankruptcy*. If your former spouse files chapter 13 bankruptcy, he or she gets three to five years to catch up on all the past-due spousal support and/or child-support payments that he or she may owe you. During those years, your ex must make all his or her current support payments in full and on time. If your former spouse files chapter 7 bankruptcy, you're entitled to collect any past-due child support and/or spousal support that your ex may owe you by using any or all of the collection options already described in this chapter. In chapter 7 bankruptcy, your former spouse must still stay up-to-date on all of his or her support obligations to you.

Your ex spouse can use bankruptcy to wipe out many of his or her debts, including some of the debts he or she may be obligated to pay you as part of your divorce. For example, in your divorce, your former spouse may have agreed to pay you money over time in exchange for taking more of your marital property than he or she would normally be entitled to. If this were the case, your ex would be able to use bankruptcy to get rid of that debt unless your attorney filed an adversary asking that the debt not be discharged. (We discuss the adversary process earlier in this section.) However, in most instances, your former spouse cannot use bankruptcy to get rid of his or her obligations to pay child support or spousal support because these particular types of obligations are considered to be *priority* debts in bankruptcy. In other words, your former spouse must pay them in full, except in three situations:

✔ If your former spouse fell behind on his or her child-support or spousal support payments and you turned those debts over to a private collection agency. By turning them over to a collection agency, you're not owed the money any more — the collection agency is. Therefore, the debts cease being priority debts, which means that they don't have to be paid in full. However, your former spouse is still legally obligated to make all *future* support payments to you in full and on time.

✔ When the bankruptcy court rules that your ex's spousal support debt to you is really another type of divorce-related financial obligation — a debt related to your property settlement, for example.

✔ When your ex owns a business and the court believes that your ex won't have enough money to continue running it if he or she has to continue paying you child or spousal support.

When your former spouse files for bankruptcy, quick action is required on your part in order for your rights to be protected. Unfortunately, if you and your ex are not communicating, staying up-to-date on the status of your ex's finances may be hard, if not impossible, to do.

Canceling divorce obligations using bankruptcy isn't all that easy

Former spouses used to be able to use bankruptcy to void certain divorce-related obligations, including promises to pay off marital debts or to make certain payments over time in exchange for keeping certain assets from your marriage. If your ex did either of these things, you may have ended up with considerably more debt to pay than you had anticipated when your divorce became final and possibly not enough money to pay it. Ironically, your ex-spouse's bankruptcy could force you into bankruptcy as well!

Since 1994, however, former spouses have had a much harder time using bankruptcy to wipe

out certain kinds of financial obligations. If the court believes that your former spouse has sufficient resources to pay for his or her basic living expenses and meet his or her financial obligations to you, your ex's bankruptcy probably won't have any effect on his or her divorce-related obligations to you, especially if the judge believes that you would suffer more than your former spouse would benefit if the court released your former spouse from his or her obligations.

Your Children Begin Having Emotional Problems

Children often experience some emotional upset during and after their parents' divorce. After all, their definition of a family has been changed, their sense of security has been shaken, and their lives have been altered in fundamental ways. In most instances, your children get through their emotional upset and are okay, assuming that you keep the lines of communication open, that you reassure them through your words and actions that you still love them and that things will be okay, and that you and your spouse don't have a bitter divorce and an angry, antagonistic post-divorce relationship. Nevertheless, some children experience serious emotional problems after their parents get divorced. For this reason, be familiar with the more common signs of serious emotional distress in children and stay alert for them in your own kids. If you see any of those signs in your children, you can intervene as soon as possible before things go from bad to worse. The following behaviors are signs that your children are hurting and need your help:

Toddlers to kindergarten-age children may

- ✔ Become fearful of leaving you
- ✔ Begin having temper tantrums
- ✔ Develop behavioral problems at home or with other children
- ✔ Have trouble sleeping in their own room or have nightmares
- ✔ Revert to infantile behavior, such as bedwetting, thumb-sucking, biting, and crying

Elementary-age children may

- ✔ Begin spending more time alone in their rooms and less time playing with friends
- ✔ Choose one parent to be angry with and choose another to cling to for comfort
- ✔ Cry a lot
- ✔ Get sick more than usual (headaches and stomachaches are particularly common) or act sick so that they can stay home from school
- ✔ Lose interest in activities they used to enjoy
- ✔ Participate less in classroom discussions and activities

Adolescents and preteens may

- ✔ Develop nonspecific illnesses or nervous habits, such as nail-biting and facial tics

- ✔ Develop behavioral problems (such as getting into fights) at school, outside of school, or at home

- ✔ Engage in rebellious behavior, such as shoplifting or vandalism, skipping school, smoking, drinking, doing drugs, or becoming sexually promiscuous

- ✔ Express anger toward the parent they think is responsible for the divorce

- ✔ Spend more time alone in their rooms

- ✔ Try to play surrogate spouse to the parent they feel has been wronged

- ✔ Withdraw from friends and family

WARNING!

Girls are more likely than boys to become extremely withdrawn and to lose interest in the things they used to enjoy and/or find important.

If one of your children exhibits some of the previous behaviors, talk with your ex about what is going on and try to come to an agreement about what to do. You both may need to spend more time with your troubled child, have a conversation about what is bothering him or her, and talk with your child's school counselor and/or with other adults who play an important role in your child's life. You should also schedule an appointment with a mental health professional who specializes in working with children — especially with children of divorce. The therapist may suggest that your child go into a support group for kids with divorced parents so that he or she can talk about his or her feelings with other kids and listen to them talk about their own problems and feelings. Or the therapist may advise one-on-one therapy for a while or family therapy. Also, the therapist can advise you about what to do if your child is doing drugs, using alcohol, has developed a serious eating disorder, and so on.

Your Finances Are Falling Apart

Many people, women in particular, struggle to pay their bills or live paycheck to paycheck after their divorce and cannot put any money away as a safety net for emergencies or for the future. They may have financial problems because

- ✔ They don't have good money-management skills, maybe because when they were married, their former spouse always took care of the money. Chapters 3 and 17 in this book provide information that can help you increase your financial IQ.

✔ They're not receiving their court-ordered child support/and or spousal support or are receiving only sporadic payments. The "The Child-Support Payments Don't Arrive" and "Your Ex-spouse Owes You Spousal Support" sections of this chapter tell you what to do if these problems apply to you.

✔ They're not making enough money in their job. For advice and resources on how to make more money, see Chapter 17.

Getting your financial act together

Strategies for getting your finances under control include

✔ Preparing a budget if you don't already have one. If you have a budget, review it and look for additional reductions in your expenses. For example, you may need to move into less-expensive housing and/or sell your car and purchase one that costs less. If you reduce your expenses as much as possible and you still can't make ends meet, knowing which ones to pay and which ones to let slide for now is important. In such a situation, be sure to put these expenses at the top of your to-be-paid list:

- Your home mortgage or rent.

- Your utility bills.

- Groceries for your family.

- Your property taxes and homeowners insurance.

- Your car payments, assuming you need a car to get to and from work.

- Your court-ordered child-support and spousal support payments.

- Any debts you secured with your home — for example, a home-equity loan.

- Your heath insurance.

- Your income taxes. If you can't pay them, contact the IRS and ask for an installment plan or an Offer in Compromise, but don't just ignore your tax obligation. The IRS can take just about whatever it wants to collect your past-due taxes. If you work with a CPA, you may want him or her to contact the IRS for you. You may get a better deal.

- Federal student loans. If you ignore this obligation, the IRS can take any tax refunds you are entitled to in order to collect what you owe or it may order your employer to take the money out of your paychecks.

If you're able to pay your most important expenses and debts and have money left over, use that money to pay your unsecured debts — the debts that you didn't collateralize with one of your assets. Focus on those debts that have the highest interest rates. Credit card debts are the most common example of unsecured debts.

✔ If you continue to struggle even after you've done what you can to reduce your expenses, contact your creditors right away to try to negotiate more affordable debt-payment plans. If you think your financial situation will improve soon, you may want to ask for a temporary reduction in your monthly payments or to make only interest payments for a while. However, if you believe that the downturn in your financial situation will be long-lived, try to negotiate a permanent reduction in your payments. If you want help negotiating with your creditors, schedule an appointment with a reputable nonprofit debt-counseling organization in your area. This organization can also help you develop a long-term plan of action for dealing with your debts.

Don't enter into negotiations with your creditors until you have a clear idea of exactly how much you can afford to pay on your debts each month. If you're unable to pay the new reduced amounts you've negotiated with them, your creditors are unlikely to agree to additional reductions.

Other options for dealing with your debts

If you earn a stable income and you feel that your job is secure, one way to take the financial pressure off is to consolidate your debts by borrowing money in order to pay off some or all of them — get a home-equity loan, for example. Be sure that the loan you get to consolidate your debts has a lower interest rate than the debts you intend to pay off with the loan proceeds.

Do not borrow against your home unless you're absolutely sure that you can repay the loan! Otherwise you risk losing your home.

If your problem is too much credit card debt, another option is to transfer some or all of that debt to a card that has a lower interest rate. However, make sure that the interest rate on that card isn't a teaser rate, unless you're certain that you can pay off the transferred debt before the term of the teaser rate expires. Otherwise, the rate on the remaining debt that you transferred may be higher than the rates were on the original debts.

You may also want to deal with your debts by

✔ Borrowing against your life insurance policy

✔ Getting a loan from a friend or relative

✔ Refinancing your mortgage and getting cash out

However, each of these options has serious drawbacks, so don't pursue any of them without talking with your CPA or financial advisor first. Weighing the benefits of each option against its drawbacks is important.

When you see no light at the end of the financial tunnel despite your best efforts to pare back your spending, increase your income, and deal with your debts, you may have to consider bankruptcy. You should always consider it if you're being threatened with foreclosure on your house, repossession of your car, the loss of utility services (assuming you have no way to come up with the money you need to keep your water, heat/air conditioning, and lights on), or garnishment of your wages.

If you're in danger of repossession, foreclosure, or if the IRS or another creditor is preparing to seize the funds in your bank account, garnish your wages, or take any of your property, schedule an appointment with a bankruptcy attorney immediately.

Bankruptcy is a complicated legal process, so don't file for it without the help of a consumer bankruptcy attorney. The attorney should evaluate your finances to determine whether you can take steps to avoid bankruptcy. For a detailed explanation of the consumer bankruptcy process and information to help you decide whether bankruptcy is your best option, read my book, *The Bankruptcy Kit,* 3rd Edition (Dearborn).

Depending on your financial situation, you file either a chapter 7 liquidation bankruptcy or a chapter 13 reorganization bankruptcy (see the earlier section "Your Ex-spouse Files for Bankruptcy"). Either type of bankruptcy protects you from most creditor collection actions, gives you time to figure out what to do about the money you owe, and helps you get rid of some or all of your unsecured debts.

If you file chapter 13 bankruptcy, your payments to your creditors are reduced to amounts you can afford and you get three to five years to pay off what you owe them. You may also be able to reduce the total amount of money that you owe to your secured creditors and get rid of some of your debts.

When you owe so much that you simply cannot afford to pay your debts, you file a chapter 7 liquidation bankruptcy rather than a chapter 13 bankruptcy. In a chapter 7 bankruptcy, you lose many of your assets so they can be sold, and the proceeds pay off your creditors. Your priority creditors (like your ex who you owe spousal or child-support payments, any past-due taxes you may owe, as well as the wages you may owe to your employees if you're self-employed) are first in line for the money. Most likely, your unsecured creditors — credit card companies, for example — will get little or nothing in your bankruptcy. At the end of your chapter 7 bankruptcy, your unpaid unsecured debts are wiped out, which means that you won't have to pay them.

You Want to Make Some Changes to Your Divorce Agreement

As time goes on after you're divorced, you may decide that the terms of your divorce no longer work for you given changes in your life or in your children's lives. For example, your employer is in financial trouble and has asked everyone to take a reduction in salary or your children have gotten older and require more expenses. Or maybe you've never been happy with the terms of your divorce and, although you've done your best to live with them, you've decided now is the time to try to get them changed.

If you and your former spouse see eye to eye on the changes, modifying your agreement or the judge's court order should be relatively hassle-free, assuming that the court shares your perspectives. Just as you did when you got your divorce, you must draw up a revised agreement with the help of your attorneys to be certain that you do not create any problems for yourselves. Then the attorney of whoever wanted to change the agreement files the agreement with the court so that the new agreement can be court ordered. However, if you want things changed and your spouse doesn't, or vice versa (which is more likely), you may be in for a replay of your divorce battles.

If you and your spouse don't see eye to eye about the changes one of you wants to make to the terms of your divorce and you don't want to minimize your legal expenses, try mediation. Mediation is a good way to avoid the expense and emotional upset of hiring attorneys and possibly having to go to court again. See Chapter 15 to find out more about mediation.

Courts are more open to changing the terms of custody, child-support, or spousal support agreements than they are to changing the terms of a property settlement agreement. In fact, many states prohibit such a change. States that do allow modifications of property settlement agreements usually provide only a very short window of opportunity — typically 30 days after your divorce — for requesting the change.

Demonstrating a change in your circumstances

If you want a change in your divorce agreement and you and your ex don't agree on the change and you can't resolve your differences outside of court, it's time to hire a divorce attorney (if you haven't already done so). Your attorney, working with the attorney representing your ex, may be able to resolve your differences but, if not, he or she will file a motion with the court, and a hearing will be held. At the hearing, your attorney will present evidence to the court justifying the need for the change you are seeking, and your ex's attorney will argue against the change. The judge isn't going to okay a change just because you don't like the terms of your divorce.

Changing how you and your former spouse manage custody and visitation

If you want to modify the terms of your custody and visitation agreement, you must demonstrate a legitimate need for the change due to significant changes in your life, in your former spouse's life, or in the lives of your children. Those changes might include the following:

✔ You're moving a long distance from your former spouse or your ex is the one who's moving far away.

✔ The income of the spouse who's paying child support has increased or decreased.

✔ Your children aren't being properly supervised when they're with their other parent. Perhaps your former spouse has a substance abuse problem; your spouse is having to spend longer hours at work and, as a result, your children are being left alone for long stretches of time; your spouse has turned into a party animal and isn't spending enough time with your kids or isn't providing them with enough supervision; and so on.

✔ One of your children has become seriously ill and you need more financial assistance to help pay for the child's care and treatment.

✔ Your ex has developed a serious physical or mental illness, has developed a serious addiction to drugs or alcohol, has been arrested for a violent crime, or has been accused of child molestation or child abuse and, therefore, you want to change your current custody and visitation arrangement.

✔ You and your teenage son or daughter are in constant conflict and you're having problems controlling him or her. You feel that having your child live with his or her other parent would be in his or her best interest.

✔ You believe that your ex's new spouse is trying to usurp your position as parent to your children, is giving your children advice that contradicts the values you're trying to instill in them, or is allowing them to do things that you would never permit. As a result, you feel that your children are being harmed and are not being raised in a positive way.

✔ You believe that your former spouse is physically abusing or sexually molesting your children.

✔ The arrangements in your divorce agreement or judgment are simply not working out.

Regardless of what reason(s) you give to the court to justify your request for a modification, the judge bases his or her decision on what is in your children's best interests.

Changing how you and your ex handle child support

You or your former spouse may also want to make changes in your child-support court order. If you receive child support, you probably want more money and, if you pay child support, you probably want to reduce how much money you must pay. What a surprise!

If you request a modification in your child-support court order, you must provide the court with proof that changes in your life and/or in your ex's life or changes in the lives of one or more of your children merit the modification. Depending on exactly why you're asking for the change, this proof may include check stubs showing that you're no longer making as much money as you once made or medical records indicating that you have a serious health problem that limits your ability to earn money. If the court denies your request, your state's law probably limits your ability to file a new child-support modification request.

Securing a court order if you change your divorce agreement yourselves

If you and your ex-spouse decide to change your child-custody and visitation agreement, be sure to put the terms of your new agreement in writing and to get a new court order that reflects all the changes. Otherwise, despite what you and your spouse agree to, the new provisions of your agreement aren't legally enforceable because, from the court's perspective, your original court-ordered agreement is still in force. Also, get an attorney's help to make certain that the new agreement is enforceable and worded accurately. Finally, make sure that you and your ex each get a copy.

A judge may not consider the child-support-related changes you and your ex agree to as being in the best interest of your children. If that's the case and the changes involve reducing, suspending, or completely ending your child-support payments, the court can find the spouse who's legally obligated to make the payments in contempt of court. As a result, that parent can end up in legal hot water. To be legally safe, enter a new court order when you want to modify the terms of your child-support court order.

Chapter 19

Thinking Ahead: Prenuptial and Postnuptial Agreements

After you've divorced, sooner or later, you'll probably meet someone new, fall in love, and maybe even think about tying the knot again. Having gone through at least one divorce, you know that marriage can be something of a gamble and that it can drain your emotions as well as your pocketbook if it ends. So you may be wondering whether you can do anything to make splitting up a little bit easier, just in case things don't work out the way you hope they will the next time around.

Well, you can do something to help alleviate your concerns: sign a prenuptial agreement. A *prenuptial agreement* is a legal document that allows you and your future spouse to work out some of the details of your potential divorce *before* you get married. Although it may seem somewhat cynical (not to mention unromantic) to discuss a prenuptial agreement with your spouse-to-be, drafting one may make good just-in-case sense given today's divorce rate.

In this chapter, we tell you all about what a prenuptial agreement can do (and can't do), what makes such an agreement legally binding, and the role that attorneys play in drafting the prenuptial agreement. We also offer you some advice for raising the subject with your future spouse.

In this chapter, you also find information about another kind of legal agreement that you can prepare *after* you're married — the *postnuptial agreement*. Although people use this agreement less often than prenuptial agreements, postnuptial agreements serve the same purpose as prenups.

Rich or Not, Plan on a Prenup

Traditionally, prenuptial agreements have been associated with wealthy people, especially when a wealthy person marries someone with a lot less wealth or earning power. But today, people of more average means are using these agreements, too, including

- ✔ People who've already gone through a difficult and expensive divorce and want to make any future split easier and cheaper.

- ✔ Spouses-to-be who own their own businesses and want to protect their enterprise from the potential repercussions of a divorce.

- ✔ Older professionals headed into marriages with a substantial amount of real estate, stocks, bonds, and other valuable assets.

- ✔ Couples, especially older ones, who want to write their own inheritance rules so they can ensure that their children from a previous marriage, and not their future spouse's children, inherit certain assets when they die. (By law in most states, when a spouse dies, the remaining spouse has a legal right to a certain portion of the deceased's estate, no matter what his or her will says.)

- ✔ Couples who want to negotiate the rules of their marriage — how they will share the housework, what religion their children will be, and other issues related to the management of their marriage and family life. (However, most courts don't enforce such lifestyle provisions.)

Using a prenup to negotiate the terms of your marriage

You can use a prenuptial agreement for more than just setting the terms of your divorce. You can also use a prenup to establish the "rules" of your marriage, even though most courts don't enforce such lifestyle provisions. Still, spending time discussing many of the seemingly minor issues that often scuttle a marriage can help solidify your married relationship. For example, your agreement may address the following potential marriage-busters:

- ✔ Will you have children? If so, how many and how soon?

- ✔ Will one of you stay home to care for the children?

- ✔ If one or both of you have children from a previous marriage and the children will be living with you or visiting periodically, what are your expectations of each other regarding the care of the other's kids? Also, if your individual children are adults, how do you feel about giving or loaning them money?

- ✔ When is borrowing money okay, and how much debt do you feel comfortable with? How do you feel about credit-card debt in particular?

- ✔ How much will you put into savings each month? Are you going to buy a home together or rent a place to live?

✔ Will you share a checking account?

✔ How will you share your bills?

✔ How will you share housework, yard work, the management of your finances, and other household activities?

✔ If you both own your own homes and furniture, where will you live and how will you blend your household items?

✔ If you reach a decision-making impasse or are having trouble getting along in general, will you agree to get counseling?

✔ Where will you spend important holidays — with your family, with your spouse's family, or somewhere else?

✔ If one of you is close to retirement age, what are your plans for the future when you stop working?

Talking out these issues before you get married can increase your confidence in the success of your marriage. On the other hand, if you and your intended don't see eye to eye on the really important issues, you may begin to question the long-term potential of your relationship and rethink the idea of marrying.

Although you may feel like you're tempting fate by having a prenup, negotiating such an agreement is a smart way to minimize the potential negative financial and emotional repercussions of a divorce. Doing most of the end-of-your-marriage negotiating at the start of your relationship — when everything's still rosy — can make your divorce easier, less emotional, and cheaper and can help protect important assets in the aftermath of divorce (should one occur). Read the sidebar in this chapter, "Using a prenup to negotiate the terms of your marriage," for suggestions about the kinds of issues you may want to address in your prenup.

Broaching the Subject to Your Future Spouse (Delicately)

You like the idea of a prenuptial agreement, but you're wondering about the best way to bring up that subject to your intended. After all, your soon-to-be spouse may not consider negotiating such an agreement an auspicious way to begin a marriage.

There's no risk-free way to broach the subject. What works for one person may be disastrous for someone else. The right approach for you depends on your individual personalities and on the degree of trust and communication that you've already established with one another. Nevertheless, here are some general ground rules for opening the prenup discussion:

✔ Be honest — without being hurtful — about your reasons for wanting a prenuptial agreement. If you sound as though you're being evasive or lying or if you appear to be acting out of greed, deceitfulness, or distrust, you may have a tough time getting to the negotiation stage, and you may even derail your marriage before it's begun.

✔ Be absolutely clear that your desire for a prenuptial agreement says nothing about your love for, and commitment to, your future spouse.

✔ Clearly explain how your spouse will benefit from the prenuptial agreement.

✔ Don't become defensive or angry if your future spouse becomes upset about the fact that you want a prenuptial agreement.

If you're nervous about bringing up the idea of a prenuptial agreement, consider getting some advice from a marriage counselor, therapist, or your religious advisor. Or, if emotions get in the way of a calm discussion, a session with one of those advisors may help you and your future spouse work through your emotions so you can work toward an understanding about the terms of the agreement.

If having a prenuptial agreement is really important to you, be prepared to offer your spouse a financial incentive for going along with what you want. Make the incentive a part of the agreement.

If you and your future spouse try to draft your own prenuptial agreement and reach a stalemate, consider scheduling a session or two with a trained mediator. (We discuss mediation in detail in Chapter 15.) If mediation helps you resolve your differences and you end up with an agreement, you should each hire separate attorneys to review it to make certain that it complies with your state's legal requirements for prenuptial agreements and to make sure that you haven't overlooked anything important. If the agreement doesn't comply with your state's legal requirements, it won't be legally enforceable.

Depending on your state, unless you and your spouse-to-be both use attorneys to help you prepare your prenuptial agreement, the agreement may not be legally enforceable.

Creating an Agreement that Meets Your Needs

The provisions you include in your agreement should reflect your individual interests and financial concerns. You may have some ideas already about what you want to include but, to make sure that you've thought of everything, ask yourself the following questions:

- How will you be compensated if you agree to be a stay-at-home parent during your marriage, especially if you'd rather work outside the home?

- If you're making a sacrifice by agreeing to give up your career to help build up your spouse's career or business, how will you be compensated?

- How will you treat the income each of you earns during your marriage?

- How will you share expenses during your marriage?

- How will you be compensated if your spouse-to-be has bad credit and, therefore, during (at least) the early years of your marriage, all credit has to be in your name? (You will be responsible for that debt, even if your spouse agrees to pay off some of it if you get divorced.)

- If you intend to support your spouse while he or she attends law school, medical school, and so on, how will you be compensated if your marriage ends?

- Who will pay the legal fees if you get divorced?

- Will one of you pay the other spousal support if your marriage ends? If so, how much will the payments be and how long will they last?

- Who will get the house and any other significant property if you get divorced?

- How will you deal with inheritance issues if one of you dies during your marriage?

- What will you do about your marital debts if you get divorced?

- How will you deal with the assets from your marriage in the event of a divorce and how will you title any real estate (houses, raw land, office buildings, and so on) that you may purchase during your marriage?

- How will your spouse be compensated for any contribution he or she may make to your business if your marriage ends in divorce?

- Will your spouse have any interest in your business if you get divorced?

- What will you do with your business if you get divorced?

Depending on your state, you may not be able to include provisions for spousal support in your premarital agreement. Also, state family courts aren't bound by provisions in such an agreement related to the custody and support of any children you may have during your marriage. Courts don't consider such provisions in the best interest of young children.

Negotiating the terms of your prenuptial agreement may have an unexpected effect. Depending on what you learn about your future spouse by going through the process or whether your negotiations deteriorate in acrimony and bad feelings that one or both of you can't get beyond, you may decide to call off your marriage instead of signing on the dotted line.

After you've prepared your prenuptial agreement, read it periodically to make sure that it continues to reflect your interests and your needs. If things change, you and your spouse can agree to amend the agreement or to void it. The amending, or voiding, process depends on your state's laws, so talk with an attorney if you and your spouse are thinking about doing either.

Making Your Prenuptial Agreement Legally Binding

Every state has its own property laws, which guide judges when they're making decisions about how to divide up a divorcing couple's marital debts. Chapter 3 discusses those laws. If you and your future spouse write a prenuptial agreement, you can also write your own rules for what to do with those assets and debts (with the provisos we state next) as long as they're acceptable to both of you.

Like other important agreements related to love, marriage, and divorce, every state has rules for what makes a prenuptial agreement legally binding and enforceable by the court. Those rules usually include the following:

✔ The agreement must be in writing. Unless whatever you agree to is in black and white, if you and your spouse decide to divorce, you may have different memories of what you agreed to. As a result, you may have to go to court to resolve your disagreement, which would defeat one of the main reasons of having a prenup.

✔ You must both sign your prenuptial agreement. Both of you must sign your agreement because you want to, not because you're being threatened or coerced.

Many attorneys videotape couples signing their prenuptial agreements because the tape provides additional proof that the agreement was something that both parties desired and entered into willingly.

✔ Depending on your state, the agreement must be notarized. Getting a document notarized provides proof that the person signing the document is, in fact, the person who is supposed to sign it.

✔ You and your future spouse should negotiate and finalize the agreement well before the date of your marriage.

Doing so lessens the likelihood that either of you will feel pressured by your pending marriage to agree to your partner's requests. The more distance you can put between the date of your marriage and the signing of the agreement, the better.

✔ You must both be involved in negotiating the agreement, although you can use attorneys to do the negotiating for you.

We highly advise using attorneys because their involvement greatly increases the enforceability of your agreement if, down the road, your spouse tries to contest its legitimacy.

✔ You and your future spouse must be 100 percent forthcoming with one another about what you each own and owe coming into your marriage. Detail all your assets — homes and land, vehicles, stocks and mutual funds, insurance policies, and so on — as well as their values. Also, be frank about how much you owe and who you owe the money to, even if you're embarrassed by your debt.

✔ Don't try to hide assets to gain an advantage over your future spouse in the event that your marriage ends. For example, don't minimize the amount of investment property you own with the idea that if your marriage ends and your spouse doesn't know about the property, you won't have to pay him or her as much spousal support as you would if you were totally honest. If your spouse finds out that you hid the property and brings that fact to the court's attention during your divorce, the court will view your action as fraud, and it may invalidate your prenuptial agreement.

If your spouse contests the legality of your prenuptial agreement and can prove that one or more of the characteristics we just listed were missing from your prenuptial agreement negotiations, the court may change or reverse certain provisions in the agreement or, after holding a hearing, it may void your prenuptial agreement entirely.

If your prenuptial agreement overwhelmingly favors you to the detriment of your spouse, he or she may be successful at getting the court to declare that the agreement is invalid. Your state may provide other legal defenses that you or your spouse can use to contest the legality of your agreement in the future. Asking your attorney about these defenses when your prenuptial agreement is being drafted is a good idea. The agreement should be drafted with those defenses in mind.

Getting Legal Help with Your Agreement

Your state may require that each of you hire your own attorneys to help you during the prenuptial agreement negotiation process. Even if that's not a requirement in your state, hiring your own attorneys is a good idea because it has important potential implications for your financial well-being.

Your attorney can help you ensure that the agreement is fair to you and can explain how the agreement can affect you if your marriage ends in divorce. He or she can also make certain that the agreement meets the letter of the law in your state.

The attorney you hire should be a family law practitioner with specific experience in the area of prenuptial planning (not all attorneys have this expertise). Depending on the circumstances, you may also need the assistance of a lawyer with special expertise outside the area of family law or the help of other professionals. For example, if you own a business, you may want a business law specialist or a business valuation expert involved in your prenuptial planning. Or, if you want to set up a trust as part of your planning, the assistance of an estate-planning attorney is advisable.

You and your future spouse should discuss your prenuptial goals and concerns and what each of you thinks is fair before you meet with your attorneys. Then you can determine whether writing a prenuptial agreement is even possible. You'll need to identify and categorize the issues you agree on, the issues that need legal clarification, and what you want your attorneys to help negotiate. The more you do together, the less your attorneys will have to do, which means that your prenuptial agreement will cost less to draft than if you involve your attorneys from start to finish.

Using an attorney to help you work out the terms of your prenuptial agreement can cost you anywhere between $1,000 and $100,000, depending on where you live, the complexity of the issues you address in the agreement, and the value of the assets involved. For most couples, the attorney fees are at the low end of the scale. If you consider the cost of a litigated divorce, spending money now on a prenuptial agreement may save you some dollars in the long run.

After You're Married: Drafting a Postnuptial Agreement

Just as its name implies, a *postnuptial agreement* is one that you and your spouse draft after you're married. Although this type of agreement isn't as common as a prenuptial agreement, it has been growing in popularity.

Understanding how you can use a postnup agreement

You can use a postnuptial agreement pretty much the same way that you can use a prenuptial agreement. For example:

✔ If you or your spouse decides to start a business after you get married, you can spell out in a postnuptial agreement what will happen to the business if you get divorced or if you die while you're still married.

For example, assume that you're going to open a shop. You and your spouse may agree that all the income your store earns will remain in a business checking account for three months in order to pay the bills. Then, after the three months are up, the income will be divided 50/50 into two separate personal property accounts — one for you and one for your spouse. Or, perhaps you want to word your agreement to ensure that the full value of the business goes to your children when you die and that your spouse will not get any of it.

✔ You can use the postnuptial agreement to ensure that all your estate goes to your children when you die instead of a portion of it automatically going to your spouse.

✔ You can use a postnuptial to work out most of the details of your divorce (child custody and child support not included).

Making the postnup agreement legally binding

State laws regarding what makes a postnuptial agreement legally binding tend to be less well-defined than those that apply to prenuptial agreements. Generally, however, the laws of both agreements tend to mirror each other. So when you negotiate your postnuptial agreement, abide by all the same rules that apply to prenuptials in your state, including full disclosure, no coercion, and honesty.

Now it belongs to me: The partition agreement

A *partition agreement* is a narrowly focused legal agreement that married couples can use to legally convert specific marital assets into separate property. With this type of agreement, one spouse gives the other his or her legal interest in the value of a certain marital asset. If the marital asset you partition is real property (such as a house), be sure that all ownership documents (the deed of record if it's real estate) are changed to reflect the new ownership. A partition agreement is normally used in community property states when one spouse is about to enter into a financially risky business. If the business fails, the agreement helps protect the assets that were transferred into the name of the spouse who does not own the business from the business's creditors. In other words, those assets are not subject to the creditors' collection actions.

If you want your postnuptial agreement to be legally valid, you're better off negotiating it while your marriage is still on solid ground, not after your relationship begins to fall apart. Otherwise, if you do split up and one of you later contests the legal validity of the agreement, the court may view the postnup as little more than an effort by one of you to defraud the other. Also, if you file for divorce too soon after you finalize your postnuptial agreement (and what constitutes "too soon" is up to a judge to decide), the agreement may not hold up in court if your soon-to-be-ex challenges it.

Even if your state doesn't require that you and your spouse use separate attorneys, doing so is a very good idea. Because a postnuptial agreement is relatively rare, using separate attorneys can help ensure that your agreement will stand up in court if one of you contests its legality down the road.

Most states will invalidate a postnuptial agreement if you can prove that the agreement is an attempt to defraud creditors.

Part VI
The Part of Tens

The 5th Wave   By Rich Tennant

"When we met, we seemed to be on the same track, so we hitched up. Then, just when I thought the relationship was gaining steam, something derailed it. I don't know. Maybe I was sending the wrong signals."

In this part . . .

The Part of Tens contains quick and handy bits of advice and information, packaged ten to a chapter, including

- ✔ Divorce-related Web sites. These sites provide information that's specific to your state, offer additional detail on the subjects we cover in this book, and can put you in touch with other people who are going through a divorce or who can offer expert advice on divorce.
- ✔ Suggestions for how to help make your children's lives as happy and stable as possible after your divorce.
- ✔ Tips for putting your divorce behind you, getting on with your life, and having a social life again.

And, because you'll probably encounter a lot of terms that you're unfamiliar with as you go through your divorce, this part also includes a handy glossary.

Chapter 20

Ten Great Divorce Web Sites

In This Chapter

▶ Surfing the Web for info about the financial, legal, and emotional aspects of divorce

▶ Chatting with other divorcing or divorced folks

▶ Getting the lowdown on the divorce laws in your particular state

Although surfing the Net is no substitute for solid legal advice, you can go to divorce-related Web sites to bone up on the issues in your divorce, to get advice, and to chat it up with other people facing the same challenges as you are in you own divorce. In this chapter, we recommend some of the best Web sites dedicated to divorce.

Divorce Central

Divorce Central (www.divorcecentral.com) covers the legal, emotional, and financial aspects of divorce and offers information about parenting during and after divorce. Specifically, it offers The DC Legal Center, The DC Lifeline (for emotional support), The DC Parenting Center, and The DC Financial Center. Within each category, you find information, bulletin boards for posting questions and comments, informative articles, checklists, links, and other divorce-related tools.

If you want to meet other people who are in your same situation, you can register to join Divorce Central's DC Community, which is a secure Web site, or you can just click on Chat with Friends, which isn't secure.

The site also features a bookstore, a newsletter you can sign up to receive, an online parenting handbook to help you help your kids cope with your divorce, and even a personals section if you're ready to begin dating again.

Divorce Doc

The founder of Divorce Doc (www.divorcedoc.com) is a clinical psychologist who works with families and individuals. Although the site doesn't get rave reviews for its design, it does have some features you don't find on other sites, including a free divorce e-zine called *When Marriage Ends,* divorce crossword puzzles, contests and games, and information about celebrity divorces as well as the legal, emotional, and financial information and advice that's standard fare for most divorce Web sites.

Divorce Helpline

Started by three California attorneys, the goal of Divorce Helpline (www. divorcehelp.com) is to help divorcing couples stay out of court. To that end, Divorce Helpline offers a solid online primer about the basic issues in a divorce as well as related books and software that you can purchase online.

Divorce Info

Friendly and comprehensive, the mission of Divorce Info (www.divorceinfo. com) is to "help you survive your divorce with some money in your pocket and your dignity in tact." We can get behind that! It features sections with titles such as "Divorce Stinks," which is about the emotional aspects of divorce, and "Cutting Through the Crud," which is about how you and your spouse can get through the divorce process without strangling one another. The site also has lots of information and resources for helping your young or adult children cope with the breakup of your marriage. The site includes divorce-related information and resources for each state, downloadable forms, and recommended books to order.

DivorceNet

DivorceNet (www.divorcenet.com) claims to be the "Net's largest divorce resource." It offers lots of information to read if you're undecided about whether or not to get divorced and, if you decide that you want to, it provides state-by-state links for getting a divorce online and lists of professionals you can consult in each state. DivorceNet also provides special information and resources for members of the military and their spouses who are getting divorced. In addition, you can participate in online chats and get your questions answered by divorce experts.

Divorce Online

Sponsored by the American Divorce Information Network, a group of professionals who support an interdisciplinary approach to divorce and other family law issues, Divorce Online (www.divorceonline.com) features informative articles on financial, real estate, legal, emotional, and social issues related to divorce. Also featured is a "He Said . . . She Said" bulletin board for angry spouses and ex-spouses who need a place to air their gripes.

Depending on where you live, you may be able to use this site to locate financial, legal, mental health, and real estate professionals in your area who can help you with your divorce (listings are available for only some states).

Divorce Source

Divorce Source (www.divorcesource.com) describes itself as "one enormous online divorce support group that caters to people facing divorce (or related issues) who desire pertinent information and want to share questions, find answers, and learn from others' experiences."

Divorce Source features numerous divorce forums and message centers where visitors can share and get information on every aspect of planning for, going through, and getting over a divorce. The site also offers forms, books, and software to download as well as a state-by-state directory of divorce-related professionals.

Divorce Wizards

Although the focus of Divorce Wizards (www.divorcewizards.com) is on helping divorcing couples in California get an online divorce, it offers plenty of information for non-Californians, too — information that isn't available on most other divorce Web sites. For example, this site features a discussion of sex, infidelity, divorce, a "Can Your Marriage Be Saved?" quiz, advice about how to make joint custody work, tips for being a great divorced dad, and more.

Flying Solo

Flying Solo (www.flyingsolo.com) helps you transition from being part of a couple to being on your own. It addresses all aspects of getting a divorce, remarrying and dealing with stepchildren, estate planning, retirement planning, and so on. It also provides links to a wide variety of sites not found on other divorce Web sites.

Womans Divorce

As its name implies, Womans Divorce (www.womansdivorce.com) is just for women. It lays out the issues women should consider before they get divorced, discusses the financial aspects of divorce, and provides detailed information for financial survival after divorce. It also helps women look to the future with inspiration and information about dealing with stress, building self-esteem, coping with anger, feeling good again, and other starting-over issues. The site also offers women a Job Toolkit and a Divorce Survival newsletter as well as message boards, links, books, and other resources that they can use not just to survive their divorce but also to thrive afterward.

Chapter 21

Ten Ways to Help Your Kids Cope

In This Chapter

▶ Letting your kids know that you still love them

▶ Cooperating with your former spouse on child-rearing

▶ Making your children's lives feel safe and secure

Children of divorce often feel as if their lives have been turned upside down and that everything that they knew and loved has been taken from them. In other words, your divorce is your children's divorce, too. So, as a parent, you're responsible for helping your kids cope with the profound changes that are happening in their lives. In this chapter, we provide suggestions for how you can do that. If you would like to talk with other parents in your same situation, visit the award-winning Web site www.parentsoup.com.

Show Your Children That You Love Them

As you go through your divorce, spend time with your kids, show them affection, and be willing to listen when they want to talk about their feelings with you. Try to do something special alone with each of your children. If you live too far away from your children to see them regularly, write or call them at least once a week.

If you are a noncustodial parent and dread seeing your children because telling them goodbye and returning them to their other parent at the end of each visit is painful, try to take comfort in the fact that, over time, those things will get easier. Don't let these feelings prevent you from seeing your children. It's important for you to continue to be a part of their lives.

Encourage Your Kids to Respect and Love Their Other Parent

Give your children permission to love their other parent. Don't paint such a negative picture of your ex that they feel guilty loving their mom or dad. Instead, speak positively about your ex. Help make your children feel comfortable talking about their other parent in front of you. Tell them funny or touching stories about your ex; share photos from your wedding day, photos of your children with their other parent, or photos of all of you in happier times. By sharing stories and photos, you demonstrate to your children that you're comfortable talking about their other parent and give them permission to talk with you about him or her. You also provide your kids with a sense of family history, something that all children need.

At first, following this advice may be hard to do but eventually it should get easier. If months go by and you still can't talk about your ex-spouse or look at a picture of the two of you without getting emotional, consider counseling.

Avoid Making Your Problems Their's

Don't treat your children like grown-ups. Although they may assume more responsibilities after your divorce, never forget that they're still kids. Don't burden them with your problems or share your worries with them; you've got close friends and adult family members for that. Your children may sense that you're going through a tough time, but assure them through your words and actions that everything will be all right.

Reach an Understanding with Your Ex about Basic Child-rearing Rules

If you and your former spouse share custody, coming to an understanding with one another about how to handle such child-rearing issues as discipline, homework, bedtime, and curfews is important. Living by one set of rules in your home and by a totally different set of rules in your ex's can confuse children and make their lives needlessly complicated. On the other hand, if your former spouse doesn't parent your children as you do, don't complain about it to your kids or argue about it with your ex in front of or within earshot of them. However, you should speak to your ex if you feel that his or her parenting style is clearly harming your children emotionally or putting them at risk for physical harm.

Make Your Children Feel At Home

Because of your divorce, you may have to move out of your home and into a new home or apartment. If you do, try to make your children feel comfortable in their new home. (If they live with you only part of the time, giving them a place to call their own is particularly important because, otherwise, they may not want to spend time at your place.) If your finances allow, let your kids decorate their new space or at least select a few items for it. And agree with your ex to maintain a supply of clothes, toiletries, and toys for your kids at each of your homes. Then your children won't have to pack and unpack items every time they move from one parent's place to the other's.

Act Like a Grown-Up

Don't argue with your ex in front of your children, don't use your kids as go-betweens if you just don't want to communicate with him or her, and don't try to prevent your ex from seeing your kids. If your ex starts dating, don't try to sabotage that relationship or make your children think that it's not okay if they like your ex's new beau. These days, kids can't have too many caring adults in their lives. Also, if you act angry or resentful about your ex's new love interest, you inadvertently give your children a lesson in jealousy.

Live Up to Your Promises

Make your children's lives as predictable and secure as possible by keeping the promises you make to them. Doing so is always important, but especially after a divorce when they may be feeling very insecure. Therefore, if you tell your kids that you'll pick them up at a certain time, be there. And if you tell them you're going to do something with them — like go to the movies — do it. If you're not able to keep a promise, let your children know as soon as possible and make an alternative plan with them. Also, don't make big promises to your children to try to buy their affection, drive a wedge between them and your ex, or to assuage your guilt about the changes that your divorce has created in their lives. Building up their hopes about something that you know won't happen is unfair and emotionally cruel.

Delay Dating

Don't bring home dates in the months immediately after your divorce is final. When you first begin dating, your children may resent the time you spend with your dates or may feel threatened by them. Also, at first, try to schedule your dates for a time when your children will be with their other parent.

Make Your Children's Lives Predictable

Children thrive on predictability so, after your divorce, try to maintain the routines, rules, and traditions that they're used to. For example, try to eat at the same time, let them keep their pets, expect them to perform the same household chores, and take them to religious services. And, as much as possible, make holidays and other special days like they've always been. Also, don't try to end or interfere with your children's relationships with their other parent, siblings, and other relatives of your former spouse. Your children have already experienced a significant loss — don't compound it by attempting to ruin the important relationships in their lives.

Avoid the "Super Parent" Syndrome

If you feel guilty about the effect your divorce may have on your kids or if you're angry because your spouse has custody, don't try to deal with your feelings by becoming a "Disneyland Dad" (or Mom), lavishing them with gifts and money. Try to maintain the same relationship with your children that you had before the divorce. Right now, your kids don't need grand gestures; they need predictability, stability, and love.

Reading up

Here's a list of some helpful books that you may want to check out:

✔ *My Parents Are Divorced Too: A Book for Kids* by Jan Blackstone-Ford, Annie Ford, Stephen Ford, Melanie Ford, and Steven Ford (Magination Press): Written by kids for kids to help your preteens/early teens talk about their feelings about your divorce.

✔ *Vicki Lansky's Divorce Book for Parents: Helping Your Children Cope with the Aftermath of Divorce* (Book Peddlers): This book provides practical advice about how to help your children cope with your divorce while it's happening and afterward.

✔ *What About the Kids? Raising Your Children Before, During and After Divorce* by Judith S. Wallerstein and Sandra Blakeslee (Hyperion): This resource contains great advice for helping your kids deal with your divorce.

✔ *Surviving the Breakup: How Children and Parents Cope with Divorce* by Judith Wallerstein and Joan Berlin Kelly (Basic Books) and *Second Chances: Men, Women and Children a Decade after Divorce* by Judith Wallerstein and Sandra Blakeslee (Houghton Mifflin Company): These books chronicle the results of Wallerstein's groundbreaking study conducted on how divorce affects children.

Chapter 22

Ten Tips to Help You Move On

*L*ife goes on after a divorce and, believe it or not, things get better (sooner rather than later, we hope). Who knows, you may even fall in love again, and your next marriage may be everything you've ever dreamed of. To help boost your spirits a bit and encourage you to look toward the future, we offer ten practical tips for getting on with your life and planning for happier times.

Find an Adult Shoulder to Lean On

When your marriage ends, you'll probably want someone to honestly share your thoughts and emotions with. Whoever you choose should be a good listener — someone you trust, and someone who has given you good advice in the past. But don't rely on your special confidant so much that you jeopardize your relationship with him or her. And don't dump your worries, frustrations, and anger on your kids. They're likely to be dealing with their own problems as a result of your divorce and don't need yours, too.

Write It All Down

Keeping a journal is a great way to get a handle on your emotions. Writing down how you feel or what has happened to you each day can make you feel better about your life and less reliant on friends and family to help you get your head on straight.

Try not to be self-conscious when you write. Remember, your journal is just for you. It's not to share with anyone unless you want to, and you aren't going to be graded on your prose. Write as though you were talking to your best friend or to yourself. You may even want to draw pictures to illustrate your thoughts.

Every week, read what you wrote the previous week. You may be surprised at the depth (or the silliness) of your emotions, or you may discover that, in just a week, your feelings about something have changed considerably.

Get Counseling If You Need It

If you're crying all the time, constantly full of anger toward your ex, or struggling with depression, schedule an appointment with a therapist or social worker. This person can give you the advice and feedback you need to get on with your life. If you don't already have a good mental health professional, get a referral to one from your family physician, your divorce attorney, or from a trusted friend or relative.

If you have a good relationship with your religious advisor, you may want to talk with him or her rather than a mental health professional.

Fight the Urge to Go Back to Your Ex

If you become desperately lonely after your divorce, don't start dating your ex or begin living together again. Although it may be tempting to resume a relationship with him or her, it's time to move on. Spending time together isn't the way to end your pain or ease your loneliness since the reasons behind your divorce probably still exist. This doesn't mean that you and your ex can't ever be together again. But for now, you're both better off focusing on the future and addressing whatever issues contributed to your divorce.

Get More Involved in Your Job

Your professional life may have suffered while you were going through your divorce because it took every ounce of your energy and concentration just to accomplish the most basic tasks at work. Now that you're divorced, refocusing your energies on your job can help take your mind off your troubles and provide the structure and routine you may need in your life right now. Plus, your professional accomplishments can make you feel good about yourself and may even land you a pay raise or a promotion.

Working hard can be good temporary therapy, but don't turn into a workaholic to fill a void in your life or to avoid facing your emotions. Finding balance in your life and building some pleasure into it are important now more than ever.

Focus on Your Spiritual Life

Don't be ashamed to pray to a higher power for guidance or begin attending religious services. Meditation or yoga are other options for connecting to your spiritual side and gaining a sense of peace. Pick up a copy of *Meditation For Dummies* by Stephan Bodian (Wiley) or *Yoga For Dummies* by Georg Feuerstein, Larry Payne, and Lilias Folan (Wiley). Or try reading *Mind Like Water: Keeping Your Balance in a Chaotic World* by Jim Ballard (Wiley) to help you stay centered and calm when your life feels like it's falling apart.

Deal with Your Debts

If you have a lot of debt, pay it off as quickly as you can. Worries about unpaid bills and debt collectors are the last thing you need right now. Also, the sooner you get out of debt, the sooner you can start stashing away money for your future. Chapter 5 provides advice and information about how to develop a household budget so you can allocate your money wisely. It is a useful tool when you are trying to live on your monthly income and pay off your debts as quickly as you can.

Be Adventurous — Try Something New

Pursue activities that you can enjoy as a newly single person or that you've always wanted to try. Those activities may include taking a dancing or cooking class where you can meet new people, training for a marathon, skydiving, joining a rock-climbing club, or taking that cross-country drive you've always dreamed about. (A change of scenery may be just what the doctor ordered!) If you're not an outdoor person, discover the artist in you. Painting, sculpting, weaving, making pottery, taking up photography, or working on the novel you always wanted to write keeps your hands and your mind busy. In the process, you may dicover a new talent and passion.

Share Your Space

If money is tight, consider a roommate. Sharing your home or apartment with another adult will reduce some of your monthly expenses and may make your living space seem less lonely. Of course, before you get a roommate, make certain that the two of you are compatible.

Sharing your space with a roommate isn't out of the question if you have kids, but be sure that the person you're considering living with likes being around children and has no problem with the noise and mess that they can create. You may even want a roommate with children who are about the same age as your's. Such an arrangement can make it easier for both of you to be single parents.

Energize Your Social Life

Get out of the house and meet new people. Join a support group or a singles' club for divorcees. Doing fun things with other divorced people is good therapy, not to mention a way to meet people you may want to date.

To find a support group for divorced people in your area, visit `www.divorcehq.com/spprtgroup` and click on your state. Another resource, `www.divorcecare.com`, offers support groups and seminars for people recovering from divorce. Use DivorceCare's "group finder" to locate the support group nearest you.

If you used to enjoy entertaining but stopped when your marriage began to fall apart or while your divorce was occurring, invite some friends over for brunch or dinner. If you're living on a shoestring budget, make the meals potluck.

At some point, you may want to begin dating. Avoid dating too soon, however. Most mental health professionals suggest waiting for at least a year after your divorce is final. Once you're ready to begin dating, you may be in a quandary about how to meet new people, especially if you've been out of the dating scene for some time, didn't date a lot before your marriage, or if you're older. Chapter 17 suggests how to find some people you may enjoy going out with.

Glossary

When getting divorced, you may hear new words that you're not familiar with. Not knowing what those words mean can only add to the anxiety and confusion that you may already be feeling. But we're here to help you out. In this glossary, we define the words that you're most likely to encounter in plain English, not lawyer-speak.

Abandonment: When one spouse moves out of the home the couple shares without the consent of, or against the wishes of, the other spouse.

Action: The legal term for a lawsuit (also called a *cause of action*).

Adversarial divorce: Occurs when a married couple can't come to an agreement about the terms of their divorce.

Affidavit: A written statement of facts relating to a lawsuit. The statement is made under oath and is notarized.

Alimony: See *spousal support*.

Alimony pendente lite: A temporary court order for support while a couple's divorce is pending (also called *temporary spousal support*).

Annulment: A court action declaring a marriage legally invalid. States vary in regard to what makes a marriage invalid. Also, some religions provide annulments, but a religious and a legal annulment are not the same.

Answer: A formal response to a petition for divorce, separation, or annulment. In the response, the person who's served with the petition admits or denies the allegations made by the petitioner and may also make allegations against the petitioner.

Appeal: The process by which the losing party in a divorce asks a higher court to review the decision of the lower court to determine whether a legal reason exists to order a new trial or to change some aspect of the lower court's decision.

Arbitration: A legally binding resolution to a dispute achieved through a non-judicial process.

Arrearage: Child support or spousal support that's past due.

Assets: Property of value including, but not limited to, cash, real estate, vehicles, securities and other investments, fine jewelry, artwork, and other valuables.

Automatic wage deduction: A court order that requires the employer of the parent who's obligated to pay child support to deduct those payments from the parent's paycheck and to send them to the court so it can distribute the money to the parent who's entitled to the support.

Cause of action: See *action*.

Change of venue: A change in the location of a trial, usually from one county to another county within the same state.

Child support: Money one spouse pays to the other spouse to help meet the financial needs of their minor children. The support usually continues until a child turns 18 or 21, depending on the state, although a parent may have to provide support while a child is a full-time college student or attends trade school.

Citation: See *summons*.

Claim: A charge by one spouse against the other.

COBRA: A federal law that allows individuals who are covered on their employer's health insurance policy to remain on the policy for a limited period of time after they stop working for their employer and for the spouse of that former employee to continue coverage for a limited period of time after their marriage ends, assuming the spouse was covered during the period of the employee's employment. The children of a former employee are also covered by COBRA under the same circumstances.

Collaborative divorce: A noncourt process that involves a divorcing couple and their respective attorneys working out the terms of their divorce together in a friendly manner without the assistance of a neutral third party like there is in mediation.

Common-law marriage: A relationship between a man and a woman that some states recognize as a marriage even though no formal ceremony occurred and no license was issued. Common-law marriages are formally ended by divorce.

Community property: Property, including money and other assets that a couple acquires during their marriage. Each spouse is legally entitled to half the value of that property. This ownership concept applies only in states with community property laws.

Complaint: The written document or pleading filed with a court to initiate a divorce. It cites a wrong (or *grounds*), names the person(s) who allegedly committed the wrong, specifies whether any minor children are involved, and describes the relief sought and other relevant information (also called a *petition*). In a no-fault divorce, the complaint doesn't allege wrongdoing on the part of a spouse, but it typically states *incompatibility* or *irreconcilable differences* as the reason for divorce.

Contempt of court: A willful and deliberate violation of a court order, judgment, or decree (for example, nonpayment of child support or spousal support). The court may punish spouses who are in contempt of court.

Contested divorce: A divorce in which the spouses cannot agree on how to resolve the issues involved. The court may resolve the issues if the parties have not settled them by the date of their divorce trial.

Court order: A written document issued by a court and signed by a judge that orders someone to do something.

Cross-examination: The questioning of a witness by the attorney representing the opposing party to ascertain the truthfulness of a witness's testimony or to further develop that testimony. Witnesses are cross-examined during a trial.

Custody: The legal right and responsibility of a parent to raise a minor child and to make decisions on her or his behalf.

Decree: The final written order in a divorce.

Deed: A legal document that conveys ownership in real estate or other real property.

Default judgment: An order or judgment made on the basis of the plaintiff's information because the defendant failed to respond, didn't respond on time, or didn't appear in court.

Defendant: The person sued for divorce; also known as the *respondent*.

Deposition: Testimony taken outside of court and under oath and subject to examination by all parties to a lawsuit. A stenographer records the testimony and types it verbatim. The deposition may also be videotaped.

Direct examination: The questioning of a witness on the stand by the attorney representing the spouse on whose behalf the witness is testifying.

Discovery: A process attorneys use to get at the facts in a divorce prior to trial. Most often discovery gets at financial facts but, depending on the jurisdiction, attorneys may also use it to explore other issues, such as how good a parent you are or whether you and your spouse are battling over custody of your children. Also, if you're divorcing in a state that allows for fault divorces and one of you filed a fault divorce, attorneys use discovery to help prove (or disprove) the alleged fault. The tools of discovery include depositions, interrogatories, and the production of documents, among other tools.

Dissolution: The end of a marriage (in other words, a divorce). The term doesn't include annulments.

Divorce agreement: See *marital settlement agreement.*

Emancipation: The age at which a child becomes a legal adult and his or her parents are no longer responsible for his or her care. In most states, the age is 18 but, in some states, children are emancipated at 21. A child may become a legal adult at a younger age if he or she marries; joins the military; goes to work full time; or petitions the court to declare him or her an emancipated minor, and the court agrees to do so.

Equitable distribution: A legal system of dividing up the value of a divorcing couple's marital property based on what's fair to each of them.

Evidence: Relevant testimony, documents, videos, tape recordings, e-mails, and other information that attorneys offer to and get accepted by the court to prove or disprove an allegation.

Ex parte: An attempt by an attorney representing one side of a lawsuit to contact the court about an issue in the lawsuit without the knowledge of the attorney for the other side, usually in an effort to influence the judge. Ex parte communications aren't allowed, and the judge presiding over the lawsuit will refuse to be a party to such communication.

Fault divorce: A kind of divorce in which the spouse who initiates the divorce provides a very specific reason for the divorce, such as mental cruelty, adultery, and so on. Not all states allow fault divorces.

Garnishment: The legal taking of a debtor's money or bank account to pay his or her debt. In a divorce, a court can garnish a parent's wages for nonpayment of child support, assuming that the state of the debtor spouse permits wage garnishment.

Grounds: The legal basis or reason for a divorce.

Guardian ad litem: A court-appointed adult, usually a trained social worker, counselor, or other professional, who represents the interests of minor children in a couple's divorce.

Hearing: A proceeding before the court that attempts to resolve an issue through testimony, legal arguments, and the introduction of evidence.

Hold harmless: A situation in which one spouse agrees to assume full responsibility for paying the other spouse's debts and promises to protect that spouse from any loss or expense associated with the debts. *Indemnification* is the same thing as holding someone harmless.

Injunction: A court order prohibiting someone from acting in a way that's likely to harm someone else, financially, emotionally, or physically.

Interrogatories: Written questions that one party formally serves to someone else (that other person may or may not be the other spouse) in a divorce. Interrogatories are used to gain information and establish facts related to the issues under dispute in a divorce. Those who provide answers to the interrogatories must do so under oath within a set period of time, usually a month.

Joint custody: A situation in which divorced (or separated) parents share custody of their minor children. The parents may share *legal custody* (the right and obligation to make important decisions for their children about matters such as medical care and treatment and what school they will attend), *physical custody* (the right and obligation to have their children reside with them), or legal and physical custody.

Joint property: Property legally owned by two or more persons; for example, a husband and wife.

Judgment of divorce: A formal written document that states that a man and a woman are divorced. Also called a *divorce decree* or *decree of dissolution*.

Jurisdiction: The authority of a court to rule on a particular legal matter. Different types of courts have different jurisdictions; for example, state family courts hear issues related to family law, and federal bankruptcy courts hear consumer and business bankruptcy cases.

Legal custody: The right and obligation of one or both parents to make decisions on their children's behalf about important matters such as their religious upbringing, medical care, education, and so on.

Legal separation: A legal agreement or court judgment formally authorizing a couple to live apart and spelling out the terms for their living apart. The couple is still married to one another. Not all states recognize legal separations.

Maintenance: Another word for *alimony* or *spousal support*.

Marital property: Property acquired by or earned by a couple during the couple's marriage.

Marital settlement agreement: A written agreement between spouses that spells out their decisions in regard to the division of their marital property and in regard to child support and visitation and spousal support. Also referred to as a *divorce agreement*.

Mediation: A popular nonlegal means of resolving a divorce-related dispute with the assistance of a neutral third party. Decisions made in a mediation session are arrived at by mutual agreement and are not ordered by a judge.

Motion: A written or oral application to the court asking the court to take a certain action, such as ordering temporary support, custody, or visitation rights, or preventing a spouse from taking or spending assets.

Motion to modify: A written request to the court to change an earlier court order regarding child custody, support, alimony, or other divorce-related decisions.

No-fault divorce: A divorce granted without the spouse who initiates the divorce having to allege and prove marital misconduct on the part of the other spouse.

Noncustodial parent: The parent who doesn't have physical custody of his or her children. Ordinarily, this parent is obligated to pay child support and has visitation rights.

Order: A ruling the court makes on a motion that requires the parties in a divorce to do something or not to do something or that establishes the parties' rights and responsibilities.

Petition: The legal document filed to initiate a divorce (also called a *complaint*).

Petitioner: The person who files a petition or initiates a couple's divorce proceedings (also called the *plaintiff*).

Physical custody: The right and obligation of one or both divorced or separated parents to have their children reside with them for a certain amount of time.

Plaintiff: See *petitioner*.

Pleading: Formal written application to the court setting forth what you would like the court to do for you. Pleadings can include petitions, answers, and motions, among other things.

Postnuptial agreement: A binding legal agreement between spouses that spells out their present and future rights and responsibilities if they divorce, separate permanently, or if one spouse dies.

Prenuptial agreement: A binding legal agreement between a couple before they marry that spells out their rights in the event that they later divorce, get a permanent separation, or one of them dies during their marriage.

Pro se: A plaintiff or defendant who represents himself or herself in a lawsuit rather than hire an attorney.

Qualified Domestic Relations Order (QDRO): A court order that requires a portion of one spouse's retirement benefits to be awarded to the other spouse. The order is directed to the administrator of the retirement benefits.

Real property: Homes, other buildings, and land and any liens on those assets.

Respondent: See *defendant.*

Response: A formal written reply by a defendant to respond to or answer a complaint.

Retainer: Money paid to an attorney to begin work on a case.

Separate property: Property legally owned by one spouse and not by both spouses.

Settlement: A written agreement between spouses resolving the issues in their divorce.

Sole custody: When only one parent has custody of the children.

Spousal support: The payment of money by one spouse to another (also called *alimony*). Spousal support is usually provided for only a limited period of time but can end earlier than the specified period if one spouse dies or remarries. Spousal support is taxable income for the spouse who receives it and provides a tax deduction for the spouse who pays it.

Subpoena: A legal document served to a witness requiring that he or she appear in court. Ignoring a subpoena can result in punishment by the court.

Summons: A written notification to the defendant in a divorce that his or her spouse has filed for divorce and that the defendant has a right to file a response to the lawsuit.

Temporary spousal support: See *alimony pendente lite*.

Testimony: Statements provided by a witness under oath during a deposition or in court.

Transcript: A typed record of a trial or a deposition.

Trial: A formal court hearing presided over by a judge to resolve the issues in a lawsuit.

Uncontested divorce: A divorce in which the two spouses don't have any outstanding issues to resolve.

Visitation: The legal right of the noncustodial parent to spend time with his or her children.

Index

  automatic wage withholding for child
    support, 193–194
  credit history and, 11, 49
  education/training, 286–288
  finding, 285–286, 288–289
  focusing on your job, 112, 342–343
  part-time, 48
  pre-divorce planning and, 12
  rehabilitative support, 143
  self-employment and child support, 194
  spousal support and, 145
  updating job skills, 12, 48, 79
  work-at-home schemes, 48
Employment Retirement Security Act
    (ERISA), 130
Equal Credit Opportunity Act (ECOA), 54
Equifax (credit reporting agency), 42, 49, 52
equitable distribution, 348
equitable distribution state, 42, 43, 44, 121
ERISA (Employment Retirement Security
    Act), 130
estate planning, 189, 278–281
etiquette, separation, 66–68
evidence, trial, 262, 348
ex parte, 256, 348
executor, 280
exercise, 111
expenses, 81, 82–83
Experian (credit reporting agency), 42, 49, 52
expert witnesses, 263

• F •

facilitator, mediation, 20
Fair and Accurate Credit Transactions Act
    (FACTA), 52
Fair, Isaac, Inc., 51, 53
fair market value, 120, 135–136
fair share, 121, 138
family, 113, 114, 293–294
Family and Child Services, Inc., 30
father's rights organization, 221
fault divorce
  abandoning your marriage and, 59
  contested divorce, 17
  definition, 348
  filing for, 72
  grounds, 15
  separation period and, 72
  spousal support and, 146
fears, of children, 101

Federal Consumer Information Center (Web
    site), 46
Federal Information Center, 288
Federal Parent Locator Service, 307
Federal Trade Commission, 46, 47, 48, 52
Feuerstein, Georg *(Yoga For Dummies),* 343
FICO score, 51, 53
final settlement, 242
financial advisor, 38
Financial Fine Points icon, 6
financial issues
  credit history, building positive, 49–55
  disability insurance, 190
  documents, 41–42
  education, 47, 286–287
  health insurance, 190
  information sources, 45–46
  inventory of financial situation, 39–42
  knowledge of family's finances, 38–42
  legal separation and, 33
  post-divorce, 283–285, 314–317
  providing financial documentation to
    attorney, 225–226, 233–234
  safeguarding your money, 83–85
  separation and, 59, 63, 65–66
  what you owe, 40–41
  what you own, 39–40
financial planner, 206, 284
financial planning
  budget, 80–83, 283–285, 315
  cash, identifying sources of, 85
  estate planning, 189, 278–283
  locating financial information, 79–80
  pre-divorce, 11–12
  protecting mutual assets, 85
  questions to ask, 78–79
  realistic goals, 78
finpipe.com (Web site), 46
Fisher, Dr. Bruce *(Rebuilding: When Your
    Relationship Ends),* 291
flat fee, 220
Flying Solo (Web site), 336
Folan, Lilias *(Yoga For Dummies),* 343
Ford, Annie *(My Parents are Divorced, Too: A
    Book for Kids by Kids),* 98, 340
Ford, Melanie *(My Parents are Divorced, Too:
    A Book for Kids by Kids),* 98, 340
Ford, Steven *(My Parents are Divorced, Too: A
    Book for Kids by Kids),* 98, 340
foreclosure, 41, 277, 317
foreperson, jury, 267
free consultation, requesting free attorney,
    222–223